Southern Living
OUR BEST
ONE-DISH MEALS

Southern Living

OUR BEST

ONE-DISH MEALS

Compiled by
Jean Wickstrom Liles

Edited by Lisa A. Hooper

Oxmoor
House®

Library of Congress Catalog Card Number: 95-69353

ISBN: 0-8487-1438-5

Manufactured in the United States of America

First Printing 1995

Editor-in-Chief: Nancy J. Fitzpatrick

Senior Foods Editor: Susan Carlisle Payne

Senior Editor, Editorial Services: Olivia Kindig Wells

Art Director: James Boone

■ **Southern Living** Our Best One-Dish Meals

Editor: Lisa A. Hooper

Copy Editor: Cecilia C. Matthews

Editorial Assistant: Alison Rich Lewis

Director, Test Kitchens: Kathleen Royal Phillips

Assistant Director, Test Kitchens: Gayle Hays Sadler

Test Kitchen Home Economists: Susan Hall Bellows, Julie Christopher, Iris Crawley, Michele Brown Fuller, Natalie E. King, Elizabeth Tyler Luckett, Jan A. Smith

Menu and Recipe Consultant: Jean Wickstrom Liles

Senior Photographer: Jim Bathie

Photographer: Ralph Anderson

Senior Photo Stylist: Kay E. Clarke

Photo Stylist: Virginia R. Cravens

Designer: Melissa Jones Clark

Publishing Systems Administrator: Rick Tucker

Production and Distribution Director: Phillip Lee

Production Manager: Gail H. Morris

Associate Production Manager: Theresa L. Beste

Production Assistant: Marianne Jordan

Cover: *Chinese Sweet-and-Sour Shrimp (page 109)*

Back cover: *Huevos Rancheros (page 18)*

Page 2: *Chicken Cacciatore (page 136)*

Contents

Welcome

■ No time to cook? When you find yourself short on time, one-dish meals are a perfect solution. ■ Because fast-paced lifestyles and busy schedules are the rule and not the exception for today's families, *Our Best One-Dish Meals* places emphasis on ease in cooking. ■ Along with the best all-in-one-dish recipes from the test kitchens of *Southern Living,* you'll find a menagerie of make-ahead and freezing instructions, helpful hints from our test kitchen home economists, and page after page of colorful photographs to inspire you with creative garnishing and serving ideas.

Our Best One-Dish Meals isn't just a book of casserole recipes. ■ We've filled the pages with rich egg and cheese combos, refreshing salads, hearty soups and sandwiches, classic international favorites, and our best bets for the oven and the cooktop. ■ We've even included a chapter that will have you dusting off those convenient cooking appliances—electric slow cookers, microwave ovens, and pressure cookers—so that supper's ready when you are.

Calzones with Herbed Tomato Sauce (page 62)

We'd like to invite you to put *Our Best One-Dish Meals* to the test. ▪ It's a handpicked collection of the best from *Southern Living* since its 1966 debut. ▪ Whether you're an experienced cook or not, our one-dish favorites will help make your time spent in the kitchen a little easier. ▪ From cover to cover, *Our Best One-Dish Meals* promises to be your best friend.

Jean Wickstrom Liles

While compiling *Our Best One-Dish Meals*, Jean Wickstrom Liles spent weeks sifting through the *Southern Living* recipe files, selecting the food staff's one-dish favorites from 1966 to the present. Each recipe selected by Jean was retested and updated to reflect today's package sizes and cooking techniques. Jean, former foods editor at *Southern Living*, is a consultant for Oxmoor House, the book publishing division of Southern Progress Corporation.

Not Just for Breakfast

■ The next time you're planning a quick lunch or casual dinner, try our breakfast main dishes as an appealing option. ■ Recipes such as Huevos Rancheros and Swiss Alpine Quiche are as welcome for a relaxed Sunday supper as they are for a hearty breakfast. ■ While many of these recipes can be prepared at a moment's notice, some have make-ahead features. ■ Brunch for a Bunch and Chile 'n' Cheese Breakfast Casserole are ideal choices for cooks who like to get an early start on meal preparation. ■ Enjoy breakfast anytime with these classics that will take you from dawn to dusk with surprising ease.

Cheese Soufflé Roll (page 26)

HAM AND EGGS À LA SWISS

To hard-cook eggs, place them in a single layer in a saucepan. Cover with cold water at least one inch above eggs. Cover and bring to a boil; remove from heat. Let stand, covered, 15 minutes; pour off water. Run cold water over the eggs to stop the cooking process.

4 English muffins
3 tablespoons butter or margarine, softened
½ pound thinly sliced cooked ham
4 hard-cooked eggs, sliced
½ cup sour cream
½ cup mayonnaise
1 cup (4 ounces) shredded Swiss cheese
Paprika

Split English muffins; spread cut surfaces of muffin halves with butter. Place muffin halves, cut side up, on a baking sheet. Broil 3 inches from heat (with electric oven door partially opened) 1 minute or until lightly browned.

Divide ham evenly among muffin halves; top evenly with egg slices. Combine sour cream and mayonnaise; spoon mixture evenly over egg slices. Top evenly with cheese, and sprinkle with paprika. Broil 3 inches from heat (with electric oven door partially opened) 1 minute or until cheese melts. Yield: 4 servings.

TEXAS BRUNCH

Need to slice or halve hard-cooked eggs? Here's a tip: roll them over halfway through cooking to help keep the yolk centered.

3 tablespoons butter or margarine
3 tablespoons all-purpose flour
2 cups milk
6 hard-cooked eggs, chopped
½ cup mayonnaise
¼ teaspoon salt
⅛ teaspoon pepper
Buttermilk Cornbread (facing page)
1¼ cups (5 ounces) shredded Cheddar cheese
8 slices bacon, cooked and crumbled
⅓ cup chopped green onions

Melt butter in a heavy saucepan over low heat; add flour, stirring until smooth. Cook, stirring constantly, 1 minute. Gradually add milk; cook over medium heat, stirring constantly, until mixture is thickened and bubbly. Stir in chopped egg and next 3 ingredients; cook, stirring constantly, until mixture is thoroughly heated.

Cut Buttermilk Cornbread into 6 rectangles; remove from pan, and split each rectangle in half horizontally. Cut each half into 2 triangles. Arrange 4 cornbread triangles, cut side up, on each individual plate. Spoon egg mixture evenly over cornbread triangles; sprinkle evenly with cheese, bacon, and green onions. Yield: 6 servings.

Buttermilk Cornbread

1 cup yellow cornmeal
⅓ cup all-purpose flour
1 teaspoon baking powder
¼ teaspoon baking soda

½ teaspoon salt
1 large egg, lightly beaten
1 cup buttermilk

Combine first 5 ingredients in a large bowl; make a well in center of mixture. Combine egg and buttermilk; add to dry ingredients, stirring just until moistened. Spoon batter into a well-greased 8-inch square pan. Bake at 400° for 20 minutes or until golden. Yield: 6 servings.

Wedges of Buttermilk Cornbread add dramatic flair to Texas Brunch, a rich egg dish as tempting for supper as it is on the morning menu.

EGGS SARDOU

Created at Antoine's restaurant in New Orleans and named for the French dramatist Victorien Sardou, Eggs Sardou consists of artichokes topped with poached eggs, Hollandaise sauce, and sometimes ham. Our version is served over a creamy spinach mixture.

3 tablespoons chopped green onions
1 tablespoon butter or margarine, melted
2 (10-ounce) packages frozen chopped spinach, thawed and well drained
1⅓ cups sour cream
⅓ cup grated Parmesan cheese
⅓ cup whipping cream
¼ teaspoon salt
¼ teaspoon ground nutmeg
⅛ teaspoon pepper
3 (14-ounce) cans artichoke bottoms, drained
Poached Eggs
Hollandaise Sauce
Paprika

Cook green onions in butter in a Dutch oven over medium-high heat until tender. Reduce heat to low; stir in spinach and next 6 ingredients. Cook, stirring constantly, until thoroughly heated (do not boil).

Arrange 12 artichoke bottoms on a baking sheet, reserving any extra for another use. Bake at 350° for 5 to 8 minutes or until thoroughly heated.

Spoon spinach mixture evenly onto 6 individual plates; top each with 2 artichoke bottoms. Place 1 Poached Egg on each artichoke bottom. Top evenly with Hollandaise Sauce; sprinkle with paprika. Yield: 6 servings.

Poached Eggs

12 large eggs

Lightly grease a large saucepan; add water to depth of 2 inches. Bring to a boil; reduce heat, and maintain at a simmer. Working with 4 eggs at a time, break eggs, one at a time, into a saucer; slip egg into water. Simmer 5 minutes or to desired degree of doneness. Remove with a slotted spoon; trim edges, if desired. Repeat with remaining eggs. Yield: 12 eggs.

Hollandaise Sauce

4 egg yolks
¼ teaspoon salt
⅛ teaspoon ground red pepper
2½ tablespoons lemon juice
⅔ cup butter or margarine, divided

Combine first 3 ingredients in top of a double boiler; gradually add lemon juice, stirring constantly. Add about 3½ tablespoons butter to egg mixture; cook over hot (not boiling) water, stirring constantly with a wire whisk until butter melts.

Add about 3½ additional tablespoons butter to egg mixture, stirring constantly. As egg mixture thickens, stir in remaining butter. Cook, stirring constantly, until mixture is thickened and temperature reaches 160°. Serve immediately. Yield: 1 cup.

CROISSANT EGGWICHES

4 large eggs, lightly beaten
3 tablespoons milk
¼ teaspoon salt
Dash of pepper
⅓ cup diced cooked ham
1 to 2 tablespoons minced
   green onions

1 tablespoon butter or
   margarine
4 croissants, sliced horizontally
2 (1-ounce) slices process
   American cheese, cut in
   half diagonally

Combine first 4 ingredients; stir with a wire whisk or fork until blended. Stir in ham and green onions. Heat a large nonstick skillet over medium heat until hot enough to sizzle a drop of water. Add butter, and tilt pan to coat bottom. Pour egg mixture into skillet. Cook without stirring until mixture begins to set on bottom. Draw a spatula across bottom of pan to form large curds. Continue cooking until eggs are thickened, but still moist; do not stir constantly.

Spoon egg mixture evenly onto cut surfaces of croissant bottoms; top evenly with cheese and croissant tops. Place sandwiches on a baking sheet; bake at 350° for 8 minutes or until cheese melts and croissants are heated. Yield: 4 servings.

■ ■ ■ ■ ■ ■ ■ ■ ■ ■ □

Scramble eggs until they are set and cooked throughout, but still moist. Remove the skillet from the heat a minute before you think the eggs are completely cooked — the residual heat will continue to cook them.

BREAKFAST TACOS

1 large potato, peeled and cubed
6 (7-inch) flour tortillas
8 slices bacon
4 green onions, sliced
3 large eggs, lightly beaten
¼ cup plus 2 tablespoons half-
 and-half
½ teaspoon Worcestershire
 sauce
¼ teaspoon salt
¼ teaspoon pepper
Sour cream
Picante sauce

Cook potato in boiling salted water to cover 10 to 12 minutes or until tender; drain. Set aside. Wrap tortillas tightly in aluminum foil; bake at 350° for 15 minutes or until heated. Set aside, and keep warm.

Cook bacon in a large skillet until crisp; remove bacon, reserving 2 tablespoons drippings in skillet. Crumble bacon, and set aside. Cook potato and green onions in drippings over medium heat 5 minutes or until potato is browned, stirring frequently. Drain off excess drippings.

Combine eggs and next 4 ingredients; pour over mixture in skillet. Cook over medium heat, stirring gently, until eggs are set. Stir in bacon.

Work with 1 tortilla at a time, keeping remaining tortillas covered and warm. Spoon about one-sixth of egg mixture down center of tortilla. Fold bottom third of tortilla over filling; fold sides in toward center, leaving top open. Repeat procedure with remaining filling and tortillas. Serve with sour cream and picante sauce. Yield: 6 servings.

FAMILY-SIZE POTATO OMELET

6 large eggs, lightly beaten
2 tablespoons water
½ teaspoon salt
2 cups chopped, cooked red
 potato
1 cup chopped onion
½ cup chopped green pepper
¼ cup chopped fresh chives
3 tablespoons vegetable oil
½ teaspoon salt
½ teaspoon coarsely ground
 pepper
Sour cream

Combine first 3 ingredients; stir with a wire whisk or fork until blended. Set aside.

Cook potato and next 3 ingredients in hot oil in a 12-inch nonstick skillet over medium-high heat, stirring constantly, until vegetables are tender and potato is lightly browned. Stir in ½ teaspoon salt and pepper.

Reduce heat to medium; pour egg mixture over vegetable mixture in skillet. As mixture starts to cook, gently lift edges of omelet with a spatula, and tilt pan so uncooked portion flows underneath. Cover and cook 5 to 6 minutes to allow uncooked portion on top to set. Cut into wedges; serve with sour cream. Yield: 4 servings.

PUFFY VEGETABLE OMELET

5 large eggs, separated
2 tablespoons water
¼ teaspoon salt
Dash of ground white pepper
2 tablespoons butter or
   margarine
⅔ cup peeled, chopped avocado

½ teaspoon lemon juice
⅔ cup chopped tomato
⅔ cup alfalfa sprouts
Cheese Sauce
Garnishes: plum tomato slices,
   fresh parsley sprigs

Combine egg yolks and next 3 ingredients; stir with a whisk or fork until blended. Beat egg whites until stiff but not dry; fold into yolk mixture.

Heat an ovenproof 10-inch omelet pan or nonstick skillet over medium heat until hot enough to sizzle a drop of water. Add butter, and tilt pan to coat bottom. Pour egg mixture into skillet, and gently smooth surface. Cook omelet, uncovered, 5 to 7 minutes or until puffy and lightly browned on bottom. Bake, uncovered, at 325° for 12 to 15 minutes or until a knife inserted in center comes out clean.

Loosen omelet with a spatula; gently slide omelet onto a serving plate. Toss chopped avocado with lemon juice. Sprinkle avocado, tomato, and alfalfa sprouts over top of omelet. Pour Cheese Sauce over vegetables. Garnish, if desired. Yield: 4 servings.

Cheese Sauce

1 tablespoon butter or
   margarine
1 tablespoon all-purpose flour
½ cup milk

¼ cup (1 ounce) shredded
   Cheddar cheese
⅛ teaspoon salt
Dash of ground white pepper

Melt butter in a heavy saucepan over low heat; add flour, stirring until smooth. Cook, stirring constantly, 1 minute. Gradually add milk; cook over medium heat, stirring constantly, until thickened and bubbly. Add cheese, salt, and pepper; stir until cheese melts. Yield: ⅔ cup.

■■■■■■■■■□
For a puffy omelet, beat the egg whites and yolks separately, and then fold them together. Cook the mixture briefly on the range, and then bake until the omelets are done. Sprinkle the omelets with toppings and serve flat, or fill and carefully fold them in half.

Treat someone special to a delightful breakfast featuring a Ham and Cheese Omelet and Cloud Biscuits (page 208).

HAM AND CHEESE OMELETS

6 large eggs, lightly beaten
¼ cup chopped green onions
2 tablespoons water
¼ teaspoon salt
Dash of pepper
2 teaspoons butter or
    margarine, divided

½ cup chopped cooked ham,
    divided
3 slices process American
    cheese, cut in half

Combine first 5 ingredients; stir with a wire whisk or fork until blended.

Heat an 8-inch omelet pan or nonstick skillet over medium heat until hot enough to sizzle a drop of water. Add 1 teaspoon butter, and tilt pan to coat bottom. Pour half of egg mixture into skillet. As mixture starts to cook, gently lift edges of omelet with a spatula, and tilt pan so uncooked portion flows underneath. Sprinkle ¼ cup ham over half of omelet; arrange 3 pieces of cheese over ham. Fold omelet in half, and transfer to a serving plate. Repeat procedure with remaining ingredients. Yield: 2 servings.

OMELETS WITH SAUSAGE FILLING

½ pound ground pork sausage
1 cup sliced fresh mushrooms
2 tablespoons butter or
    margarine
2 tablespoons all-purpose flour
¾ cup milk
2 (3-ounce) packages cream
    cheese, cubed

¼ teaspoon salt
⅛ teaspoon pepper
8 large eggs, lightly beaten
3 tablespoons water
½ teaspoon salt
¼ teaspoon pepper
1 tablespoon plus 1 teaspoon
    butter or margarine, divided

Brown sausage in a 10-inch omelet pan or nonstick skillet, stirring until it crumbles; drain, reserving drippings in pan. Pat sausage dry with paper towels.

Cook mushrooms in drippings over medium-high heat, stirring constantly, until tender. Drain and pat dry with paper towels. Wipe drippings from skillet with a paper towel.

Melt 2 tablespoons butter in a heavy saucepan over low heat; add flour, stirring until smooth. Cook, stirring constantly, 1 minute. Gradually add milk; cook over medium heat, stirring constantly, until mixture is thickened and bubbly. Add cream cheese, ¼ teaspoon salt, and ⅛ teaspoon pepper; stir until cream cheese melts. Stir in sausage and mushrooms. Set aside, and keep warm.

Combine eggs and next 3 ingredients; stir with a wire whisk or fork until blended. Heat omelet pan or nonstick skillet over medium heat until hot enough to sizzle a drop of water. Add 2 teaspoons butter, and tilt pan to coat bottom. Pour half of egg mixture into pan. As mixture starts to cook, gently lift edges of omelet with a spatula, and tilt pan so uncooked portion flows underneath.

Spoon half of sausage mixture evenly over half of omelet. Fold omelet in half; transfer to a serving plate. Repeat procedure with remaining ingredients. Serve immediately. Yield: 4 servings.

Omelets cook quickly and should be served immediately. Have the filling ingredients chopped and, if needed, cooked, before adding to the eggs.

BROCCOLI-CHEESE FRITTATA

3 large eggs, lightly beaten
3 tablespoons milk
1/4 teaspoon salt
Dash of ground red pepper
1 (10-ounce) package frozen chopped broccoli, thawed and well drained

1 small onion, finely chopped
1 small clove garlic, crushed
2 tablespoons butter or margarine, melted
1½ cups (6 ounces) shredded Swiss or Cheddar cheese

Combine first 4 ingredients in a small bowl; stir with a wire whisk or fork until blended.

Cook broccoli, onion, and garlic in butter in a 10-inch nonstick skillet over medium heat, stirring constantly, until onion is tender. Remove from heat; stir in egg mixture, and sprinkle with cheese. Cover and cook over low heat 10 minutes or until egg mixture is set. Cut frittata into wedges, and serve immediately. Yield: 4 servings.

HUEVOS RANCHEROS

6 (6-inch) corn tortillas
1 cup chopped onion
1 cup chopped green pepper
2 cloves garlic, minced
3 tablespoons olive oil
1 tablespoon all-purpose flour
2 (16-ounce) cans whole tomatoes, drained and chopped
1 (4.5-ounce) can chopped green chiles

1/4 cup dry white wine
½ teaspoon dried oregano
½ teaspoon ground cumin
½ teaspoon chili powder
1/4 teaspoon salt
1/8 teaspoon pepper
6 large eggs
1 cup (4 ounces) shredded sharp Cheddar cheese
1/4 cup sliced ripe olives

Wrap tortillas tightly in aluminum foil; bake at 350° for 15 minutes or until thoroughly heated. Set aside, and keep warm.

Cook onion, green pepper, and garlic in hot oil in a large skillet over medium heat, stirring constantly, 5 to 10 minutes or until vegetables are tender. Add flour; cook, stirring constantly, 1 minute. Add tomato and next 7 ingredients; stir well. Bring to a boil over medium heat, stirring constantly; cook, uncovered, 10 minutes or until mixture is thickened, stirring frequently.

Line a lightly greased 11- x 7- x 1½-inch baking dish with warm tortillas, letting tortillas extend up sides of dish. Pour tomato mixture into dish; spread evenly over tortillas. Make 6 indentations in tomato mixture using the back of a spoon; carefully break 1 egg into each indentation. Bake, uncovered, at 350° for 20 minutes or just until eggs are set. Sprinkle with cheese and olives; bake 5 additional minutes or until cheese melts. Yield: 6 servings.

The full-bodied flavors of Mexico come your way with Huevos Rancheros, a baked egg casserole.

CHEESY COUNTRY HAM PUFF

3 large eggs, lightly beaten
4 slices white bread, torn into
    bite-size pieces
2 cups milk
½ teaspoon spicy brown
    mustard
⅛ teaspoon paprika
Dash of garlic powder
2 cups (8 ounces) shredded
    Cheddar cheese

1½ cups diced country ham*
½ cup chopped onion
2 tablespoons chopped fresh
    parsley or 2 teaspoons dried
    parsley flakes
4 slices bacon, cooked and
    crumbled

Combine first 6 ingredients in a large bowl; stir with a wire whisk or fork until mixture is almost smooth. Add cheese and remaining ingredients; stir well.

    Pour mixture into a lightly greased 11- x 7- x 1½-inch baking dish. Bake at 375° for 35 to 40 minutes or until puffed and golden. Let stand 10 minutes before serving. Yield: 6 servings.

*Cooked ham may be substituted for country ham.

CHILE 'N' CHEESE BREAKFAST CASSEROLE

■ ■ ■ ■ ■ ■ ■ ■ □
To make Chile 'n' Cheese Breakfast Casserole or Brunch for a Bunch (facing page) ahead of time, prepare as directed, but do not bake. Cover and refrigerate the dish overnight. Remove from the refrigerator, and let stand, covered, 30 minutes; then uncover and bake as directed.

3 English muffins
2 tablespoons butter or
    margarine, softened
1 pound ground pork sausage
1 (4.5-ounce) can chopped green
    chiles, drained

3 cups (12 ounces) shredded
    Cheddar cheese
12 large eggs, lightly beaten
1½ cups sour cream

Split English muffins; spread cut sides of muffin halves with butter. Place muffin halves, cut side down, in a lightly greased 13- x 9- x 2-inch baking dish.

    Brown sausage in a large skillet, stirring until it crumbles; drain. Layer half each of sausage, chiles, and cheese evenly over muffin halves. Combine eggs and sour cream; stir with a wire whisk or fork until blended. Pour egg mixture evenly over cheese. Repeat layers with remaining sausage, chiles, and cheese. Bake at 350° for 40 minutes or until puffed and set. Yield: 8 servings.

Serve the gang Brunch for a Bunch before the big game. Savory sausage, hash browns, eggs, and cheese make up this winning combination.

BRUNCH FOR A BUNCH

1 pound ground hot pork
    sausage
3 cups frozen hash brown
    potatoes, thawed
3 cups (12 ounces) shredded
    Cheddar cheese

½ cup chopped green pepper
12 large eggs, lightly beaten
2 cups milk
½ teaspoon salt
Garnishes: celery leaves, tomato
    wedges, green pepper rings

Brown sausage in a medium skillet, stirring until it crumbles; drain. Place hash browns in a lightly greased shallow 3-quart baking dish. Layer cooked sausage, cheese, and chopped green pepper evenly over hash browns. Combine eggs, milk, and salt in a large bowl, stirring with a wire whisk or fork until blended; pour egg mixture over chopped green pepper layer. Bake at 350° for 50 minutes or until golden. Garnish, if desired. Yield: 8 servings.

SAUSAGE-CHEESE BAKE

1 pound ground pork sausage
¼ cup chopped green pepper
1 (8-ounce) package refrigerated
   crescent rolls
2 cups (8 ounces) shredded
   Monterey Jack cheese

4 large eggs, lightly beaten
¾ cup milk
½ teaspoon dried oregano
¼ teaspoon pepper

Cook sausage and green pepper in a large skillet over medium-high heat until sausage is browned and green pepper is tender, stirring until sausage crumbles. Drain.

Unroll crescent rolls into a lightly greased 13- x 9- x 2-inch baking dish. Press dough ½ inch up sides of dish to form a crust; seal perforations. Sprinkle sausage mixture and cheese evenly over dough.

Combine eggs and remaining ingredients; stir with a wire whisk or fork until blended. Pour egg mixture over cheese. Bake at 400° for 18 to 20 minutes or until golden. Yield: 8 servings.

HAM-AND-EGGS CRESCENT PIZZA

1 (8-ounce) package refrigerated
   crescent rolls
¼ cup chopped onion
1 tablespoon butter or
   margarine, melted
1 cup finely chopped cooked
   ham
1 cup (4 ounces) shredded
   Swiss cheese

4 large eggs, lightly beaten
½ cup milk
1 tablespoon chopped fresh or
   frozen chives
½ teaspoon salt
¼ teaspoon pepper

Unroll crescent rolls into an ungreased 13- x 9- x 2-inch pan. Press dough ½ inch up sides of pan to form a crust; seal perforations. Bake at 375° for 5 minutes on lower rack of oven; set aside.

Cook onion in butter in a small skillet over medium-high heat, stirring constantly, until tender; stir in ham. Spoon mixture evenly over dough; sprinkle with cheese.

Combine eggs and remaining ingredients; stir with a wire whisk or fork until blended. Pour mixture over cheese. Bake at 350° for 25 to 30 minutes or until mixture is set. Serve immediately. Yield: 6 servings.

SWISS ALPINE QUICHE

Pastry for 9-inch pie
1 (10-ounce) package frozen
    chopped broccoli
2 cups cubed cooked ham
2 cups (8 ounces) shredded
    Swiss cheese

3 tablespoons minced onion
3 large eggs, lightly beaten
1½ cups milk
⅛ teaspoon salt
⅛ teaspoon pepper

Line a 9-inch quiche dish with pastry; trim excess pastry around edges. Prick bottom and sides of pastry with a fork. Bake at 400° for 3 minutes; remove from oven, and gently prick with a fork. Bake 5 additional minutes. Set aside.

Cook broccoli according to package directions, omitting salt; drain well. Layer half each of broccoli, ham, and cheese in pastry shell; repeat layers. Sprinkle onion evenly over top.

Combine eggs and remaining ingredients; stir with a wire whisk or fork until blended. Pour over layers in pastry shell. Bake at 450° for 10 minutes. Reduce oven temperature to 325°, and bake 30 minutes or until set and golden. Let stand 10 minutes. Yield: one 9-inch quiche.

If you don't have time to prepare pastry for the crust of Swiss Alpine Quiche or the other quiches that follow, use a refrigerated piecrust.

GREEK SPINACH QUICHE

Pastry for 9-inch pie
3 large eggs, lightly beaten
1 cup milk
¼ cup butter or margarine,
    melted
2 tablespoons all-purpose flour
2 tablespoons grated Romano
    cheese

¼ teaspoon salt
¼ teaspoon ground white
    pepper
Dash of ground nutmeg
1 (10-ounce) package frozen
    chopped spinach, thawed
    and well drained
1 cup crumbled feta cheese

Line a 9-inch quiche dish with pastry; trim excess pastry around edges. Prick bottom and sides of pastry with a fork. Bake at 400° for 3 minutes; remove from oven, and gently prick with a fork. Bake 5 additional minutes. Set aside.

Combine eggs and next 7 ingredients; stir with a wire whisk or fork until blended. Stir in spinach and feta cheese; pour into pastry shell. Bake at 350° for 35 minutes or until quiche is set and golden. Let stand 10 minutes. Yield: one 9-inch quiche.

Press thawed and drained spinach between several layers of paper towels to remove as much excess moisture as possible.

An enticing combination of crabmeat, Swiss cheese, and green onion flavors delectable Crabmeat Quiche.

CRABMEAT QUICHE

Pastry for 9-inch pie
2 large eggs, lightly beaten
½ cup milk
½ cup mayonnaise
2 tablespoons all-purpose flour
2 cups (8 ounces) shredded
   Swiss cheese

⅓ cup chopped green onions
1 (6-ounce) package frozen
   crabmeat, thawed and
   drained
Garnish: small green onion
   bunch

Line a 9-inch quiche dish with pastry; trim excess pastry around edges. Prick bottom and sides of pastry with a fork. Bake at 400° for 3 minutes; remove from oven, and gently prick with a fork. Bake 5 additional minutes. Set aside.

Combine eggs and next 3 ingredients; stir with a wire whisk or fork until blended. Add cheese, chopped green onions, and crabmeat, stirring well. Pour mixture into pastry shell. Bake at 350° for 35 to 40 minutes or until set and golden. Let stand 10 minutes before serving. Garnish, if desired. Yield: one 9-inch quiche.

ARTICHOKE-CHEESE STRATA

½ cup sliced fresh mushrooms
½ cup sliced green onions
1 tablespoon butter or
     margarine, melted
3 slices white bread, cubed
¾ cup (3 ounces) shredded
     sharp Cheddar cheese
1 (14-ounce) can artichoke
     hearts, drained and
     quartered

1 (4-ounce) jar diced pimiento,
     drained
4 large eggs, lightly beaten
1½ cups milk
½ teaspoon dry mustard
¼ teaspoon salt
⅛ teaspoon ground white
     pepper

After a strata is assembled, it should chill at least eight hours to allow the bread to absorb the liquid ingredients. This do-ahead feature makes a strata convenient for breakfast or brunch.

Cook mushrooms and green onions in butter in a small skillet over medium-high heat, stirring constantly, until tender. Layer half each of bread, vegetable mixture, cheese, artichoke hearts, and pimiento in a lightly greased 9-inch quiche dish; repeat layers.

Combine eggs and remaining ingredients; stir with a wire whisk or fork until blended. Pour egg mixture evenly over vegetable layers; cover and chill 8 hours.

Remove from refrigerator; let stand, covered, 30 minutes. Uncover and bake at 350° for 55 to 60 minutes or until set and lightly browned. Let stand 10 minutes before serving. Yield: 6 servings.

CHEDDAR CHEESE SOUFFLÉ

2 tablespoons butter or
   margarine
3 tablespoons all-purpose flour
1 cup milk
1 cup (4 ounces) shredded
   Cheddar cheese

¼ teaspoon paprika
⅛ teaspoon salt
3 large eggs, separated

Lightly grease the bottom of a 1-quart soufflé dish; set aside.

Melt butter in a heavy saucepan over low heat; add flour, stirring until smooth. Cook, stirring constantly, 1 minute. Gradually add milk; cook over medium heat, stirring constantly, until mixture is thickened and bubbly. Add cheese, paprika, and salt, stirring until cheese melts.

Beat egg yolks at medium speed of an electric mixer until thick and pale. Gradually stir about one-fourth of hot mixture into yolks; add to remaining hot mixture, stirring constantly.

Beat egg whites at high speed until stiff peaks form; gently fold one-third of beaten egg whites into hot cheese mixture. Fold in remaining egg whites. Spoon cheese mixture into prepared dish. Bake at 350° for 40 minutes or until soufflé is puffed and golden. Serve immediately. Yield: 3 servings.

CHEESE SOUFFLÉ ROLL

⅓ cup butter or margarine
⅓ cup all-purpose flour
1¼ cups milk
1 cup (4 ounces) shredded
   Cheddar cheese, divided
½ cup grated Parmesan cheese
¾ teaspoon salt
⅛ teaspoon ground red pepper

7 large eggs, separated
¼ teaspoon cream of tartar
2 tablespoons grated Parmesan
   cheese
Spinach-Mushroom Filling
   (facing page)
Fresh spinach leaves
Garnish: cherry tomato wedges

Lightly oil bottom and sides of a 15- x 10- x 1-inch jellyroll pan; line with wax paper, allowing paper to extend beyond ends of pan. Lightly oil wax paper. Set aside.

Melt butter in a heavy saucepan over low heat; add flour, stirring until smooth. Cook, stirring constantly, 1 minute. Gradually add milk;

cook over medium heat, stirring constantly, until mixture is very thick. Add ½ cup Cheddar cheese, ½ cup Parmesan cheese, salt, and pepper, stirring until cheeses melt. Transfer mixture to a large bowl.

Beat egg yolks at high speed of an electric mixer until thick and pale. Gradually stir about one-fourth of hot cheese mixture into egg yolks; add to remaining cheese mixture, stirring well.

Beat egg whites and cream of tartar at high speed until stiff peaks form. Stir a small amount of cheese mixture into beaten egg whites. Gradually fold egg white mixture into remaining cheese mixture.

Spread batter evenly in prepared pan. Bake at 350° for 18 minutes or until puffy and firm in center (do not overcook). Loosen edges of soufflé with a knife blade or metal spatula. Turn soufflé out onto a double layer of wax paper that has been sprinkled with 2 tablespoons Parmesan cheese. Carefully peel wax paper off top of soufflé. Spread soufflé evenly with Spinach-Mushroom Filling. Starting with long side, and using wax paper for support, carefully roll up soufflé, jellyroll fashion.

Carefully slide roll, seam side down, onto a large baking sheet; sprinkle with remaining ½ cup Cheddar cheese. Broil 5½ inches from heat (with electric oven door partially opened) 1 minute or until cheese melts. Carefully transfer roll to a spinach leaf-lined serving platter. Garnish, if desired. Yield: 8 servings.

Spinach-Mushroom Filling

1 (10-ounce) package frozen
   chopped spinach
3 cups chopped fresh
   mushrooms
¼ cup finely chopped green
   onions

2 tablespoons butter or
   margarine, melted
½ cup sour cream
½ teaspoon garlic salt

Cook spinach according to package directions; drain well, pressing between layers of paper towels to remove excess moisture. Set aside.

Cook mushrooms and green onions in butter in a medium skillet over medium-high heat, stirring constantly, until tender; stir in spinach, sour cream, and garlic salt. Cook 3 minutes or until mixture is thoroughly heated. Remove from heat, and keep warm. Yield: 2½ cups.

Salad Sampler

■ For a fresh approach to the "what's-for-dinner?" dilemma, make a salad the focal point of your menu. ■ The addition of protein-rich foods such as seafood, meat, and poultry transforms plain green salads into complete meals. ■ Most of these main-dish salads are simple to prepare and make economical use of leftovers. ■ Consider serving one of our selections when you need to get dinner on the table in a jiffy.

Greek Salad (page 37)

BROILED SALMON SALAD

2 (1-inch-thick) salmon steaks
    (about ¾ pound)
Lemon-and-Herb Dressing
1 medium zucchini
1 medium-size yellow squash
1 medium carrot, scraped
½ large sweet red pepper,
    seeded
1 tablespoon chopped fresh
    cilantro or parsley

2 cups torn fresh spinach
2 cups torn Bibb lettuce
1 medium tomato, cut into
    wedges
1 small avocado, peeled, seeded,
    and sliced
Garnishes: lemon twists, fresh
    cilantro or parsley sprigs

Place salmon steaks in a large heavy-duty, zip-top plastic bag; add
¼ cup Lemon-and-Herb Dressing. Seal bag; marinate in refrigerator
1 hour, turning bag once.

Cut zucchini and next 3 ingredients into thin strips. Combine vegetable strips, chopped cilantro, and ¼ cup Lemon-and-Herb Dressing
in a medium bowl, tossing gently. Set aside.

Remove salmon steaks from marinade, discarding marinade; place on
a lightly greased rack of a broiler pan. Broil 5½ inches from heat (with
electric oven door partially opened) 5 to 6 minutes; turn salmon steaks,
and brush with 2 tablespoons Lemon-and-Herb Dressing. Broil an
additional 4 to 5 minutes or until fish flakes easily when tested with a
fork. Cool slightly.

Arrange spinach, lettuce, and vegetable mixture on individual serv-
ing plates; top with salmon steaks, tomato wedges, and avocado slices.
Garnish, if desired. Serve with remaining Lemon-and-Herb Dressing.
Yield: 2 servings.

Lemon-and-Herb Dressing

¾ cup lemon juice
½ cup vegetable oil
1½ tablespoons sugar
1 teaspoon chopped fresh
    parsley
¾ teaspoon dried basil

¾ teaspoon paprika
½ teaspoon dried tarragon
½ teaspoon seasoned salt
¼ teaspoon minced garlic
⅛ teaspoon pepper

Combine all ingredients in a jar. Cover tightly, and shake vigorously.
Yield: 1⅓ cups.

Peel shrimp, and devein, if desired. Combine shrimp, beans, green pepper, onion, celery, and cilantro in a large bowl, tossing gently. Combine picante sauce and next 4 ingredients in a small bowl; stir with a wire whisk until well blended. Pour picante sauce mixture over shrimp mixture; toss gently to combine. Cover and chill 8 hours.

Arrange shrimp around edge of a lettuce-lined serving platter; spoon bean mixture into center of platter. Yield: 4 servings.

SUPER SEAFOOD SALAD

3 cups water
1 pound unpeeled large fresh
    shrimp
¼ pound fresh lump crabmeat,
    drained
1 (2¼-ounce) can sliced ripe
    olives, drained
1 shallot, minced
½ cup sliced pimiento-stuffed
    olives
½ cup chopped green pepper
¼ cup chopped celery
2½ tablespoons chopped sweet
    pickle

1½ teaspoons minced fresh
    parsley
1 cup commercial Italian salad
    dressing
2 tablespoons walnut oil or
    olive oil
1½ teaspoons lemon juice
Leaf lettuce leaves
½ medium head iceberg lettuce,
    coarsely shredded
2 medium tomatoes, cut into
    wedges

When you need a make-ahead entrée, consider this marinated salad. The marinating time allows the flavors to blend.

Bring water to a boil; add shrimp, and cook 3 to 5 minutes or until shrimp turn pink. Drain well; rinse with cold water. Chill.

Peel shrimp, and devein, if desired. Combine shrimp, crabmeat, and next 7 ingredients in a large bowl, tossing gently. Combine salad dressing, oil, and lemon juice in a small bowl; stir with a wire whisk until well blended. Pour dressing mixture over seafood mixture; toss gently. Cover and chill 8 hours.

Line a serving platter with lettuce leaves; top with shredded lettuce. Spoon seafood mixture over shredded lettuce, using a slotted spoon. Arrange tomato wedges around seafood mixture. Yield: 4 servings.

MEXI-PEA SALAD

2 cups frozen black-eyed peas
1 pound ground chuck
1 cup chopped onion, divided
½ cup chopped green pepper
1 tablespoon chili powder
½ teaspoon salt
⅛ teaspoon pepper
2 avocados, peeled, seeded, and
    chopped
2 medium tomatoes, coarsely
    chopped
1 head iceberg lettuce, torn into
    bite-size pieces
1 (9-ounce) package corn chips
1 (8-ounce) can whole kernel
    corn, drained
1 cup (4 ounces) shredded
    Cheddar cheese
½ cup commercial creamy
    Italian salad dressing
½ cup commercial Thousand
    Island salad dressing

Cook peas according to package directions; drain. Set aside; let cool.

Cook ground chuck, ½ cup onion, and green pepper in a large skillet over medium-high heat, stirring constantly, until meat is browned and vegetables are tender. Drain; stir in chili powder, salt, and pepper. Set aside; let cool.

Combine peas, meat mixture, remaining ½ cup onion, avocado, and next 5 ingredients in a large bowl; toss gently. Combine salad dressings, and pour over salad; toss gently. Serve immediately. Yield: 8 servings.

MEXICAN CHEF'S SALAD

1 pound ground chuck
⅔ cup water
1 (1.25-ounce) package taco
    seasoning mix
8 cups torn iceberg lettuce
1 (16-ounce) can kidney beans,
    rinsed and drained
2 tomatoes, coarsely chopped
1 (2¼-ounce) can sliced ripe
    olives, drained
Guacamole Dressing
½ cup (2 ounces) shredded
    Cheddar cheese
Tortilla chips

Brown ground chuck in a skillet, stirring until it crumbles. Drain; stir in water and taco seasoning mix. Bring mixture to a boil; reduce heat, and simmer, uncovered, 5 minutes or until liquid evaporates, stirring occasionally.

Layer lettuce, beans, meat mixture, tomato, and olives on individual serving plates. Top evenly with Guacamole Dressing, and sprinkle evenly with cheese. Serve with tortilla chips. Yield: 6 servings.

Guacamole Dressing

1 avocado, peeled, seeded, and
  mashed
½ cup sour cream
2 tablespoons commercial
  Italian salad dressing

1 tablespoon lemon juice
1 teaspoon dried onion flakes
¾ teaspoon chili powder
¼ teaspoon salt
¼ teaspoon pepper

Combine all ingredients, stirring until blended. Yield: about 1½ cups.

Mexican Chef's Salad is an updated version of the usual taco salad, featuring a
smooth and creamy guacamole topping.

SALAD BY COMMITTEE

■■■■■■■■■■
This huge salad is a perfect group project. Assign each "committee" member a couple of ingredients to bring to a party, and have a fun time creating the salad.

3 (6½-ounce) jars marinated artichoke hearts, undrained
¾ cup vegetable oil
¾ cup red wine vinegar
1½ teaspoons sugar
¾ teaspoon salt
¾ teaspoon garlic powder
¾ teaspoon dry mustard
¾ teaspoon pepper
½ pound fresh mushrooms, sliced
1 pound cooked roast beef, cubed
1 pound cooked ham, cubed
1 pound cooked chicken, cubed
3 heads iceberg lettuce, torn
2 avocados, peeled, seeded, and chopped
1 pint small cherry tomatoes
1 small purple onion, sliced and separated into rings
1 (2¼-ounce) can sliced ripe olives, drained
2 cups cauliflower flowerets
1 cup sliced, unpeeled cucumber
1 cup sliced radishes
3 large hard-cooked eggs, quartered
1 pound bacon, cooked and crumbled

Drain artichoke hearts, reserving marinade. Chop artichoke hearts, and set aside. Combine artichoke marinade, oil, and next 6 ingredients in a bowl; stir with a wire whisk until well blended. Add chopped artichoke and mushrooms; cover and chill 4 hours, stirring occasionally.

Combine roast beef and next 10 ingredients in a large bowl; toss gently. Pour artichoke mixture over salad; toss gently. Arrange eggs over salad; sprinkle with bacon. Yield: 12 servings.

WESTERN-STYLE BEEF SALAD

6 cups shredded iceberg lettuce
½ pound cooked roast beef, cut into thin strips
1 (8-ounce) package Monterey Jack cheese, cut into thin strips
1 small onion, sliced and separated into rings
2 medium tomatoes, cut into wedges
1 (2¼-ounce) can sliced ripe olives, drained
1 (8-ounce) carton sour cream
½ cup commercial French salad dressing
1 teaspoon chili powder

Place lettuce on a serving platter; arrange roast beef and next 4 ingredients over lettuce. Combine sour cream, salad dressing, and chili powder; stir well, and spoon over salad. Yield: 4 servings.

GREEK SALAD

1 pound lean boneless lamb
1 cup olive oil
1 cup red wine vinegar
3 tablespoons chopped fresh mint
3 tablespoons chopped fresh parsley
1½ tablespoons Dijon mustard
1½ teaspoons dried oregano
½ teaspoon salt
½ teaspoon pepper
½ teaspoon dried rosemary, crushed

¼ pound fresh green beans, cut into ½-inch pieces
1 (14-ounce) can artichoke hearts, drained and halved
1 small purple onion, sliced and separated into rings
½ sweet red pepper, seeded and cut into thin strips
⅓ cup pitted ripe olives, halved
4 cups mixed salad greens
2 medium tomatoes, cut into wedges
½ cup crumbled feta cheese

The lamb helps make this a typical Greek Salad, but you can substitute a one-pound flank steak if you prefer beef.

Place lamb on a lightly greased rack of a broiler pan. Broil 5½ inches from heat (with electric oven door partially opened) 6 minutes on each side or to desired degree of doneness. Cool; thinly slice across grain.

Place lamb in a large heavy-duty, zip-top plastic bag. Combine olive oil and next 8 ingredients; pour over lamb. Seal bag; marinate in refrigerator 5 hours, turning bag occasionally.

Cook beans in boiling water to cover 3 minutes. Plunge in ice water; drain well. Add beans and next 4 ingredients to meat mixture. Seal bag; marinate in refrigerator 3 hours, turning bag occasionally.

Arrange mixed greens on a serving platter; top with meat mixture. Arrange tomato wedges around meat mixture, and sprinkle with feta cheese. Yield: 4 servings.

CHEF'S SALAD

2 cups torn iceberg lettuce
2 cups torn red leaf lettuce
2 cups torn romaine lettuce
¼ cup chopped green onions
4 ounces Swiss cheese, cut into very thin strips

4 (1-ounce) slices cooked ham, cut into very thin strips
4 hard-cooked eggs, coarsely chopped
8 cherry tomatoes, halved

Combine all ingredients in a large bowl, tossing gently. Serve with commercial salad dressing. Yield: 4 servings.

SPICY ITALIAN HAM SALAD

Prosciutto is a spiced Italian-style ham that has been salt-cured and air-dried. Available in most delis cut in paper-thin slices, it is best eaten as is — prolonged cooking may toughen it.

½ cup vegetable oil
½ cup red wine vinegar
¼ cup water
½ pound thinly sliced black-peppered ham, cut into thin strips
½ pound thinly sliced prosciutto, cut into thin strips
4 pickled hot cherry peppers, seeded and chopped
2 stalks celery, diagonally sliced

1 medium-size green pepper, seeded and cut into thin strips
½ medium-size purple onion, thinly sliced and separated into rings
1 head Boston lettuce, torn into bite-size pieces
1 teaspoon chopped fresh oregano
Garnish: pickled hot cherry peppers

Combine first 3 ingredients in a jar. Cover tightly, and shake vigorously. Set aside.

Combine ham and next 5 ingredients in a large bowl, tossing to combine. Place lettuce evenly on 4 serving plates; top evenly with ham mixture. Shake vinegar mixture vigorously, and pour evenly over salads; sprinkle evenly with chopped oregano. Garnish, if desired. Yield: 4 servings.

LAYERED ANTIPASTO SALAD

2 (6½-ounce) jars marinated artichoke hearts, undrained
3 tablespoons olive oil
2 tablespoons white wine vinegar
1 clove garlic, minced
6 cups torn romaine lettuce
4 medium tomatoes, cut into wedges
1 (3½-ounce) package sliced pepperoni

8 ounces mozzarella cheese, cut into thin strips
½ cup whole pitted ripe olives
1 small purple onion, sliced and separated into rings
8 pickled banana peppers
4 slices bacon, cooked and crumbled
Garnish: sliced ripe olives

Drain artichoke hearts, reserving marinade; set artichoke hearts aside. Combine marinade, olive oil, vinegar, and garlic in a jar. Cover tightly, and shake vigorously. Set aside.

Layer one-third of lettuce and half of tomato in a 4-quart bowl; top with artichoke hearts and pepperoni. Layer with one-third of lettuce, cheese, whole olives, and onion; drizzle with half of vinegar mixture. Top with remaining third of lettuce, remaining half of tomato, and banana peppers. Drizzle with remaining half of vinegar mixture. Cover and chill at least 3 hours. Just before serving, sprinkle with bacon, and garnish, if desired. Yield: 8 servings.

Arrange Layered Antipasto Salad in your prettiest glass bowl for a dish that looks as sensational as it tastes.

PLENTIFUL P'S SALAD

■■■■■■■■■■
Plentiful P's Salad gets its name from the abundance of ingredients that begin with the letter P in this recipe.

4 cups canned, drained black-eyed peas
2 cups cooked rotelle macaroni
2 tablespoons minced fresh parsley
1 medium-size green pepper, seeded and chopped
1 medium-size sweet red pepper, seeded and chopped
1 medium-size purple onion, chopped
1 (6-ounce) package sliced provolone cheese, cut into strips

1 (4½-ounce) jar sliced mushrooms, drained
1 (3½-ounce) package sliced pepperoni, cut into strips
1 (2-ounce) jar diced pimiento, drained
1 (0.7-ounce) package Italian salad dressing mix
½ cup white vinegar
¼ cup sugar
¼ cup vegetable oil
¼ teaspoon pepper

Combine first 10 ingredients in a large bowl. Combine dressing mix and remaining ingredients in a jar. Cover tightly, and shake vigorously; pour over pea mixture. Toss gently. Cover and chill. Yield: 8 servings.

ITALIAN PASTA SALAD

6 ounces spaghetti, uncooked
1 (6-ounce) jar marinated artichoke hearts, undrained
1½ cups (6 ounces) shredded part-skim mozzarella cheese
¾ cup sliced zucchini
¾ cup shredded carrot
3 tablespoons grated Parmesan cheese

4 ounces sliced salami, cut into strips
3 tablespoons vegetable oil
3 tablespoons white vinegar
1 teaspoon dry mustard
¾ teaspoon dried oregano
¾ teaspoon dried basil
1 clove garlic, crushed

Break spaghetti in half; cook according to package directions, omitting salt. Drain. Rinse with cold water; drain. Drain artichoke hearts, reserving marinade. Chop artichoke hearts. Combine spaghetti, artichoke hearts, mozzarella, and next 4 ingredients in a large bowl; toss gently.

Combine artichoke marinade, oil, and remaining ingredients in a jar. Cover tightly, and shake vigorously. Pour over spaghetti mixture, and toss gently. Cover and chill 2 to 3 hours. Yield: 5 servings.

BEAN AND SAUSAGE SALAD

1 pound fresh spinach
1 pound kielbasa, sliced
1 large onion, chopped
2 cloves garlic, minced
2 tablespoons olive oil
2 (15-ounce) cans cannelloni
  beans or white beans, rinsed
  and drained

2 (2¼-ounce) cans sliced ripe
  olives, drained
1 (7.95-ounce) jar roasted red
  peppers, drained and
  chopped
¼ cup red wine vinegar
1 teaspoon hot sauce
½ teaspoon dried oregano

Remove stems from spinach; wash leaves thoroughly, and pat dry. Tear leaves into bite-size pieces. Set aside.

Cook kielbasa, onion, and garlic in hot olive oil in a Dutch oven over medium-high heat 5 minutes; drain. Add beans and remaining ingredients; stir well.

Arrange spinach on individual serving plates, and top evenly with sausage mixture. Yield: 6 servings.

Kielbasa, or Polish sausage, is usually made of pork, but sometimes contains beef. Although kielbasa has been cooked prior to packaging, the flavor improves when the sausage is heated, as we've done in Bean and Sausage Salad.

HEARTY SPINACH SALAD

1 pound fresh spinach
½ cup chopped green onions
3 large hard-cooked eggs, cut
  into wedges
2 medium tomatoes, cut into
  wedges
1 medium avocado, peeled,
  seeded, and sliced
1 cup (4 ounces) shredded
  mozzarella cheese

6 slices bacon, cooked and
  crumbled
½ cup ketchup
¼ cup vegetable oil
¼ cup red wine vinegar
1 teaspoon Worcestershire
  sauce
½ teaspoon lemon juice
⅛ teaspoon garlic powder
Dash of hot sauce

Remove stems from spinach; wash leaves thoroughly, and pat dry. Tear leaves into bite-size pieces. Place spinach on individual serving plates or a large serving platter. Arrange green onions, egg, tomato, and avocado evenly over spinach; sprinkle evenly with cheese and bacon.

Combine ketchup and remaining ingredients in a jar. Cover tightly, and shake vigorously. Serve dressing with salad. Yield: 6 servings.

Cool off a hot summer day with a relaxing lunch featuring Curried Chicken-Rice Salad accompanied by fresh fruit.

CURRIED CHICKEN-RICE SALAD

4 skinned chicken breast halves
½ teaspoon salt
1½ cups cooked long-grain rice
1 cup chopped celery
1 cup seedless green grapes, halved
½ cup chopped pecans, toasted
⅓ cup sweet pickle relish
¾ cup mayonnaise or salad dressing

1 teaspoon curry powder
½ teaspoon salt
¼ teaspoon pepper
Bibb lettuce leaves
1 pint fresh strawberries
1 fresh pineapple, cut into small, thin triangles
Garnish: celery leaves

Combine chicken and ½ teaspoon salt in a Dutch oven; add water to cover. Bring to a boil; cover, reduce heat, and simmer 30 minutes or until chicken is tender. Remove chicken from broth; let cool. Reserve broth for another use, if desired. Bone chicken, and cut meat into bite-size pieces.

Combine chicken, rice, and next 4 ingredients in a large bowl; toss gently. Combine mayonnaise and next 3 ingredients; add to chicken mixture, stirring gently. Spoon chicken mixture evenly onto individual lettuce-lined plates; arrange strawberries and pineapple evenly around chicken mixture. Garnish, if desired. Yield: 6 servings.

CHICKEN AND TORTELLINI SALAD

1 pound skinned, boned chicken breast halves, cubed
2 cloves garlic, minced
2 tablespoons olive oil, divided
1 (8-ounce) package fresh cheese-filled spinach tortellini, uncooked
6 ounces smoked Gouda cheese, cut into strips
3 stalks celery, sliced
1 medium-size sweet red pepper, seeded and cut into strips

½ small purple onion, cut into strips
½ cup olive oil
½ cup cider vinegar
1½ tablespoons honey
1½ tablespoons Dijon mustard
6 slices Canadian bacon, cut into strips

Cook chicken and garlic in 1 tablespoon hot olive oil in a medium skillet over medium-high heat, stirring constantly, until chicken is done. Remove from heat, and set aside.

Prepare tortellini according to package directions; drain. Combine cooked tortellini and 1 tablespoon olive oil in a large bowl; toss well. Add chicken, cheese, celery, red pepper, and onion; toss mixture well.

Combine ½ cup olive oil and next 3 ingredients in a jar. Cover tightly, and shake vigorously. Pour dressing mixture over tortellini mixture; toss well. Cover and chill thoroughly. To serve, add Canadian bacon to salad mixture; toss well. Yield: 6 servings.

ORIENTAL CHICKEN SALAD

■■■■■■■■■■■

If fresh snow peas aren't available, you can substitute one 6-ounce package of frozen snow peas. Let them thaw before tossing them into the salad.

1½ pounds skinned, boned chicken breasts halves, cut into bite-size pieces
⅔ cup vegetable oil
¼ cup lemon juice
¼ cup soy sauce
3 tablespoons rice wine vinegar
½ teaspoon salt
¼ teaspoon ground ginger
¼ teaspoon pepper
1 clove garlic, minced

1 tablespoon vegetable oil
½ pound fresh snow pea pods, trimmed
4 green onions, cut into 1-inch pieces
1 sweet red pepper, seeded and cut into 1-inch strips
⅔ cup fresh bean sprouts
2 cups torn fresh spinach
2 (5-ounce) cans chow mein noodles

Place chicken in a large heavy-duty, zip-top plastic bag. Combine ⅔ cup oil and next 7 ingredients in a jar. Cover tightly, and shake vigorously. Pour half of oil mixture over chicken; reserve remaining half of mixture. Seal bag; marinate in refrigerator 1 hour, turning bag once.

Remove chicken from marinade, discarding marinade. Cook chicken in 1 tablespoon hot oil in a large skillet over medium-high heat, stirring constantly, 5 minutes or until chicken is done. Drain. Combine chicken, reserved half of oil mixture, snow peas, and next 3 ingredients; cover and chill 2 hours.

Combine chicken mixture and spinach in a large bowl; toss well. Spoon mixture over chow mein noodles using a slotted spoon; serve immediately. Yield: 6 servings.

ASPARAGUS-CHICKEN SALAD

■■■■■■■■■■■

Select a bundle of firm, bright green asparagus spears that are approximately the same size and thickness to ensure even cooking.

1 pound fresh asparagus
3 cups torn iceberg lettuce
1½ cups chopped cooked chicken
¼ cup slivered almonds, toasted
¼ cup chopped fresh parsley
3 tablespoons raisins

1 medium-size Red Delicious apple, unpeeled and cut into ½-inch pieces
Leaf lettuce leaves (optional)
Creamy Blue Cheese Dressing
Garnish: apple slices

Snap off tough ends of asparagus. Remove scales with a knife or vegetable peeler, if desired. Arrange asparagus in a vegetable steamer over boiling water; cover and steam 4 to 6 minutes or until crisp-tender.

Plunge asparagus into ice water to stop the cooking process; drain. Cut asparagus into 1½-inch pieces.

Combine asparagus, torn lettuce, and next 5 ingredients; toss gently. Spoon mixture into a lettuce-lined bowl, if desired. Serve with Creamy Blue Cheese Dressing. Garnish, if desired. Yield: 4 servings.

Creamy Blue Cheese Dressing

¾ cup sour cream
¼ cup crumbled blue cheese
1 tablespoon lemon juice

¼ teaspoon garlic powder
Freshly ground pepper

Combine all ingredients in a small bowl; stir well. Yield: 1 cup.

MEXICAN CHICKEN SALAD

4 cups chopped cooked chicken
2 cups (8 ounces) shredded
    sharp Cheddar cheese
2 tablespoons chopped green
    pepper
2 tablespoons chopped sweet
    red pepper
1 (16-ounce) can red kidney
    beans, rinsed and drained
1 (4.5-ounce) can chopped green
    chiles, drained
1 (2¼-ounce) can sliced ripe
    olives, drained

1 medium onion, chopped
½ cup sour cream
½ cup mayonnaise or salad
    dressing
1 (1.25-ounce) package taco
    seasoning mix
2 medium avocados, peeled,
    seeded, and coarsely
    chopped
Shredded iceberg lettuce
2 medium tomatoes, coarsely
    chopped
Corn chips

Combine first 8 ingredients in a large bowl; toss well. Set aside.

Combine sour cream, mayonnaise, and taco seasoning mix; stir well, and pour over chicken mixture. Toss gently; cover and chill.

Gently stir avocado into chicken mixture. Place lettuce on a large serving platter; spoon chicken mixture onto lettuce. Top with tomato and corn chips. Serve immediately. Yield: 10 servings.

CHUTNEY CHICKEN SALAD

4½ cups chopped cooked
  chicken
¾ cup mayonnaise or salad
  dressing
½ cup commercial chutney

1 tablespoon lime juice
1½ teaspoons curry powder
¼ teaspoon salt
1½ cups sliced almonds, toasted
Leaf lettuce leaves (optional)

Combine first 6 ingredients; cover and chill. Just before serving, stir in almonds; spoon into a lettuce-lined bowl, if desired. Yield: 4 servings.

FRIED CHICKEN GINGER SALAD

1 carrot, scraped and cut into
  thin strips
½ cup fresh Sugar Snap peas,
  cut in half diagonally
½ pound frozen breaded
  chicken nuggets

4 cups mixed salad greens
Ginger Dressing
½ cup shredded red cabbage
½ cup sliced fresh mushrooms
1 tablespoon sliced almonds,
  toasted

Cook carrot and peas in boiling water to cover 1 minute; drain. Plunge into ice water; drain and set aside. Fry or bake chicken nuggets according to package directions. Drain on paper towels; set aside.

Combine greens and 2 tablespoons Ginger Dressing; arrange mixture on 2 serving plates. Combine carrot mixture, cabbage, mushrooms, and 2 tablespoons Ginger Dressing; arrange evenly over greens. Top evenly with chicken, and sprinkle evenly with almonds. Serve with remaining Ginger Dressing. Yield: 2 servings.

Ginger Dressing

¼ cup peanut oil
¼ cup rice wine vinegar
¼ cup soy sauce
¼ cup hoisin sauce
1 to 2 tablespoons peeled,
  grated fresh ginger

½ teaspoon sugar
½ teaspoon dry mustard
¼ teaspoon Chinese five-spice
  powder
¼ teaspoon minced garlic
¼ teaspoon chili oil

Combine all ingredients in a jar. Cover tightly, and shake vigorously. Let mixture stand at room temperature 2 hours. Pour mixture through a fine wire-mesh strainer into a small bowl, discarding ginger and garlic. Yield: 1 cup.

Note: Hoisin sauce and chili oil can be found in the ethnic foods section of most large supermarkets.

The secret to the intense Oriental flavor of Fried Chicken Ginger Salad lies in several spicy ingredients in the dressing.

Turn a traditional side salad into a main dish with Grilled Turkey Caesar Salad.

GRILLED TURKEY CAESAR SALAD

4 (¾-inch) slices French bread
¼ cup butter or margarine, melted
1 pound turkey cutlets
¼ teaspoon salt
¼ teaspoon freshly ground pepper
2 cloves garlic
1½ teaspoons anchovy paste
¼ cup olive oil

2 teaspoons lemon juice
2 teaspoons Worcestershire sauce
2 teaspoons Dijon mustard
1 large head romaine lettuce, torn (about 1½ pounds)
½ cup freshly grated Parmesan cheese
Freshly ground pepper

Cut bread into ¾-inch cubes. Cook bread cubes in butter in a medium skillet over medium heat until lightly browned, stirring frequently. Drain on paper towels.

Sprinkle turkey cutlets evenly with salt and ¼ teaspoon pepper. Grill cutlets, covered, over medium coals (300° to 350°) 3 minutes on each side or until done. Remove cutlets from grill, and let cool 5 minutes. Slice cutlets diagonally across grain into thin slices.

Press garlic into a large salad bowl, using a garlic press. Add anchovy paste; mash with the back of a spoon to combine. Add olive oil and next 3 ingredients; stir with a wire whisk until well blended. Add sliced turkey; toss to coat. Add lettuce, Parmesan cheese, and bread cubes; toss gently. Sprinkle with freshly ground pepper. Serve immediately. Yield: 4 servings.

PRIMAVERA SALAD

1 (12-ounce) package bow tie
    pasta, uncooked
Versatile Vinaigrette
1 pound fresh broccoli
1 (10-ounce) package fresh
    spinach
1 pound smoked turkey breast,
    cut into thin strips

1 pint cherry tomatoes, halved
½ cup chopped fresh basil
⅓ cup pine nuts, toasted
¼ cup chopped fresh parsley

Cook pasta according to package directions; drain. Rinse with cold water; drain. Combine pasta and Versatile Vinaigrette in a large heavy-duty, zip-top plastic bag. Seal bag; shake gently. Chill at least 2 hours.

Remove broccoli leaves, and cut off tough ends of stalks; discard. Wash broccoli thoroughly, and cut into 1-inch pieces. Cook broccoli in boiling water to cover 1 minute; drain immediately, and plunge into ice water. Drain and pat dry with paper towels; chill.

Remove stems from spinach; wash leaves thoroughly, and pat dry. Tear spinach leaves into bite-size pieces. Combine spinach, pasta mixture, broccoli, turkey, and remaining ingredients in a very large bowl; toss gently. Yield: 10 servings.

Versatile Vinaigrette

⅔ cup vegetable oil
¼ cup white wine vinegar
¼ cup water
1 tablespoon freshly ground
    pepper

1½ teaspoons salt
1 clove garlic, pressed

Combine all ingredients in a jar. Cover tightly, and shake vigorously. Yield: 1 cup.

Sandwich Sensations

■ You won't find any humdrum sandwiches in this chapter. BLT Croissant Sandwiches, Calzones with Herbed Tomato Sauce, and Peppery Chicken Pitas will satisfy your craving for the out-of-the-ordinary. ■ You'll also find many traditional favorites: Grilled Reubens, Curried Chicken Salad in a Pocket, and Hot Brown Sandwiches, just to name a few. ■ Sandwiches are fun to serve, especially during the summer when dining tends to be more relaxed. ■ And for those cold winter months, hot hearty sandwiches make a satisfying supper.

Oyster-Bacon Po' Boys (page 53)

Grilled Amberjack Sandwiches

4 (³/₄-inch-thick) amberjack
    fillets (about 1½ pounds)
Lemon-Soy Marinade
Vegetable cooking spray
⅓ cup tartar sauce

1½ tablespoons capers
4 whole wheat buns, split and
    toasted
4 leaf lettuce leaves
4 tomato slices

Place fish in a shallow dish; pour Lemon-Soy Marinade over fish. Cover and marinate in refrigerator 1 hour, turning once. Remove fish from marinade; place marinade in a saucepan. Bring to a boil; remove from heat. Coat a grill basket with cooking spray; place fish in basket. Grill, covered, over medium coals (300° to 350°) 8 minutes on each side or until fish flakes easily with a fork, basting occasionally with marinade.

Combine tartar sauce and capers; stir well. Layer bottom halves of buns evenly with lettuce, tomato, tartar sauce mixture, and fish; cover with tops of buns. Yield: 4 servings.

Lemon-Soy Marinade

¼ cup fresh lemon juice
2 tablespoons soy sauce
¼ teaspoon garlic powder

¼ teaspoon pepper
¼ teaspoon hot sauce
¼ cup olive oil

Combine first 5 ingredients in container of an electric blender; cover. With blender running, add oil in a slow, steady stream. Yield: ⅔ cup.

Hot Tuna Salad Rolls

1 (12¼-ounce) can solid white
    tuna packed in water,
    drained and flaked
1 cup chopped celery
1 cup frozen English peas,
    thawed and drained
1 cup (4 ounces) shredded
    Swiss cheese

¾ cup mayonnaise
¼ cup chopped fresh parsley
6 (6-inch) French bread rolls
¼ cup butter or margarine,
    melted
1 lemon, cut into 6 wedges
    (optional)

Combine first 6 ingredients; stir well. Cut a thin slice from top of each roll; set tops aside. Hollow out rolls, leaving ½-inch-thick shells. Brush inside of bread shells with butter; fill evenly with tuna mixture, and cover with tops.

Wrap each roll separately in aluminum foil; place on a baking sheet. Bake at 400° for 20 minutes or until thoroughly heated. Skewer lemon wedges on wooden picks, if desired. Remove rolls from foil, and secure rolls with wooden picks. Yield: 6 servings.

OYSTER-BACON PO' BOYS

8 slices bacon
⅓ cup chopped onion
¼ cup chopped green pepper
¼ cup chopped celery
1 tomato, seeded and chopped
2 tablespoons chopped fresh parsley
1 teaspoon garlic powder
½ teaspoon seasoned salt
⅓ cup mayonnaise or salad dressing
¼ teaspoon hot sauce

1 cup cracker meal*
½ cup cornmeal
¼ teaspoon seasoned salt
⅛ teaspoon pepper
1 (12-ounce) container fresh Select oysters, drained
2 large eggs, lightly beaten
Vegetable oil
4 (6-inch) French bread rolls, split horizontally and toasted
Leaf lettuce leaves

A variation of this oyster loaf originated as the famous "peacemaker" in New Orleans. The story goes that a husband who was detained downtown would make peace with his wife by bringing home one of these specialties— plump fried oysters nestled in a loaf of French bread.

Cook bacon in a large skillet until crisp; remove bacon, reserving 1 tablespoon drippings in skillet. Set bacon aside.

Cook onion, green pepper, and celery in drippings, stirring constantly, until tender. Stir in tomato and next 3 ingredients. Drain well, and transfer to a bowl. Stir in mayonnaise and hot sauce; set aside.

Combine cracker meal, cornmeal, ¼ teaspoon seasoned salt, and pepper in a medium bowl. Dip oysters in egg; dredge in cornmeal mixture. Pour oil to depth of 2 inches into a Dutch oven; heat to 375°. Fry oysters in batches 1½ to 2 minutes or until golden, turning once. Drain on paper towels.

Spread mayonnaise mixture evenly on cut surfaces of roll halves. Arrange bacon, lettuce, and oysters evenly on bottom halves of rolls; cover with top halves. Yield: 4 servings.

* As a substitute for cracker meal, process saltine crackers in a food processor until finely ground.

To enjoy Grilled Reubens at their best, serve them hot off the griddle.

GRILLED REUBENS

1 (16-ounce) bottle Thousand
    Island salad dressing
18 slices rye bread
12 slices Swiss cheese
2 cups canned sauerkraut,
    drained

2 pounds corned beef, thinly
    sliced
Softened butter or margarine
Pimiento-stuffed olives
    (optional)

Spread 1⅓ cups salad dressing evenly on one side of 12 bread slices. Layer 1 cheese slice, 2 heaping tablespoons sauerkraut, and about 4 slices corned beef over each prepared bread slice. Stack bread to make 6 (2-layer) sandwiches. Spread one side of each of remaining 6 slices with remaining dressing, and place, dressing side down, on sandwiches.

Spread butter over top of each sandwich. Place sandwiches, buttered side down, on a moderately hot griddle or skillet; cook until bread is golden. Spread butter on ungrilled side of sandwiches; turn carefully, and cook until bread is golden. Skewer olives on wooden picks, if desired, and secure sandwiches with wooden picks. Serve immediately. Yield: 6 servings.

BIG WHEEL SANDWICH LOAF

1 (8- to 9-inch) round loaf
   sourdough bread (1 pound)
2 teaspoons prepared
   horseradish
1/4 pound thinly sliced cooked
   roast beef
2 tablespoons mayonnaise or
   salad dressing
4 slices Swiss cheese
2 tablespoons prepared mustard
1/4 pound thinly sliced cooked
   ham

1 medium tomato, thinly sliced
4 slices bacon, cooked
4 slices process American
   cheese
1/2 medium-size purple onion,
   thinly sliced
1/4 cup butter or margarine,
   softened
1 tablespoon sesame seeds,
   toasted
1/2 teaspoon onion salt

Slice bread horizontally into 6 equal layers, using an electric or serrated knife. Spread cut surface of first bread layer with horseradish; top with roast beef and second bread layer.

Spread second bread layer with mayonnaise; top with Swiss cheese and third bread layer. Spread third bread layer with mustard; top with ham and fourth bread layer.

Top fourth bread layer with tomato slices, bacon, and fifth bread layer. Top fifth bread layer with American cheese, onion slices, and sixth bread layer.

Combine butter, sesame seeds, and onion salt; stir well. Spread butter mixture over top and sides of entire loaf. Wrap loaf in aluminum foil, and place on a baking sheet. Bake at 400° for 25 to 30 minutes or until loaf is thoroughly heated. To serve, slice loaf into wedges using an electric or serrated knife. Yield: 8 servings.

HEARTY ROAST BEEF SANDWICHES

⅓ cup sour cream
2 tablespoons Dijon mustard
2 teaspoons prepared
 horseradish
4 (6-inch) French rolls, split
 horizontally

1 pound thinly sliced cooked
 roast beef
4 slices provolone cheese,
 halved
1 cup alfalfa sprouts

Combine first 3 ingredients; stir well. Spread sour cream mixture on cut surfaces of rolls. Layer roast beef and cheese evenly on bottom halves of rolls; cover with top halves. Wrap sandwiches in aluminum foil, and place on a baking sheet. Bake at 350° for 25 minutes or until sandwiches are thoroughly heated.

Remove roll tops, and arrange alfalfa sprouts evenly over roast beef; replace roll tops. To serve, cut each sandwich in half crosswise. Serve immediately. Yield: 4 servings.

TACO PITAS

1 pound ground chuck
1 (10-ounce) can tomatoes and
 green chiles, drained
1 (7-ounce) can whole kernel
 corn, drained
1 (1.25-ounce) package taco
 seasoning mix

¾ cup water
5 (6-inch) pita bread rounds
1 cup shredded iceberg lettuce
¾ cup (3 ounces) shredded
 Cheddar cheese

Brown ground chuck in a large skillet, stirring until it crumbles; drain. Stir in tomatoes and green chiles, corn, taco seasoning mix, and water. Bring to a boil; reduce heat, and simmer, uncovered, 15 minutes, stirring occasionally.

Cut pita bread rounds in half crosswise, and place on a 12-inch round glass platter; cover with paper towels. Microwave at HIGH 15 to 20 seconds or until bread is warm and pliable, giving platter a half-turn after 10 seconds.

Fill each pita pocket about half full with meat mixture; top evenly with lettuce and cheese. Serve immediately. Yield: 5 servings.

Lamb Pockets with Cucumber Topping

½ cup plain low-fat yogurt
¾ teaspoon minced fresh
   dill or ¼ teaspoon dried
   dillweed
¼ teaspoon seasoned salt
1 medium cucumber, thinly
   sliced
1½ cups chopped tomato
½ cup sliced green onions

1 pound lean ground lamb
¼ cup chopped onion
2 cloves garlic, minced
½ teaspoon salt
¼ teaspoon pepper
4 (6-inch) whole wheat pita
   bread rounds
8 leaf lettuce leaves

Combine first 3 ingredients in a small bowl, stirring well. Stir in cucumber slices. Cover and chill. Combine tomato and green onions; set aside.

Cook lamb, chopped onion, and garlic in a skillet over medium-high heat until meat is browned and onion is tender, stirring until meat crumbles; drain. Stir in ½ teaspoon salt and pepper.

Cut pita bread rounds in half crosswise, and place on a 12-inch round glass platter; cover with paper towels. Microwave at HIGH 15 to 20 seconds or until bread is warm and pliable, giving platter a half-turn after 10 seconds.

Line each pita pocket with a lettuce leaf; spoon meat mixture evenly into pockets. Top evenly with cucumber mixture and tomato mixture. Serve immediately. Yield: 4 servings.

Sloppy Dogs

½ pound ground chuck
1 cup chopped onion
2 (8-ounce) cans tomato sauce
1 teaspoon chili powder
1 teaspoon steak sauce
⅛ teaspoon salt

⅛ teaspoon ground cumin
8 frankfurters, cooked
8 hot dog buns
Chopped onion (optional)
Shredded Cheddar cheese
   (optional)

Try grilling the frankfurters for Sloppy Dogs—they'll have more flavor.

Cook ground chuck and 1 cup onion in a large skillet over medium-high heat until meat is browned and onion is tender, stirring until meat crumbles; drain. Stir in tomato sauce and next 4 ingredients. Bring to a boil; reduce heat, and simmer, uncovered, 15 minutes, stirring occasionally.

Spoon beef mixture evenly over frankfurters in buns. If desired, sprinkle with additional chopped onion and cheese. Yield: 8 servings.

GRILLED BACON-SWISS SANDWICHES

■ ■ ■ ■ ■ ■ ■ ■ ■ ■

When you make either of
these sandwiches that
spotlight bacon, pour off
the drippings as the
bacon cooks to make it
crisper and to help
reduce spatters.

½ cup (2 ounces) shredded
    Swiss cheese
2 tablespoons butter or
    margarine, softened
⅔ cup sliced fresh mushrooms
1 teaspoon butter or
    margarine, melted
8 slices sandwich bread

12 slices bacon, cooked and
    crumbled
3 large eggs, lightly beaten
⅓ cup milk
2 tablespoons butter or
    margarine, melted and
    divided

Combine cheese and 2 tablespoons softened butter in a small bowl; stir well, and set aside.

Cook mushrooms in 1 teaspoon butter in a small skillet over medium-high heat, stirring constantly, until tender; drain.

Spread cheese mixture evenly on one side of 4 bread slices, leaving a ½-inch margin around edges of bread; sprinkle evenly with mushrooms and bacon. Top with remaining bread slices; press gently to make sandwiches hold together.

Combine eggs and milk; carefully dip sandwiches into egg mixture. Cook 2 sandwiches in 1 tablespoon melted butter in a large skillet over medium heat 2 minutes on each side or until golden and cheese is melted. Repeat procedure with remaining 2 sandwiches and remaining 1 tablespoon melted butter. Serve immediately. Yield: 4 servings.

BLT CROISSANT SANDWICHES

1 (3-ounce) package cream
    cheese, softened
1 (3-ounce) package goat
    cheese, softened
¼ cup chopped commercial
    oil-packed dried tomatoes

1 teaspoon dried basil
6 large croissants, split
    horizontally
12 slices bacon, cooked
3 plum tomatoes, sliced
6 Bibb or red leaf lettuce leaves

Combine cream cheese and goat cheese, stirring until smooth; stir in chopped tomato and basil. Cover and chill 8 hours, if desired, to develop stronger flavor. Let mixture stand at room temperature to soften slightly before spreading on bread.

Spread cheese mixture evenly over cut surfaces of croissant halves. Place croissant halves, cheese side up, on an ungreased baking sheet.

Bake, uncovered, at 325° for 5 to 7 minutes or until cheese mixture is thoroughly heated. Place 2 strips bacon on bottom half of each croissant; top evenly with tomato slices, lettuce leaves, and croissant tops. Serve immediately. Yield: 6 servings.

BLT Croissant Sandwich features a tangy spread of goat cheese blended with cream cheese, sun-dried tomatoes, and basil.

THE GRINDER

1 medium-size green pepper,
   seeded and cut into rings
1 clove garlic, minced
3 tablespoons olive oil
½ teaspoon onion salt
½ pound thinly sliced cooked
   ham

2 small tomatoes, thinly sliced
1 (16-ounce) loaf French bread,
   split horizontally
½ teaspoon dried oregano
2 cups (8 ounces) shredded
   part-skim mozzarella
   cheese

Cook pepper rings and garlic in hot oil in a skillet over medium-high heat, stirring constantly, until pepper rings are crisp-tender; sprinkle with onion salt. Remove pepper rings, reserving oil mixture; drain pepper rings on paper towels.

Layer ham, tomato slices, and pepper rings on bottom half of loaf. Drizzle with reserved oil mixture; sprinkle with oregano and cheese. Cover with top half of loaf.

Wrap loaf in aluminum foil; place on a baking sheet. Bake at 350° for 35 minutes or until loaf is thoroughly heated. To serve, cut into slices. Yield: 6 servings.

The Grinder makes a generous meal for six people. Have several ready for a casual gathering of friends.

HAM AND CHEESE MELTS

½ cup butter or margarine,
  softened
1 tablespoon poppy seeds
2 tablespoons minced onion
2 tablespoons Dijon mustard

8 hamburger buns
1 pound thinly sliced cooked
  ham
8 slices Swiss cheese

Ham and Cheese Melts may be wrapped and frozen up to one month before baking. Thaw the sandwiches in the refrigerator overnight, and bake them as directed.

~~mbine~~ first 4 ingredients, stirring well; spread mixture evenly on cut ~~??~~ s of buns. Arrange ham evenly on bottom halves of buns; top ~~??~~ with a cheese slice. Cover with top halves of buns. Wrap each ~~??~~ wich in aluminum foil, and place on a baking sheet. Bake at 350° ~~??~~ 20 minutes or until sandwiches are thoroughly heated. Serve immediately. Yield: 8 servings.

?PER SUBMARINE SANDWICHES

? (6-ounce) loaves French
  bread
1 (3-ounce) package cream
  cheese, softened
⅔ cup mayonnaise or salad
  dressing
2 tablespoons chopped fresh or
  frozen chives
½ pound thinly sliced cooked
  ham
½ pound thinly sliced Genoa
  salami

½ pound thinly sliced bologna
½ pound thinly sliced black-
  peppered turkey
½ pound thinly sliced summer
  sausage
4 cups torn romaine lettuce
1 medium tomato, seeded and
  chopped
⅓ cup sliced pimiento-stuffed
  olives
2 tablespoons commercial
  Italian salad dressing

Cut each bread loaf in half crosswise using an electric or serrated knife; split each half horizontally. Set aside.

Combine cream cheese, mayonnaise, and chives; stir well. Spread cut surfaces of bread evenly with cream cheese mixture. Fold meat slices in half; arrange meat slices evenly on bottom halves of bread.

Combine lettuce and remaining ingredients; toss gently. Spoon mixture evenly over meat slices. Replace bread tops. To serve, cut each sandwich in half crosswise. Yield: 8 servings.

FRENCH BREAD PIZZAS

■■■■■■■■■■
Kids love these French
Bread Pizzas, but they
may prefer that you
hold the onion.

¾ cup pizza sauce
4 (6-inch) French rolls, split
  horizontally and toasted
1 small onion, thinly sliced and
  separated into rings

1 (3½-ounce) package sliced
  pepperoni
2 cups (8 ounces) shredded
  mozzarella cheese

Spread pizza sauce evenly over cut surfaces of roll halves. Top evenly with onion and pepperoni; sprinkle evenly with cheese. Place pizzas on an ungreased baking sheet. Bake at 400° for 12 minutes. Yield: 4 servings.

CALZONES WITH HERBED TOMATO SAUCE

1 package active dry yeast
1 cup warm water (105° to 115°)
3 to 3½ cups all-purpose flour,
  divided
¼ cup vegetable oil
1 teaspoon salt
½ pound Italian sausage or
  ground pork sausage
½ pound ground chuck

½ cup chopped onion
1 (6-ounce) can tomato paste
2½ cups (10 ounces) shredded
  mozzarella cheese
1 teaspoon dried basil
1 teaspoon dried oregano
Olive oil
Herbed Tomato Sauce
Freshly grated Parmesan cheese

Combine yeast and warm water in a 1-cup liquid measuring cup; let stand 5 minutes. Combine yeast mixture, 2 cups flour, vegetable oil, and salt in a mixing bowl; beat at medium speed of an electric mixer until blended. Gradually stir in enough remaining flour to make a stiff dough.

Turn dough out onto a floured surface; knead until smooth and elastic (about 5 minutes). Place in a well-greased bowl, turning to grease top. Cover and let rise in a warm place (85°), free from drafts, 1 hour or until doubled in bulk.

Remove casings from Italian sausage, if necessary. Cook sausage, ground chuck, and onion in a large skillet over medium-high heat until meat is browned and onion is tender, stirring until meat crumbles; drain. Stir in tomato paste and next 3 ingredients. Set aside.

Punch dough down, and divide into 6 equal portions. Roll each portion to a 7-inch circle; spoon ½ cup meat mixture onto each circle. Moisten edges of circles with water; fold circles in half. Seal securely, fluting edges or pressing edges together with a fork dipped in flour.

Transfer calzones to a lightly greased baking sheet; brush with olive oil. Cover and let rise in a warm place, free from drafts, 30 minutes.

Cut slits in tops of calzones to allow steam to escape during baking. Bake at 400° for 25 minutes or until golden. Serve immediately with Herbed Tomato Sauce and Parmesan cheese. Yield: 6 servings.

Herbed Tomato Sauce

1¼ cups tomato sauce
⅓ cup tomato paste
2½ tablespoons minced onion
¾ teaspoon dried basil

¾ teaspoon dried oregano
¼ teaspoon pepper
1 clove garlic, minced

Combine all ingredients in a small saucepan; cover and cook over medium heat 10 minutes or until thoroughly heated, stirring occasionally. Serve warm. Yield: 1⅔ cups.

A Calzone with Herbed Tomato Sauce resembles a pocket pizza. Sprinkle it with freshly grated Parmesan cheese for maximum flavor.

CURRIED CHICKEN SALAD IN A POCKET

Pita, or "pocket" bread, originated in the Middle East. When making sandwiches from pita bread, the rounds are typically cut in half crosswise to form two pockets for the filling ingredients.

4 skinned chicken breast halves
4 cups water
½ teaspoon instant minced onion
Dash of garlic powder
1 bay leaf
4 medium-size sweet pickles, chopped
1 large carrot, scraped and grated
1 medium onion, chopped
1 medium Red Delicious apple, chopped

1 cup mayonnaise or salad dressing
½ cup raisins
¼ cup chopped celery
2 teaspoons curry powder
½ teaspoon salt
¼ teaspoon ground white pepper
6 (6-inch) pita bread rounds, cut in half crosswise
2 cups alfalfa sprouts

Combine first 5 ingredients in a large saucepan. Bring to a boil; cover, reduce heat, and simmer 30 minutes or until chicken is tender. Remove chicken from broth; let cool. Strain broth, and reserve for another use, if desired. Bone chicken, and cut into ½-inch pieces. Combine chicken, pickles, and next 9 ingredients; stir well. Cover and chill.

To serve, spoon chicken salad evenly into pita bread halves, and top evenly with alfalfa sprouts. Yield: 6 servings.

PEPPERY CHICKEN PITAS

Pita bread rounds can also be folded around a sandwich filling, as in this recipe. Microwaving the pita rounds helps soften them so they're less likely to crack when folded.

6 skinned, boned chicken breast halves
¼ cup teriyaki sauce
1 teaspoon dried thyme
1 teaspoon ground white pepper
1 teaspoon black pepper
½ teaspoon garlic powder
½ teaspoon ground red pepper

2 tablespoons olive oil, divided
⅓ cup mayonnaise or salad dressing
1 tablespoon prepared horseradish
6 (8-inch) pita bread rounds
2 cups shredded lettuce

Cut chicken lengthwise into ½-inch-wide strips. Place chicken in a large heavy-duty, zip-top plastic bag. Pour teriyaki sauce over chicken; seal bag. Marinate in refrigerator 2 hours, turning bag occasionally.

Remove chicken from marinade; discard marinade. Combine thyme and next 4 ingredients; sprinkle over chicken. Cook half of chicken in 1 tablespoon hot oil in a skillet over medium-high heat 5 minutes or until done, stirring frequently. Drain on paper towels; keep warm. Repeat procedure with remaining half of chicken and remaining tablespoon oil.

Combine mayonnaise and horseradish; set aside. Wrap pita rounds in heavy-duty plastic wrap; microwave at HIGH 45 seconds or until heated.

Spread pita rounds evenly with mayonnaise mixture; top evenly with lettuce and chicken. Fold sides of pita rounds over chicken, and secure with wooden picks. Serve immediately. Yield: 6 servings.

MARINATED CHICKEN SANDWICHES

⅔ cup white vinegar
⅔ cup sugar
½ cup dry mustard
1 large egg
8 skinned, boned chicken breast
  halves
1 cup soy sauce
½ cup pineapple juice

¼ cup firmly packed brown
  sugar
¼ cup sherry
¾ teaspoon minced garlic
8 slices Monterey Jack cheese
8 kaiser rolls, split horizontally
Leaf lettuce leaves
8 slices tomato (optional)

Combine first 4 ingredients in container of an electric blender; cover and process until smooth. Pour mixture into top of a double boiler; bring water to a boil. Reduce heat to low; cook, stirring constantly, 7 minutes or until smooth and thickened. Cover and chill.

Place chicken in a large heavy-duty, zip-top plastic bag. Combine soy sauce and next 4 ingredients; reserve ¼ cup of mixture for basting. Pour remaining mixture over chicken; seal bag. Marinate in refrigerator 30 minutes, turning bag once.

Remove chicken from marinade, discarding marinade. Grill chicken, covered, over medium-hot coals (350° to 400°) 4 minutes on each side, basting with reserved soy sauce mixture. Place 1 slice cheese on each chicken breast, and grill, covered, 2 additional minutes or until cheese melts. Remove chicken from grill.

Spread cut surfaces of rolls with mustard mixture. Place 1 chicken breast on bottom half of each roll; top with lettuce and a tomato slice, if desired. Cover with roll tops, and serve immediately. Yield: 8 servings.

Presenting Smoked Chicken Club Sandwiches in wax paper-lined baskets creates a nostalgic diner atmosphere.

SMOKED CHICKEN CLUB SANDWICHES

12 slices whole wheat bread, toasted

¼ to ½ cup mayonnaise or salad dressing

¾ pound thinly sliced smoked chicken breast

8 leaf lettuce leaves

8 thin slices tomato

8 slices bacon, cooked

Spread one side of each slice of bread with mayonnaise. Top 4 bread slices evenly with chicken and 4 lettuce leaves; cover each with another slice of bread. Top each evenly with remaining lettuce leaves, tomato slices, and bacon; cover with remaining slices of bread, mayonnaise side down. Cut each sandwich into 4 triangles, and secure each triangle with a wooden pick. Yield: 4 servings.

TANGY CLUB SANDWICHES

1 (3-ounce) package cream
   cheese, softened
⅓ cup crumbled blue cheese
3 tablespoons mayonnaise or
   salad dressing, divided
1 teaspoon instant minced onion
Dash of Worcestershire sauce
12 slices sandwich bread,
   toasted

½ pound thinly sliced cooked
   chicken or turkey
8 slices tomato
4 slices Swiss cheese
⅛ teaspoon salt
⅛ teaspoon pepper
8 slices bacon, cooked
4 leaf lettuce leaves

Combine cream cheese, blue cheese, 1 tablespoon mayonnaise, onion, and Worcestershire sauce in a small mixing bowl; beat at low speed of an electric mixer until well blended. Spread cheese mixture evenly over one side of 4 slices of bread; top evenly with turkey, tomato slices, and Swiss cheese. Sprinkle evenly with salt and pepper. Top each with 1 bread slice, 2 slices bacon, and a lettuce leaf.

   Spread remaining 4 bread slices evenly with remaining 2 tablespoons mayonnaise, and place, mayonnaise side down, over lettuce. Cut each sandwich into 4 triangles, and secure each triangle with a wooden pick. Yield: 4 servings.

■ ■ ■ ■ ■ ■ ■ ■ ■ □

Traditional club sandwiches consist of three bread slices spread with mayonnaise and layered with thinly sliced chicken or turkey, cooked bacon, tomato slices, and lettuce leaves. Tangy Club Sandwiches feature a cream cheese-blue cheese spread, sure to add lots of zip.

HOT BROWN SANDWICHES

¼ cup butter or margarine
¼ cup all-purpose flour
1 cup milk
1 cup turkey or chicken broth
1 cup (4 ounces) shredded
  Cheddar cheese
¾ teaspoon salt

⅛ teaspoon ground white
  pepper
8 slices sandwich bread, toasted
¾ pound sliced cooked turkey
8 slices bacon, cooked
Grated Parmesan cheese
Paprika

Melt butter in a saucepan over low heat; add flour, stirring until smooth. Cook, stirring constantly, 1 minute. Gradually add milk and broth; cook over medium heat, stirring constantly, until slightly thickened and bubbly. Stir in Cheddar cheese, salt, and pepper; cook, stirring constantly, 2 minutes or until cheese melts. Remove from heat; set aside.

Place 2 bread slices on each of 4 ovenproof plates; arrange turkey and bacon evenly over bread. Top evenly with cheese sauce, and sprinkle with Parmesan cheese and paprika. Broil 3 inches from heat (with electric oven door partially opened) 4 to 5 minutes or until cheese sauce is golden. Serve immediately. Yield: 4 servings.

OPEN-FACED GUACAMOLE SUBS

1 small avocado, peeled, seeded,
  and mashed
1 tablespoon lemon juice
1 tablespoon mayonnaise or
  salad dressing
¼ teaspoon hot sauce
1 clove garlic, minced
1 (16-ounce) loaf Italian bread

½ pound thinly sliced cooked
  turkey
1 large tomato, sliced
¼ cup chopped green onions
6 slices Monterey Jack cheese,
  cut in half
  diagonally
¼ cup sliced ripe olives

Combine first 5 ingredients; stir well, and set aside.

Cut bread loaf in half crosswise; slice each piece in half horizontally. Lightly toast cut surfaces of bread; spread cut surfaces evenly with avocado mixture. Top bread pieces evenly with turkey and tomato; sprinkle evenly with green onions, and top evenly with cheese pieces.

Place sandwiches on an ungreased baking sheet, and broil 5½ inches from heat (with electric oven door partially opened) 1 minute or until cheese melts. Sprinkle with olives. Yield: 4 servings.

A Turkey Open-Facer, served with fresh melon cutouts, makes a delightful entrée for a ladies' luncheon.

TURKEY OPEN-FACERS

1 (10-ounce) package frozen asparagus spears, thawed
1/4 cup commercial French salad dressing
1 tablespoon chopped onion
1/8 teaspoon pepper
2 tablespoons butter or margarine, softened
1 tablespoon plus 1 teaspoon mayonnaise
4 slices sandwich bread, toasted
1/2 pound thinly sliced cooked turkey
4 slices Swiss cheese, cut in half diagonally

Place asparagus in a small saucepan. Combine salad dressing, onion, and pepper; pour over asparagus. Cook over medium heat 3 to 4 minutes or until mixture comes to a boil; remove from heat.

Combine butter and mayonnaise; spread evenly over one side of bread slices. Top bread slices evenly with turkey and asparagus mixture; top evenly with cheese slices. Place sandwiches on an ungreased baking sheet. Broil 5½ inches from heat (with electric oven door partially opened) until cheese melts. Serve immediately. Yield: 4 servings.

Put on a Pot of Soup

Soup's on! And what could be more satisfying than a bowl of hot soup, especially on a cold, blustery day? From soups and stews to chilis, chowders, and gumbos, our top choices include Hearty Bean-and-Barley Soup, Ham and Black-Eyed Pea Stew, Chuck Wagon Chili, Cheesy Potato-Corn Chowder, and Spicy Seafood Gumbo. Many of our selections can be made ahead and frozen, which is sure to come in handy for a busy evening. Whether it's chili with the family or gumbo with a group of friends, our favorites will warm you from head to toe.

Baked Potato Soup (page 78)

CRAB AND LEEK BISQUE

1½ pounds leeks (2 or 3)
1 clove garlic, minced
½ cup butter or margarine, melted
½ cup all-purpose flour
4 cups chicken broth
½ cup dry white wine
½ pound fresh crabmeat, drained and flaked
2 cups half-and-half
¼ teaspoon salt
¼ teaspoon ground white pepper
Garnish: sliced leeks

Remove roots, tough outer leaves, and green tops from leeks. Split white portion of leeks in half; wash and cut halves into thin slices.

Cook leeks and garlic in butter in a Dutch oven over medium heat, stirring constantly, until leeks are tender. Add flour; cook, stirring constantly, 1 minute. Gradually add chicken broth and wine; cook, stirring constantly, until mixture is thickened and bubbly.

Stir in crabmeat and next 3 ingredients; cook, stirring constantly, until thoroughly heated (do not boil). Ladle soup into bowls; garnish, if desired. Yield: 2 quarts.

GULF COAST CIOPPINO

20 fresh mussels
20 fresh clams
2 cups chopped celery
2 cups chopped green pepper
1 cup chopped green onions
2 cloves garlic, pressed
¼ cup butter or margarine, melted
1 tablespoon olive oil
1 (16-ounce) can crushed tomatoes
1 (15-ounce) can tomato sauce
1 to 1½ tablespoons dried Italian seasoning
1½ teaspoons paprika
1 teaspoon sugar
1 teaspoon salt
1 teaspoon ground red pepper
½ teaspoon black pepper
2 (14½-ounce) cans ready-to-serve chicken broth
1 pound grouper, amberjack, or sea bass fillets, cut into bite-size pieces

Scrub mussels with a brush, removing beards. Wash clams. Discard any opened or cracked mussels and clams. Set aside.

Cook celery, green pepper, green onions, and garlic in butter and hot oil in a Dutch oven over medium-high heat, stirring constantly, until vegetables are tender. Stir in crushed tomatoes and next 7 ingredients;

cook 3 minutes, stirring occasionally. Add chicken broth. Bring to a boil; reduce heat, and simmer, uncovered, 45 minutes, stirring occasionally.

Stir in mussels, clams, and fish; cook 4 minutes, stirring occasionally. (Mussels and clams should open during cooking.) Discard any unopened mussels and clams. Serve immediately. Yield: about 3 quarts.

SHRIMP ENCHILADA SOUP

5 cups chicken broth
4 ounces corn tortilla chips
   (about 3 cups)
1½ pounds unpeeled medium-
   size fresh shrimp
1 (10-ounce) can diced tomatoes
   and green chiles, undrained
   and chopped
2 (4.5-ounce) cans chopped
   green chiles, undrained

1 medium onion, chopped
2 cloves garlic, minced
2 tablespoons butter or
   margarine, melted
1 (8-ounce) carton sour cream
¼ cup chopped fresh cilantro
Shredded mozzarella cheese
Shredded Cheddar cheese

Bring chicken broth to a boil in a large Dutch oven; add tortilla chips. Remove from heat, and let stand, uncovered, 10 minutes.

Peel shrimp, and devein, if desired. Set aside.

Position knife blade in food processor bowl; add half of broth mixture. Process until smooth, stopping once to scrape down sides. Transfer processed mixture to another container. Repeat procedure with remaining half of broth mixture. Return entire processed mixture to Dutch oven; stir in tomatoes and green chiles and chopped green chiles. Set mixture aside.

Cook shrimp, onion, and garlic in butter in a large skillet over medium-high heat, stirring constantly, 3 to 4 minutes or until shrimp turn pink; drain.

Stir shrimp mixture into broth mixture; cook over medium heat until mixture is thoroughly heated, stirring occasionally (do not boil). Stir in sour cream and cilantro. Ladle soup into bowls, and sprinkle with cheeses. Yield: 2½ quarts.

Sample the bounty of Vegetable-Beef Soup, brimming with colorful vegetables and tender chunks of beef.

VEGETABLE-BEEF SOUP

3 pounds beef short ribs
2 quarts water
2 teaspoons salt
1 teaspoon pepper
1 bay leaf
4 medium-size round red
    potatoes, peeled and cubed
4 medium carrots, scraped and
    chopped

2 medium onions, chopped
2 (8-ounce) cans tomato sauce
1 dried red chile pepper
½ small cabbage, coarsely
    chopped
1 (10-ounce) package frozen
    whole kernel corn
1 (10-ounce) package frozen
    lima beans

Combine first 5 ingredients in a large Dutch oven. Bring to a boil; cover, reduce heat, and simmer 1 hour. Remove ribs from stock, reserving stock in Dutch oven; remove and discard bay leaf. Let ribs cool. Remove meat from bones; discard fat and bones. Chop meat. Skim fat from stock.

Add chopped meat, potato, and next 4 ingredients to stock. Bring to a boil; cover, reduce heat, and simmer 30 minutes. Add cabbage, corn, and beans; cover and simmer 15 minutes or until vegetables are tender. Remove and discard chile pepper. Yield: 5½ quarts.

BLACK BEAN SOUP

1 (16-ounce) package dried
  black beans
1 quart water
1 (10½-ounce) can beef
  consommé, undiluted
1 large meaty ham hock
6 black peppercorns
3 cloves garlic, halved
2 bay leaves
1 dried red chile pepper, cut in
  half crosswise
1 medium onion, chopped
1 medium carrot, scraped and
  chopped

1 small green pepper, seeded
  and chopped
1 stalk celery, chopped
1½ teaspoons ground cumin
1½ teaspoons ground coriander
¼ cup dry sherry
1 teaspoon salt
½ teaspoon freshly ground
  pepper
½ teaspoon hot sauce
Sour cream
Seeded, chopped tomato
Chopped green onions

Sort and wash beans; place in a Dutch oven. Cover with water 2 inches above beans; let soak 8 hours. Drain beans, and return to Dutch oven. Add 1 quart water, consommé, and ham hock.

Place peppercorns, garlic, bay leaves, and chile pepper on an 8-inch square of cheesecloth; tie with string. Add cheesecloth bag to bean mixture. Bring to a boil; cover, reduce heat, and simmer 1 hour.

Add onion and next 5 ingredients to bean mixture; cover and cook over medium-low heat 45 to 50 minutes or until beans are tender.

Remove and discard cheesecloth bag. Remove ham hock; let cool slightly. Remove meat from bone; discard fat and bone. Chop meat.

Add chopped meat, sherry and next 3 ingredients; cook until thoroughly heated, stirring gently. Serve soup with sour cream, chopped tomato, and chopped green onions. Yield: 2 quarts.

Hearty Bean-and-Barley Soup

■■■■■■■■■
Hearty Bean-and-Barley
Soup is very thick. For a
thinner consistency, add a
little water. The soup may
be frozen in an airtight
container up to
three months.

2 pounds dried Great Northern
  beans
1 pound ground chuck
2 quarts water
2 cups coarsely chopped cooked
  ham
1 cup fine barley
6 carrots, scraped and sliced
4 cloves garlic, minced
1 large onion, chopped
1 large meaty ham hock
4 (10½-ounce) cans beef
  consommé, undiluted
¼ cup Worcestershire sauce
1 teaspoon salt
1 teaspoon pepper
½ teaspoon hot sauce
2 fresh jalapeño peppers, seeded

Sort and wash beans; place in a large Dutch oven. Cover with water 2 inches above beans; let soak 8 hours. Drain beans; return to Dutch oven.

Brown ground chuck in a large skillet, stirring until it crumbles. Drain. Add meat, 2 quarts water, and next 7 ingredients to beans. Bring to a boil; cover, reduce heat, and simmer 2 hours, stirring occasionally.

Remove ham hock; let cool slightly. Remove meat from bone; discard fat and bone. Chop meat. Add chopped meat, Worcestershire sauce, and remaining ingredients to Dutch oven. Bring to a boil; cover, reduce heat, and simmer 30 minutes, stirring occasionally. Remove and discard jalapeño peppers. Yield: 5 quarts.

Guadalajara Soup

1¼ cups dried pinto beans
3½ to 4 pounds country-style
  pork ribs
2 tablespoons vegetable oil
1 cup finely chopped onion
2 cloves garlic, minced
4 cups water
2 (14½-ounce) cans condensed
  beef broth, undiluted
2 teaspoons chili powder
1 teaspoon dried oregano
1 teaspoon ground cumin
4 cups thinly sliced carrot
1 (7-ounce) jar baby corn on the
  cob, drained
½ teaspoon salt
¼ teaspoon pepper
Sour cream (optional)
Jalapeño salsa (optional)
Chopped fresh cilantro
  (optional)

Sort and wash beans; place in a Dutch oven. Cover with water 2 inches above beans. Cover and bring to a boil; boil 2 minutes. Remove beans from heat; let stand, covered, 1 hour. Drain beans, and set aside.

Brown short ribs in hot oil in Dutch oven over medium heat. Remove short ribs, reserving drippings in Dutch oven. Cook onion and garlic in drippings over medium-high heat, stirring constantly, until onion is tender. Add beans, short ribs, 4 cups water, and next 4 ingredients to Dutch oven. Bring to a boil; cover, reduce heat, and simmer 1½ hours or until short ribs are tender, stirring occasionally. Remove short ribs; let cool slightly. Remove meat from bones; discard fat and bones. Chop meat. Skim fat from broth mixture.

Add chopped meat, carrot, corn, salt, and pepper to Dutch oven. Bring to a boil; cover, reduce heat, and simmer 30 minutes or until carrot is tender. If desired, serve soup with sour cream, jalapeño salsa, and chopped cilantro. Yield: about 3 quarts.

Jalapeño salsa, cilantro, and sour cream add south-of-the-border character to Guadalajara Soup.

BAKED POTATO SOUP

You might think at first that you're eating a loaded baked potato when you spoon into Baked Potato Soup. If you prefer thinner soup, stir in a little milk.

4 large baking potatoes
⅔ cup butter or margarine
⅔ cup all-purpose flour
6 cups milk
¾ teaspoon salt
½ teaspoon pepper
1½ cups (6 ounces) shredded Cheddar cheese, divided
12 slices bacon, cooked, crumbled, and divided
4 green onions, chopped and divided
1 (8-ounce) carton sour cream

Wash potatoes; prick several times with a fork. Bake at 400° for 1 hour or until done; let cool. Cut potatoes in half lengthwise; scoop out and reserve pulp. Discard shells.

Melt butter in a Dutch oven over low heat; add flour, stirring until smooth. Cook, stirring constantly, 1 minute. Gradually add milk; cook over medium heat, stirring constantly, until thickened and bubbly.

Stir in potato, salt, pepper, 1 cup cheese, ½ cup bacon, and 2 tablespoons green onions; cook until heated (do not boil). Stir in sour cream; cook just until heated (do not boil). Serve with remaining cheese, bacon, and green onions. Yield: 2½ quarts.

LIME SOUP

Besides tangy fresh juice, much of the flavor in Lime Soup comes from cilantro, the aromatic leaves of the coriander plant. Cilantro is a common ingredient in Southwestern cuisine.

1 (3- to 3½-pound) broiler-fryer
1 medium onion, quartered
1 stalk celery, halved
3 fresh cilantro or parsley sprigs
6 black peppercorns
6 cups water
2 teaspoons salt
½ teaspoon dried thyme
1 medium-size green pepper, seeded and chopped
1 medium onion, chopped
2 tablespoons vegetable oil
2 large tomatoes, peeled and chopped
1½ teaspoons grated lime rind
⅓ cup fresh lime juice
3 tablespoons chopped fresh cilantro or parsley
¼ teaspoon salt
¼ teaspoon pepper
8 (6-inch) corn tortillas*
Vegetable oil
Garnishes: lime slices, fresh cilantro or parsley sprigs

Combine first 8 ingredients in a large Dutch oven. Bring to a boil; cover, reduce heat, and simmer 1 hour or until chicken is tender. Remove chicken from broth, reserving broth. Remove vegetables and pepper-corns from broth, and discard. Let chicken cool; skin, bone, and chop chicken. Skim fat from broth.

Cook green pepper and chopped onion in 2 tablespoons hot oil in Dutch oven over medium-high heat, stirring constantly, until tender. Add tomato; cook 5 minutes, stirring occasionally. Add broth, lime rind, lime juice, and 3 tablespoons chopped cilantro. Bring to a boil; reduce heat, and simmer, uncovered, 20 minutes. Stir in chopped chicken, ¼ teaspoon salt, and ¼ teaspoon pepper. Bring to a boil; reduce heat, and simmer, uncovered, 10 minutes.

Cut each tortilla into 8 wedges. Pour oil to depth of 1 inch into a large heavy skillet. Fry tortilla wedges in hot oil over medium heat until crisp. Drain on paper towels.

To serve, place 8 tortilla wedges in each individual soup bowl; ladle soup into bowls. Garnish, if desired. Serve immediately. Yield: 2 quarts.

* Commercial tortilla chips may be substituted for fried tortilla wedges.

CREAMY CHICKEN SOUP

4 chicken breast halves (about 2 pounds)
4 cups water
2 medium carrots, scraped and minced
2 stalks celery, minced
1 teaspoon salt
½ teaspoon pepper
3 tablespoons all-purpose flour
1 cup milk

Combine chicken and water in a large saucepan. Bring to a boil; cover, reduce heat, and simmer 30 minutes or until chicken is tender. Remove chicken from broth, reserving 3 cups broth. Reserve remaining broth for another use, if desired. Let chicken cool; skin, bone, and cut chicken into bite-size pieces. Skim fat from broth.

Combine reserved broth, chopped chicken, carrot, and next 3 ingredients in pan. Bring to a boil; cover, reduce heat, and simmer 1 hour.

Combine flour and milk, stirring until smooth. Gradually add flour mixture to chicken mixture, stirring well. Cook over medium heat 15 minutes or until thickened, stirring occasionally. Yield: about 1½ quarts.

BEEF STEW WITH DUMPLINGS

2 pounds beef stew meat, cut
    into 1-inch pieces
⅓ cup all-purpose flour
1½ teaspoons salt
¼ teaspoon pepper
3 tablespoons vegetable oil
5 cups water
1 medium onion, sliced
1 clove garlic, minced
1 bay leaf
4 large carrots, scraped and
    quartered

6 small boiling onions, peeled
3 large potatoes, peeled and
    quartered
3 stalks celery, quartered
1 cup biscuit and baking mix
1 large egg, lightly beaten
3 tablespoons milk
1 tablespoon chopped fresh
    parsley

Combine first 4 ingredients in a zip-top plastic bag. Seal bag; shake well.
Remove meat from bag; reserve any remaining flour mixture.

    Brown meat in hot oil in a Dutch oven over medium-high heat. Stir
in remaining flour mixture, water, and next 3 ingredients. Bring to a
boil; cover, reduce heat, and simmer 1 hour. Add carrot; cover and simmer 30 minutes. Add boiling onions, potato, and celery; cover and simmer 30 minutes. Remove and discard bay leaf.

    Combine biscuit mix and remaining ingredients; stir just until moist-
ened. Drop dough by tablespoonfuls on top of simmering stew. Cook,
uncovered, 10 minutes; cover and cook 10 minutes. Yield: 2½ quarts.

LAMB STEW

2 pounds lean boneless lamb,
    cut into 1-inch pieces
½ cup all-purpose flour
1 teaspoon salt
½ teaspoon pepper
2 tablespoons vegetable oil
3 cups water
¼ cup tomato puree
1 teaspoon dried thyme

2 cloves garlic, minced
1 bay leaf
1 (10½-ounce) can condensed
    beef broth, undiluted
8 small boiling onions, peeled
4 medium-size round red
    potatoes, peeled and cubed
4 medium carrots, scraped and
    cut into 1-inch pieces

Combine first 4 ingredients in a zip-top plastic bag. Seal bag; shake well.
Remove meat from bag; reserve any remaining flour mixture.

Brown meat in hot oil in a Dutch oven over medium-high heat. Stir in remaining flour mixture, water, and next 5 ingredients. Bring to a boil; cover, reduce heat, and simmer 1 hour.

Add onions, potato, and carrot to Dutch oven; cover and simmer 45 minutes. Uncover and simmer 30 to 40 minutes or until meat and vegetables are tender, stirring occasionally. Remove and discard bay leaf. Yield: 2½ quarts.

PANCHO VILLA STEW

½ pound chorizo, casings removed
2 pounds boneless pork loin, cut into 1-inch cubes
¼ cup all-purpose flour
2 tablespoons vegetable oil
3 (14½-ounce) cans ready-to-serve chicken broth
3 (4.5-ounce) cans diced green chiles, undrained
3 cloves garlic, crushed
1 (14½-ounce) can whole tomatoes, drained and chopped
1 large purple onion, thinly sliced and separated into rings

1 (2-inch) stick cinnamon
2 teaspoons ground cumin
2 teaspoons cocoa
1 teaspoon dried oregano
¼ teaspoon salt
2 (15-ounce) cans black beans, rinsed and drained
1 (15½-ounce) can white hominy, rinsed and drained
1 (10-ounce) package frozen whole kernel corn
½ cup tequila or beer
Flour tortillas
Butter or margarine

Chorizo, a coarsely ground pork sausage that's seasoned with lots of garlic and chili powder, provides much of this soup's spicy taste. Chorizo is often used in Mexican and Spanish recipes.

Brown chorizo in a Dutch oven, stirring until it crumbles; drain well, and set aside.

Dredge pork in flour. Brown pork in hot oil in Dutch oven over medium heat. Stir in sausage, chicken broth, and next 9 ingredients. Bring to a boil; cover, reduce heat, and simmer 1 hour. Stir in black beans, hominy, corn, and tequila; cover and simmer 30 minutes. Remove and discard cinnamon stick.

Wrap tortillas tightly in aluminum foil; bake at 350° for 15 minutes or until thoroughly heated. Spread warm tortillas with butter, and serve with stew. Yield: 1 gallon.

Note: Stew may be frozen in an airtight container up to 3 months.

Rich in flavor and high in protein, Ham and Black-Eyed Pea Stew will warm up your wintertime menu.

HAM AND BLACK-EYED PEA STEW

1 (16-ounce) package dried
   black-eyed peas
1 meaty ham hock
1 (10½-ounce) can beef
   consommé, undiluted
2 bay leaves
6 cups water, divided
3 stalks celery, chopped
1 large onion, chopped

1 large green pepper, seeded
   and chopped
2 cups chopped cooked ham
2 tablespoons ketchup
1 tablespoon Worcestershire
   sauce
1 cup thinly sliced green onions
½ teaspoon pepper
¼ teaspoon hot sauce

Sort and wash peas. Combine peas, ham hock, consommé, bay leaves, and 4 cups water in a Dutch oven. Bring to a boil; cover, reduce heat, and simmer 1 hour, stirring occasionally.

Add remaining 2 cups water, celery, and next 5 ingredients to pea mixture. Cover, reduce heat, and simmer 1 hour and 15 minutes or until peas and vegetables are tender.

Remove ham hock from stew; let cool slightly. Remove meat from bone; discard fat and bone. Chop meat, and return to stew. Remove and discard bay leaves. Stir in green onions, ½ teaspoon pepper, and hot sauce; cook just until thoroughly heated. Yield: about 3 quarts.

BRUNSWICK STEW

1 (2½- to 3-pound) broiler-fryer

1½ pounds beef stew meat, cut into 1-inch pieces

1 pound pork tenderloin

3 (16-ounce) cans whole tomatoes, undrained and chopped

1 (16-ounce) package frozen white corn

1 (6-ounce) can tomato paste

6 medium-size round red potatoes, peeled and cubed

3 medium jalapeño peppers, seeded and chopped

4 cups frozen lima beans

4 cups chopped onion

2 cups sliced carrot

2 cups frozen sliced okra

1 cup frozen English peas

1 cup chopped cabbage

1 tablespoon sugar

3 tablespoons Worcestershire sauce

2 tablespoons lemon juice

2 teaspoons salt

½ to 1 teaspoon pepper

Brunswick County, Virginia, claims the origin of this thick stew. Brunswick stew usually contains two or more meats and an abundance of vegetables, including lima beans, okra, corn, and tomatoes.

Combine chicken, beef, and pork in a large Dutch oven; add water to cover. Bring to a boil; cover, reduce heat, and simmer 2 hours or until chicken and meats are tender. Remove chicken and meats from stock, reserving stock. Let chicken and meats cool. Skin, bone, and coarsely chop chicken. Coarsely chop beef and pork. Skim fat from stock, reserving 7 cups stock. Reserve any remaining stock for another use, if desired.

Combine reserved 7 cups stock, chopped chicken, chopped meats, tomato, and next 10 ingredients in Dutch oven. Bring to a boil; cover, reduce heat, and simmer 2 hours. Stir in sugar and remaining ingredients. Yield: 2 gallons.

Note: Stew may be frozen in an airtight container up to 3 months.

CHUCK WAGON CHILI

Whether or not the claim is valid, chili owes much of its popularity to the introduction of chili powder in the 1890s by a Texan named William Gebhardt. This chili, with its chunks of beef instead of ground beef, is typically Texan.

1 (2-pound) boneless chuck
  roast
2 tablespoons vegetable oil
1 cup chopped onion, divided
1 cup chopped green pepper
2 cloves garlic, crushed
1 (28-ounce) can whole
  tomatoes, undrained and
  chopped

1 (6-ounce) can tomato paste
1 cup water
3 tablespoons chili powder
1 tablespoon salt
1 teaspoon dried oregano
½ teaspoon pepper
Shredded Monterey Jack cheese

Trim fat from roast; cut roast into ½-inch cubes. Brown meat in hot oil in a Dutch oven over medium-high heat. Remove meat, reserving drippings in Dutch oven.

Cook ¾ cup onion, green pepper, and garlic in drippings over medium-high heat, stirring constantly, until tender. Stir in meat, tomato, and next 6 ingredients. Bring to a boil; cover, reduce heat, and simmer 1½ hours or until meat is tender, stirring occasionally. Ladle chili into bowls, and top with remaining ¼ cup onion and cheese. Yield: 2 quarts.

HOTTO LOTTO CHILI

Even in the Southwest, there's widespread disagreement on what constitutes an authentic chili: Should it have chopped meat or ground, beans or no beans, tomatoes and other vegetables or no vegetables at all? You should find a chili to suit your taste in this chapter.

1 pound ground chuck
1 pound ground hot pork
  sausage
1 clove garlic, minced
1 (16-ounce) can kidney beans,
  undrained
1 (15-ounce) can hot Mexican-
  style chili beans, undrained
1 (10-ounce) can diced tomatoes
  and green chiles, undrained
  and chopped

1 (7½-ounce) can whole
  tomatoes, undrained and
  chopped
1 (5½-ounce) can tomato juice
¼ cup dry red wine
2 tablespoons chili powder
¾ teaspoon salt
1 bay leaf

Cook first 3 ingredients in a Dutch oven over medium-high heat until meats are browned, stirring until they crumble. Drain; stir in kidney beans and remaining ingredients. Bring to a boil; cover, reduce heat, and simmer 1 hour, stirring occasionally. Remove and discard bay leaf. Yield: 9 cups.

FRIDAY NIGHT CHILI

2 pounds ground chuck
2 large onions, chopped
3 large cloves garlic, minced
2 (16-ounce) cans kidney beans, undrained
1 (16-ounce) can whole tomatoes, undrained and chopped
1 (8-ounce) can tomato sauce
2 cups water
2 tablespoons chili powder
2 teaspoons garlic salt
1½ teaspoons ground cumin
1 teaspoon dried oregano
1 teaspoon black pepper
½ teaspoon ground red pepper
¼ teaspoon hot sauce
Corn chips (optional)
Shredded sharp Cheddar cheese (optional)
Sliced green onions (optional)

Cook ground chuck, chopped onion, and garlic in a Dutch oven over medium-high heat until meat is browned and onion is tender, stirring until meat crumbles. Drain; stir in beans and next 10 ingredients. Bring to a boil; reduce heat, and simmer, uncovered, 1 hour, stirring occasionally. If desired, serve chili with corn chips, cheese, and green onions. Yield: 9 cups.

For a TGIF treat, try Friday Night Chili. Top each bowlful with corn chips, Cheddar cheese, and green onions for extra flavor and crunch.

VENISON CHILI

½ pound salt pork, quartered
2 pounds ground venison
2 medium onions, chopped
1 clove garlic, minced
1 (16-ounce) can whole
   tomatoes, undrained and
   coarsely chopped

2 or 3 large green chiles, diced
1 cup water
¾ cup dry red wine
3 tablespoons chili powder
¾ teaspoon dried oregano
½ teaspoon cumin seeds,
   crushed

Brown salt pork in a Dutch oven over medium heat. Add venison, onion, and garlic; cook until venison is browned and onion is tender, stirring until venison crumbles. Drain; stir in tomato and remaining ingredients. Bring to a boil; reduce heat, and simmer, uncovered, 1 hour, stirring occasionally. Remove and discard salt pork before serving. Yield: 1½ quarts.

CHEESY POTATO-CORN CHOWDER

6 slices bacon
3 cups fresh corn cut from cob
½ cup chopped onion
½ cup chopped celery
½ cup chopped green pepper
2½ cups water
2 cups peeled, chopped red
   potato

1 teaspoon salt
¼ teaspoon pepper
¼ teaspoon ground thyme
¼ cup all-purpose flour
3 cups milk, divided
2 cups (8 ounces) shredded
   Cheddar cheese
Garnish: fresh parsley sprigs

Cook bacon in a Dutch oven until crisp; remove bacon, reserving drippings in Dutch oven. Crumble bacon, and set aside. Cook corn and next 3 ingredients in drippings over medium-high heat, stirring constantly, until corn is tender.

Add water and next 4 ingredients to Dutch oven. Bring to a boil; cover, reduce heat, and simmer 20 minutes or until potato is tender, stirring occasionally.

Combine flour and 1 cup milk, stirring until smooth; gradually add to corn mixture, stirring constantly. Stir in remaining 2 cups milk. Cook, over medium heat, stirring constantly, until mixture is thickened and bubbly. Add cheese, stirring until cheese melts. Ladle chowder into bowls, and sprinkle with bacon. Garnish, if desired. Yield: 9 cups.

Manhattan-Style Seafood Chowder is chockful of good things from the sea.

MANHATTAN-STYLE SEAFOOD CHOWDER

4 medium onions, chopped
1 large green pepper, seeded
    and chopped
¼ cup vegetable oil
2 tablespoons all-purpose flour
3 (14½-ounce) cans stewed
    tomatoes, undrained
1 tablespoon celery salt
1 teaspoon garlic powder
1 teaspoon hot sauce

½ teaspoon pepper
2 pounds unpeeled medium-size
    fresh shrimp
½ pound fresh crabmeat,
    drained and flaked
½ pound firm white fish fillets,
    cut into bite-size pieces
1 (12-ounce) container
    Standard oysters, drained

■■■■■■■■■
There are basically two
types of chowders—
Manhattan-style
(left), which is
tomato based, and New
England-style (following
page), which is milk or
cream based.

Cook onion and green pepper in hot oil in a Dutch oven over medium-high heat, stirring constantly, until tender. Add flour; cook, stirring constantly, 1 minute. Stir in tomato and next 4 ingredients. Bring to a boil; cover, reduce heat, and simmer 15 minutes.

    Peel shrimp, and devein, if desired. Add shrimp, crabmeat, fish, and oysters to Dutch oven; cover and simmer 15 minutes. Yield: 3 quarts.

New England Clam Chowder

3 cups water
2 chicken-flavored bouillon cubes
4 medium-size round red potatoes, finely diced
2 (6½-ounce) cans minced clams, undrained
4 slices bacon, cut into 1-inch pieces
¾ cup chopped onion
3 tablespoons butter or margarine
¼ cup plus 2 tablespoons all-purpose flour
4 cups milk
¾ teaspoon salt
¼ teaspoon pepper

Combine water and bouillon cubes in a Dutch oven; bring to a boil. Add potato; cover and simmer 10 minutes or until tender. Drain potato, and set aside. Drain clams, reserving juice. Set clams and juice aside.

Cook bacon and onion in a medium skillet over medium-high heat, stirring constantly, until bacon is crisp and onion is tender. Remove bacon and onion, reserving 2 tablespoons drippings. Set bacon and onion aside.

Combine reserved drippings and butter in Dutch oven; cook over low heat until butter melts. Add flour, stirring until smooth. Cook, stirring constantly, 1 minute. Gradually add reserved clam juice and milk; cook over medium heat, stirring constantly, until mixture is thickened and bubbly. Remove from heat; stir in potato, clams, bacon mixture, salt, and pepper. Cook, stirring constantly, until mixture is thoroughly heated (do not boil). Yield: 2 quarts.

Turkey Chowder

2 tablespoons butter or margarine
2 tablespoons all-purpose flour
2 cups milk
1 teaspoon chicken-flavored bouillon granules
1 (16-ounce) loaf process cheese spread, cubed
1 (10-ounce) package frozen mixed vegetables, thawed
2 cups chopped cooked turkey
1½ cups cubed cooked potato
½ teaspoon instant minced onion
¼ teaspoon dry mustard
⅛ teaspoon pepper

Melt butter in a large saucepan over low heat; add flour, stirring until smooth. Cook, stirring constantly, 1 minute. Gradually add milk and bouillon granules; cook over medium heat, stirring constantly, until mixture is thickened and bubbly. Add cheese and remaining ingredients. Cook over medium-low heat until cheese melts and mixture is thoroughly heated, stirring occasionally. Yield: 1½ quarts.

SPICY SEAFOOD GUMBO

1 cup vegetable oil
1 cup all-purpose flour
8 stalks celery, chopped
4 medium onions, chopped
3 cloves garlic, minced
4 (14½-ounce) cans ready-
    to-serve chicken broth
2 (28-ounce) cans whole
    tomatoes, undrained and
    chopped
2 (10-ounce) packages frozen
    sliced okra
1 pound crab claws
½ cup minced fresh parsley
¼ cup Worcestershire sauce
1 tablespoon hot sauce

2 teaspoons dried thyme
2 teaspoons dried basil
2 teaspoons dried oregano
2 teaspoons rubbed sage
1 teaspoon pepper
5 bay leaves
2 pounds unpeeled medium-size
    fresh shrimp
2 (12-ounce) containers
    Standard oysters, undrained
1 pound fresh crabmeat,
    drained and flaked
1 pound firm white fish fillets,
    cut into 1-inch cubes
Hot cooked rice
Gumbo filé (optional)

Combine oil and flour in a large stockpot; cook over medium heat, stirring constantly, until roux is chocolate colored (about 20 minutes). Stir in celery, onion, and garlic; cook 10 minutes, stirring frequently. Add chicken broth and next 12 ingredients. Bring to a boil; reduce heat, and simmer, uncovered, 2 hours, stirring occasionally.

Peel shrimp, and devein, if desired. Add shrimp, oysters, crabmeat, and fish to stockpot. Bring to a boil; reduce heat, and simmer, uncovered, 10 minutes or until seafood is done. Remove and discard bay leaves. Serve gumbo over rice; sprinkle with gumbo filé, if desired. Yield: 2 gallons.

CHICKEN-SEAFOOD GUMBO

Most gumbos are thickened with a roux, a browned flour-fat mixture. The roux's richness and color is determined by the amount of time it cooks.

1 (2½- to 3-pound) broiler-fryer
6 cups water
⅓ cup vegetable oil
⅓ cup all-purpose flour
4 cloves garlic, minced
2 medium onions, chopped
1 (16-ounce) package frozen sliced okra
2½ cups chopped celery
½ cup chopped green pepper
6 live blue crabs, steamed and broken in half
1 (12-ounce) container Standard oysters, undrained
1 (8-ounce) can tomato sauce
¼ pound chopped cooked ham
1 tablespoon chopped fresh parsley
1½ tablespoons Worcestershire sauce
1 tablespoon lemon juice
1 tablespoon browning-and-seasoning sauce
2 teaspoons Creole seasoning
1 teaspoon dried thyme
¼ teaspoon garlic powder
¼ teaspoon liquid smoke
2 bay leaves
Hot cooked rice
Gumbo filé (optional)

Combine chicken and water in a Dutch oven. Bring to a boil; cover, reduce heat, and simmer 1 hour or until chicken is tender. Remove chicken from broth, reserving broth. Let chicken cool. Skin, bone, and coarsely chop chicken. Skim fat from broth; reserve 4 cups broth. Reserve any remaining broth for another use, if desired. Set chicken and 4 cups reserved broth aside.

Combine oil and flour in Dutch oven; cook over medium heat, stirring constantly, until roux is caramel colored (about 15 minutes). Add garlic and next 4 ingredients; cook 30 minutes or until vegetables are tender, stirring occasionally.

Add 4 cups reserved chicken broth, chicken, crabs, and next 12 ingredients. Bring to a boil; reduce heat, and simmer, uncovered, 2½ hours, stirring occasionally. Remove and discard bay leaves. Serve over rice; sprinkle with gumbo filé, if desired. Yield: 3½ quarts.

DOVE AND SAUSAGE GUMBO

15 dove breasts
1 (10½-ounce) can beef
    consommé, undiluted
1 beef-flavored bouillon cube
½ cup vegetable oil
½ cup all-purpose flour
1½ cups finely chopped onion
1 cup finely chopped celery
2 cloves garlic, minced
1 or 2 bay leaves
2 tablespoons Worcestershire
    sauce
½ teaspoon dried basil

¼ teaspoon poultry seasoning
¼ teaspoon freshly ground
    black pepper
⅛ teaspoon ground red pepper
⅛ teaspoon ground allspice
⅛ teaspoon ground cloves
¾ pound smoked sausage, cut
    into ¼-inch slices
¼ cup dry red wine
⅛ teaspoon hot sauce
Hot cooked rice
Gumbo filé (optional)

Place dove breasts in a Dutch oven; add water to cover. Bring to a boil; cover, reduce heat, and simmer 10 minutes. Remove dove from broth, reserving broth. Let dove cool. Bone and coarsely chop dove; set aside. Add enough water to reserved broth to measure 3 cups, if necessary.

Combine broth, consommé, and bouillon cube in a medium saucepan; cook over medium heat until bouillon cube dissolves. Set aside.

Brown dove in hot oil in Dutch oven over medium heat. Remove dove, reserving drippings in Dutch oven; add flour to drippings. Cook over medium heat, stirring constantly, until roux is caramel colored (about 15 minutes). Gradually add 1½ cups broth; cook over medium heat, stirring constantly, until mixture is thickened and bubbly. Add onion and celery; cook 5 minutes or until vegetables are tender, stirring occasionally. Add remaining broth, garlic, and next 8 ingredients to roux mixture; stir well.

Brown sausage in a large skillet over medium heat. Add sausage and dove to roux mixture. Bring to a boil; cover, reduce heat, and simmer 1½ hours, stirring occasionally. Stir in wine and hot sauce. Remove and discard bay leaves. Serve over rice; sprinkle with gumbo filé, if desired. Yield: 5 cups.

Note: Gumbo may be frozen in an airtight container up to 3 months.

TURKEY GUMBO

1 pound smoked sausage, cut
   into ½-inch slices
¼ cup vegetable oil
¼ cup all-purpose flour
3 stalks celery, chopped
2 medium onions, chopped

2 cups cubed cooked turkey
3 cups water
½ teaspoon salt
¼ teaspoon pepper
Hot cooked rice
Gumbo filé (optional)

Brown sausage in a large skillet over medium heat; drain and set aside.
   Combine oil and flour in a Dutch oven; cook over medium heat, stirring constantly, until roux is the color of a copper penny (about 10 minutes). Add celery and onion; cook until tender, stirring frequently. Add sausage, turkey, and water. Bring to a boil; reduce heat, and simmer, uncovered, 2 hours, stirring occasionally. Stir in salt and pepper. Serve over rice; sprinkle with gumbo filé, if desired. Yield: 1½ quarts.

The compliments you'll receive on Gumbo Ya Ya will make this Creole dish worth the effort.

Gumbo Ya Ya

1 (4- to 5-pound) dressed
    duckling
1 (3- to 3½-pound) broiler-fryer
1 gallon water
1½ teaspoons salt
½ teaspoon pepper
1 pound smoked sausage, cut
    into ½-inch slices
6 stalks celery, chopped
3 large onions, chopped
2 large green peppers, seeded
    and chopped
2 cloves garlic, minced

1 tablespoon vegetable oil
1 cup bacon drippings
1 cup all-purpose flour
1 (10-ounce) can diced tomatoes
    and green chiles, undrained
2 teaspoons salt
1 teaspoon seasoned pepper
1 teaspoon hot sauce
1 (16-ounce) package frozen
    sliced okra, thawed
Hot cooked rice
Gumbo filé (optional)

Don't skip the step of chilling Gumbo Ya Ya for eight hours. The refrigeration not only enables you to remove the solidified fat from the surface, but also allows the rich flavors of the gumbo to blend and intensify.

Combine first 5 ingredients in a large Dutch oven or stockpot. Bring to a boil; cover, reduce heat, and simmer 1 hour or until duck and chicken are tender. Remove duck and chicken from broth, reserving broth. Let duck and chicken cool. Transfer broth to another container; set aside. Skin, bone, and coarsely chop duck and chicken; set aside.

Cook sausage and next 4 ingredients in hot oil in Dutch oven over medium-high heat, stirring constantly, until sausage is browned and vegetables are tender. Remove sausage and vegetables from Dutch oven; drain and set aside.

Combine bacon drippings and flour in Dutch oven; cook over medium heat, stirring constantly, until roux is chocolate colored (about 20 minutes). Gradually add reserved broth, stirring constantly. Stir in chopped meat, sausage mixture, tomatoes and green chiles, 2 teaspoons salt, seasoned pepper, and hot sauce. Bring to a boil; cook over medium heat, uncovered, 3 hours, stirring occasionally. Add okra; cook, uncovered, 30 minutes, stirring occasionally. Remove from heat; let cool almost to room temperature, stirring occasionally. Cover and chill at least 8 hours.

Remove from refrigerator; skim as much solidified fat from top of gumbo as possible. Cook over medium heat until mixture is thoroughly heated, stirring frequently. Serve over rice; sprinkle with gumbo filé, if desired. Yield: 5 quarts.

International Flair

▪ Today's cuisine is a virtual melting pot of the food heritages of other countries. ▪ With all the choices in this chapter, you can travel worldwide while savoring quick-and-easy family fare or specialty recipes for company. ▪ Sample an array of Italian pasta dishes from Shrimp and Tortellini to Special Manicotti, or try succulent stir-frys like Sukiyaki and Mongolian Beef. ▪ And to satisfy that craving for spicy Mexican treats, enjoy our Beef-and-Bean Chimichangas and Chiles Rellenos with Red Sauce. ▪ You'll savor a feast of foreign flavors—and you won't even need your passport.

Chinese Sweet-and-Sour Shrimp (page 109)

MINESTRONE

Pasta, beans, and cheese give Minestrone, a traditional Italian soup, enough protein to be a complete meal.

1 cup thinly sliced carrot
1 cup thinly sliced celery
1 cup chopped onion
1 clove garlic, crushed
2 tablespoons butter or margarine, melted
9 medium tomatoes, peeled and chopped
2 teaspoons salt
1 teaspoon dried oregano
1 teaspoon dried basil
½ teaspoon pepper
2 (14½-ounce) cans ready-to-serve beef broth

1 (16-ounce) can navy beans, undrained
1 (15-ounce) can kidney beans, undrained
1 large zucchini, cut in half lengthwise and sliced
1 cup elbow macaroni, uncooked
¼ cup chopped fresh parsley
Freshly grated Parmesan cheese (optional)

Cook first 4 ingredients in butter in a Dutch oven over medium-high heat, stirring constantly, until crisp-tender. Add tomato, salt, oregano, basil, and pepper. Bring to a boil; cover, reduce heat, and simmer 15 minutes, stirring occasionally.

Stir in beef broth and next 5 ingredients. Bring to a boil; cover, reduce heat, and simmer 15 minutes or until macaroni is tender. Serve with Parmesan cheese, if desired. Yield: 3½ quarts.

SHRIMP AND TORTELLINI

Tortellini is available filled with meat, sun-dried tomatoes, or cheese, the type called for in this recipe.

1 pound unpeeled medium-size fresh shrimp
1 (9-ounce) package fresh cheese-filled tortellini, uncooked
1 shallot, minced
2 tablespoons chopped fresh basil or 2 teaspoons dried basil

⅓ cup butter or margarine, melted
½ cup grated Parmesan cheese
Garnish: fresh basil sprigs

Peel shrimp, and devein, if desired; set aside.

Cook tortellini according to package directions; drain and set aside.

Cook shrimp, shallot, and chopped basil in butter in a large skillet over medium-high heat, stirring constantly, 5 minutes or until shrimp turn pink. Add tortellini and Parmesan cheese; toss gently. Garnish, if desired. Yield: 4 servings.

LASAGNA SUPREME

12 lasagna noodles, uncooked
1 pound ground chuck
1 small onion, chopped
1 clove garlic, minced
2 (6-ounce) cans tomato paste
1 (16-ounce) can whole
   tomatoes, undrained and
   chopped
1½ cups water
1 tablespoon dried basil
1 teaspoon sugar
1 teaspoon salt
½ teaspoon dried rosemary
2 bay leaves

2 large eggs, lightly beaten
1 (8-ounce) carton sour cream
2 cups ricotta cheese
¼ cup chopped fresh parsley or
   2 tablespoons dried parsley
½ teaspoon salt
¼ teaspoon pepper
1 cup (4 ounces) shredded
   Cheddar cheese
½ cup grated Parmesan cheese
½ cup grated Romano cheese
2 (6-ounce) packages mozzarella
   cheese slices

■■■■■■■■■■
Let lasagna stand 10 minutes before serving. This allows the lasagna to cool slightly and gives the layers time to firm up before being cut.

Cook lasagna noodles according to package directions; drain well, and set aside.

Cook ground chuck, onion, and garlic in a large skillet over medium-high heat until meat is browned and onion is tender, stirring until meat crumbles. Drain; return mixture to skillet. Combine tomato paste and next 7 ingredients; add to mixture in skillet. Bring to a boil; reduce heat, and simmer, uncovered, 1 hour and 15 minutes, stirring frequently. Remove and discard bay leaves.

Combine eggs and next 5 ingredients; stir well, and set aside.

Arrange 4 lasagna noodles in bottom of a lightly greased 13- x 9- x 2-inch baking dish; layer with one-third each of meat mixture, egg mixture, and Cheddar, Parmesan, and Romano cheeses. Repeat layers twice. Bake at 350° for 30 to 35 minutes or until bubbly. Arrange mozzarella slices over top; bake 5 additional minutes or until cheese melts. Let stand 10 minutes before serving. Yield: 8 servings.

The thick meat sauce that tops Special Manicotti makes it just that—special.

SPECIAL MANICOTTI

■■■■■■■■■■
Wondering how to stuff manicotti shells? It's easy. Just use a pastry bag fitted with a large round tip or a heavy-duty, zip-top plastic bag with ¼ inch cut from one corner of the bag.

½ pound Italian sausage
1 pound ground chuck
2 medium onions, chopped
5 cloves garlic, minced
2 (15-ounce) cans tomato sauce
1 (16-ounce) can whole
    tomatoes, undrained and
    chopped
1 (12-ounce) can tomato paste
1½ teaspoons dried oregano
1¼ teaspoons dried basil
1 teaspoon sugar
½ teaspoon black pepper
½ teaspoon dried thyme
½ teaspoon dried rosemary
¼ teaspoon salt
¼ teaspoon dried marjoram

⅛ teaspoon ground red pepper
1 (8-ounce) package manicotti
    shells
1 (15-ounce) container ricotta
    cheese
1 (8-ounce) package cream
    cheese, softened
1 (3-ounce) package cream
    cheese with chives, softened
4 cloves garlic, pressed
4 cups (16 ounces) shredded
    mozzarella cheese
½ cup grated Parmesan cheese
½ teaspoon dried thyme
½ teaspoon dried oregano
½ teaspoon black pepper
Garnish: fresh oregano sprigs

Remove casings from sausage, if necessary. Cook sausage, ground chuck, onion, and garlic in a large Dutch oven over medium-high heat until meat is browned and onion is tender, stirring to crumble meat.

Drain; add tomato sauce and next 11 ingredients. Bring to a boil; cover, reduce heat, and simmer 2½ hours, stirring occasionally.

Cook manicotti shells according to package directions; drain. Combine ricotta cheese and remaining ingredients in a large bowl; stir well. Stuff shells with cheese mixture.

Pour 1 cup meat sauce into each of 2 lightly greased 11- x 7- x 1½-inch baking dishes. Arrange stuffed shells over sauce; spoon remaining meat sauce evenly over stuffed shells. Cover and bake at 350° for 30 to 40 minutes or until bubbly and thoroughly heated. Let stand 5 minutes before serving. Garnish, if desired. Yield: 8 servings.

Note: Special Manicotti may be prepared ahead and frozen. Prepare as directed above, but do not bake. Cover and freeze up to 3 months. Remove from freezer, and bake, covered, at 350° for 2 hours or until bubbly. (Manicotti may be thawed in refrigerator 24 hours and baked, covered, at 350° for 1 hour.)

THICK-AND-SPICY SPAGHETTI

2 pounds ground chuck
2 large onions, chopped
2 medium-size green peppers, seeded and chopped
2 or 3 cloves garlic, minced
1 cup chopped celery
1 (16-ounce) can whole tomatoes, undrained and coarsely chopped
3 (8-ounce) cans tomato sauce
3 (6-ounce) cans tomato paste
1 (4-ounce) can sliced mushrooms, undrained
3 drops hot sauce

2 bay leaves
½ cup water
½ cup dry red wine
2 tablespoons Worcestershire sauce
2 teaspoons dried oregano
2 teaspoons chili powder
1 teaspoon salt
1 teaspoon dried Italian seasoning
1 teaspoon ground cinnamon
2 teaspoons white vinegar
Hot cooked spaghetti
Grated Parmesan cheese

Cook first 5 ingredients in a large Dutch oven over medium-high heat until meat is browned and vegetables are tender, stirring until meat crumbles. Drain; add tomato and next 14 ingredients. Bring to a boil; cover, reduce heat, and simmer 1 hour, stirring occasionally. Remove and discard bay leaves. Serve sauce over spaghetti; sprinkle with Parmesan cheese. Yield: about 3½ quarts.

THICK 'N' CRUSTY PEPPERONI PIZZAS

■■■■■■■■■■■
You can store these pizzas in the freezer unbaked and tightly wrapped up to one month. When you're ready to serve the pizzas, remove them from the freezer, and let stand 15 minutes. Remove the wrapping, and bake the pizzas at 450° for 20 minutes or until the cheese melts.

1 package active dry yeast
¼ cup warm water (105° to 115°)
4 to 4½ cups all-purpose flour, divided
1¼ cups warm water (105° to 115°)
2 teaspoons vegetable oil
1 teaspoon salt
1 teaspoon sugar

1 medium onion, chopped
1 medium-size green pepper, seeded and diced
1 tablespoon vegetable oil
Tomato Sauce
1 (3½-ounce) package sliced pepperoni
1½ cups sliced fresh mushrooms
4 cups (16 ounces) shredded mozzarella cheese

Combine yeast and ¼ cup warm water in a 1-cup liquid measuring cup; let stand 5 minutes. Combine yeast mixture, 2 cups flour, 1¼ cups warm water, and next 3 ingredients in a large mixing bowl; beat at medium speed of an electric mixer until well blended. Gradually stir in enough of remaining flour to make a soft dough.

Turn dough out onto a lightly floured surface, and knead 3 minutes. Place in a well-greased bowl, turning to grease top. Cover and let rise in a warm place (85°), free from drafts, 15 minutes.

Punch dough down, and divide in half. Pat dough evenly into 2 lightly greased 12-inch pizza pans; prick with a fork. Bake at 450° for 5 minutes for a soft crust or 10 minutes for a crisper crust. Set aside.

Cook onion and green pepper in 1 tablespoon hot oil in a large skillet over medium-high heat, stirring constantly, until tender. Spread Tomato Sauce evenly over prepared crusts; top evenly with layers of pepperoni, vegetable mixture, mushrooms, and cheese. Bake at 450° for 10 minutes or until cheese melts. Yield: two 12-inch pizzas.

Tomato Sauce

1 (8-ounce) can tomato sauce
1 (6-ounce) can tomato paste
2 tablespoons minced fresh parsley
2 tablespoons dry red wine
1 tablespoon vegetable oil

1 tablespoon water
½ teaspoon salt
½ teaspoon sugar
½ teaspoon dried oregano
¼ teaspoon pepper
1 clove garlic, minced

Combine all ingredients in a medium saucepan. Bring to a boil; cover, reduce heat, and simmer 20 minutes, stirring frequently. Yield: 1½ cups.

GRUYÈRE-CHICKEN PIZZA

1 (8-ounce) carton sour cream
1 tablespoon all-purpose flour
1½ cups chopped cooked
    chicken
1½ cups (6 ounces) grated
    Gruyère cheese, divided
¼ teaspoon ground cumin

⅛ teaspoon hot sauce
1 clove garlic, minced
1 Crispy Pizza Crust
⅓ cup sliced ripe olives
¼ cup chopped green onions
2 tablespoons grated Parmesan
    cheese

Combine sour cream and flour in a large bowl, stirring well. Stir in chicken, 1 cup Gruyère cheese, cumin, hot sauce, and garlic. Spread chicken mixture over Crispy Pizza Crust. Top with olives, green onions, remaining ½ cup Gruyère cheese, and Parmesan cheese. Bake at 450° for 15 minutes or until cheese melts. Yield: one 12-inch pizza.

Crispy Pizza Crusts

1 package active dry yeast
1 cup warm water (105° to 115°)
3 to 3¼ cups all-purpose flour,
    divided

1 tablespoon olive oil
1 teaspoon salt
1 to 2 teaspoons cornmeal

Combine yeast and warm water in a 2-cup liquid measuring cup; let stand 5 minutes. Combine yeast mixture, 1½ cups flour, oil, and salt in a large mixing bowl; beat at medium speed of an electric mixer until mixture is well blended. Gradually stir in enough of remaining flour to make a firm dough.

Turn dough out onto a lightly floured surface, and knead until smooth and elastic (about 5 minutes). Place in a well-greased bowl, turning to grease top. Cover and let rise in a warm place (85°), free from drafts, 1 hour or until doubled in bulk.

Punch dough down; divide in half. Roll each portion to a 12-inch circle on a floured surface. Transfer dough to 2 ungreased 12-inch pizza pans sprinkled with cornmeal. Fold over edges of dough, and pinch to form a rim; prick with a fork. Bake at 450° for 5 minutes for soft crust or 10 minutes for crisper crust. Yield: two 12-inch pizza crusts.

Note: Baked Crispy Pizza Crusts may be wrapped tightly and frozen up to 1 month. To use, remove from freezer, and let stand 30 minutes. Remove wrapping; top and bake as directed above.

CHILES RELLENOS WITH RED SAUCE

8 canned whole mild green chiles (about four 4-ounce cans)
1 (8-ounce) package Monterey Jack cheese*
½ cup all-purpose flour
¼ teaspoon salt
⅛ teaspoon pepper
4 large eggs, separated
¼ cup all-purpose flour
Vegetable oil
Red Sauce

Rinse chiles, and remove seeds; pat dry. Cut block of cheese into 8 crosswise strips; place a strip of cheese inside each chile. (If chiles tear, overlap torn sides; batter will hold chiles together.)

Combine ½ cup flour, salt, and pepper in a shallow bowl; set aside. Beat egg yolks until thick and pale. Beat egg whites in a large bowl at high speed of an electric mixer until stiff peaks form. Gently fold yolks and ¼ cup flour into beaten egg white.

Pour oil to depth of 2 inches into a Dutch oven; heat to 375°. Dredge each stuffed chile in dry flour mixture; dip in egg batter. Fry chiles, a few at a time, in hot oil until golden, turning once; drain on paper towels. Serve warm with Red Sauce. Yield: 4 servings.

Red Sauce

4 cloves garlic, crushed
¼ cup butter or margarine, melted
¼ cup all-purpose flour
1 cup beef broth
1 (8-ounce) can tomato sauce
1 tablespoon chili powder
1 teaspoon rubbed sage
1 teaspoon ground cumin

Cook garlic in butter in a medium saucepan over medium heat, stirring constantly, 3 minutes; add flour, stirring until smooth. Cook, stirring constantly, 1 minute. Gradually add beef broth and tomato sauce, stirring constantly. Add chili powder, sage, and cumin; cook, stirring constantly, until mixture is thickened and bubbly. Yield: 2 cups.

*Monterey Jack with jalapeño peppers may be substituted.

MEAT-AND-BEAN BURRITOS

¾ pound boneless beef, cut into
  ½-inch pieces
¾ pound boneless pork, cut into
  ½-inch pieces
1 cup chopped onion
3 tablespoons vegetable oil,
  divided
1½ cups water
1 teaspoon salt

1 clove garlic, crushed
1 (4.5-ounce) can chopped green
  chiles, drained
10 (8-inch) flour tortillas
1 (16-ounce) can refried beans
¼ cup (1 ounce) shredded
  Cheddar cheese
Chunky salsa
Sour cream

Cook first 3 ingredients in 2 tablespoons hot oil in a Dutch oven over medium heat, stirring constantly, until meat is browned and onion is tender; stir in water, salt, and garlic. Bring to a boil; cover, reduce heat, and simmer 1½ to 2 hours or until meat is tender. Dice meat; return to Dutch oven. Stir in chiles; cook, uncovered, 15 minutes or until liquid evaporates, stirring occasionally. Set aside.

Wrap tortillas tightly in aluminum foil; bake at 350° for 15 minutes. Cook refried beans in remaining 1 tablespoon oil in a medium skillet over medium heat until thoroughly heated. Add cheese, stirring until cheese melts.

Spread about 3 tablespoons bean mixture evenly over each tortilla. Spoon a heaping ¼ cup meat mixture down center of each tortilla. Roll up tortillas, and place, seam side down, on a baking sheet; cover with aluminum foil. Bake at 325° for 15 minutes or until thoroughly heated. Serve immediately with salsa and sour cream. Yield: 10 burritos.

Spicy Tomato-Green Chile Sauce gives Beef-and-Bean Chimichangas authentic Mexican flavor.

BEEF-AND-BEAN CHIMICHANGAS

Fry a burrito, and you have a chimichanga. To prevent the filling from falling out while frying, tuck in the ends of the tortilla and secure with a wooden pick. Just be sure to remove the picks before you serve the chimichangas.

1 pound ground chuck
1 medium onion, chopped
2 cloves garlic, minced
1 (16-ounce) can refried beans
½ cup tomato sauce
1 tablespoon chili powder
¾ teaspoon ground cumin
10 (10-inch) flour tortillas
Vegetable oil
Tomato-Green Chile Sauce
2 cups (8 ounces) shredded
    Monterey Jack cheese

Cook first 3 ingredients in a large skillet over medium-high heat until meat is browned and onion is tender, stirring until meat crumbles. Drain; stir in refried beans and next 3 ingredients.

For each chimichanga, place a heaping ⅓ cup meat mixture just below center of tortilla. Fold bottom edge of tortilla over filling; fold in left and right sides. Roll up to form a rectangle; secure with a wooden pick.

Pour oil to depth of 2 inches into a Dutch oven; heat to 375°. Fry chimichangas, a few at a time, in hot oil 3 minutes or until golden, turning once. Drain on paper towels. Remove wooden picks.

Arrange chimichangas on a large ovenproof platter or baking sheet; spoon warm Tomato-Green Chile Sauce over chimichangas, and sprinkle with cheese. Broil 5½ inches from heat (with electric oven door partially opened) 1 to 2 minutes or until cheese melts. Serve immediately. Yield: 10 chimichangas.

Tomato-Green Chile Sauce

1 medium onion, finely chopped
1 clove garlic, minced
2 tablespoons butter or
    margarine, melted
2 cups tomato sauce
½ teaspoon dried oregano
½ teaspoon ground cumin
¼ teaspoon salt
1 (4.5-ounce) can chopped green
    chiles, drained

Cook onion and garlic in butter in a large saucepan over medium-high heat, stirring constantly, until tender. Stir in tomato sauce and remaining ingredients. Bring to a boil; reduce heat, and simmer, uncovered, 20 minutes or until thickened, stirring occasionally. Yield: 2½ cups.

PICADILLO

2 pounds ground chuck
2 medium onions, chopped
1 clove garlic, minced
1 (28-ounce) can whole
    tomatoes, undrained and
    chopped
2 or 3 canned jalapeño peppers,
    seeded and sliced into thin
    strips
2 cooking apples, peeled, cored,
    and chopped
½ cup raisins
¼ cup sliced pimiento-stuffed
    olives
¼ teaspoon salt
¼ teaspoon ground cinnamon
⅛ teaspoon ground cloves
⅛ teaspoon pepper
¼ cup slivered almonds
1 teaspoon olive oil
Hot cooked rice

Try this Mexican dish with black beans instead of rice, if you prefer. For a change of pace, use Picadillo as a filling for tortillas.

Cook ground chuck, onion, and garlic in a Dutch oven over medium-high heat until meat is browned and onion is tender, stirring until meat crumbles. Drain; add tomato and next 8 ingredients. Bring to a boil; cover, reduce heat, and simmer 20 minutes, stirring occasionally.

Cook almonds in hot oil in a small skillet over medium-high heat, stirring constantly, until toasted. Drain on paper towels. Spoon meat mixture over rice; sprinkle with almonds. Yield: 6 servings.

Tostadas Compuestas

■■■■■■■■■■
For your next casual
gathering, let your
guests entertain them-
selves. With Tostadas
Compuestas, they can
build their own creations
of fried tortillas with
various toppings.

1 pound ground chuck
1 medium onion, chopped
1 (16-ounce) can refried beans
¼ cup hot picante sauce
2 medium avocados
1 tablespoon lemon juice
Vegetable oil

8 (6-inch) corn tortillas
2 cups (8 ounces) shredded
 Cheddar cheese
2 cups shredded lettuce
2 large tomatoes, chopped
Hot picante sauce
Sour cream

Cook ground chuck and onion in a large skillet over medium-high heat until meat is browned and onion is tender, stirring until meat crumbles. Drain; return mixture to skillet. Stir in beans and ¼ cup picante sauce. Set aside.

Peel avocados, and remove seeds. Mash avocados; stir in lemon juice. Set aside.

Pour oil to depth of 1 inch into a large heavy skillet; heat to 375°. Fry tortillas, one at a time, 20 to 30 seconds on each side or until crisp and golden. Drain on paper towels.

Spoon meat mixture evenly onto fried tortillas; sprinkle with cheese. Place tostadas on baking sheets. Bake at 400° for 2 to 3 minutes or until cheese melts. Top with avocado mixture, lettuce, tomato, additional picante sauce, and sour cream. Yield: 8 servings.

Pollo con Calabacita

■■■■■■■■■■
Translated into English,
Pollo con Calabacita
means chicken with
zucchini. Hot cooked rice
makes a nice addition to
this main dish.

1 (3½- to 4-pound) package
 chicken pieces
¼ cup vegetable oil
2 large zucchini, cubed
1 clove garlic, minced
3 tablespoons all-purpose flour
2 tablespoons chopped onion

2 tablespoons chopped green
 pepper
1 teaspoon salt
1 teaspoon pepper
½ teaspoon ground cumin
3 cups water

Brown chicken in hot oil in a Dutch oven; drain on paper towels. Discard pan drippings. Return chicken to Dutch oven.

Combine zucchini and next 7 ingredients; toss gently. Spoon vegetable mixture evenly over chicken; add 3 cups water. Bring to a boil; reduce heat, and simmer, uncovered, 40 to 45 minutes or until chicken is tender, stirring frequently. Yield: 4 servings.

PAELLA

1 pound unpeeled medium-size
   fresh shrimp
⅓ cup olive oil
2 cloves garlic, sliced
1 (3½- to 4-pound) package
   chicken pieces
1 (28-ounce) can whole
   tomatoes, undrained and
   chopped

½ teaspoon salt
¾ cup long-grain rice, uncooked
¼ teaspoon ground saffron
¼ cup boiling water
1 cup cut fresh green beans
1 cup frozen English peas,
   thawed and drained

■ ■ ■ ■ ■ ■ ■ ■ ■ ■ ❑
Paella comes from Spain
and takes its name from
the round, shallow pan in
which it's prepared and
served. While the vegeta-
bles and meat may vary,
the saffron-flavored rice is
a constant in paella.

Peel shrimp, and devein, if desired. Set aside. Heat oil over medium-high heat in a paella pan or skillet. Add garlic; cook, stirring constantly, 1 minute. Discard garlic. Brown chicken in hot oil. Drain; add tomato and salt. Bring to a boil; cover, reduce heat, and simmer 30 minutes.

    Remove chicken; stir in rice. Combine saffron and boiling water; add to rice. Add chicken to skillet. Bring to a boil; cover, reduce heat, and simmer 20 minutes (do not stir). Sprinkle beans, peas, and shrimp over rice mixture. Cover and simmer 10 minutes (do not stir). Yield: 6 servings.

Saffron is the secret to the deep golden color of Paella.

SPICY CHICKEN ENCHILADAS

■■■■■■■■■

**Wake up your family's
usual fare with Spicy
Chicken Enchiladas. This
dish fills the bill for a
great chicken dinner:
basic ingredients imagina-
tively seasoned.**

2 canned jalapeño peppers,
   seeded and chopped
1 large tomato, finely chopped
½ cup finely chopped onion
¼ cup tomato juice
½ teaspoon salt
¼ cup butter or margarine
¼ cup all-purpose flour
2 cups chicken broth

1 (8-ounce) carton sour cream
2 canned jalapeño peppers,
   seeded and chopped
12 (6-inch) corn tortillas
2 cups chopped cooked chicken
2 cups (8 ounces) shredded
   Monterey Jack cheese,
   divided
¾ cup chopped onion

Combine first 5 ingredients; stir well. Cover and chill.

Melt butter in a medium saucepan over medium heat; add flour, stir-ring until smooth. Cook, stirring constantly, 1 minute. Gradually add chicken broth; cook, stirring constantly, until thickened and bubbly. Remove from heat; stir in sour cream and 2 chopped jalapeño peppers.

Pour half of sour cream mixture into a lightly greased 13- x 9- x 2-inch baking dish; set dish and remaining sour cream mixture aside.

Wrap tortillas tightly in aluminum foil; bake at 350° for 15 minutes.

Spoon 2 heaping tablespoons chicken and 1 tablespoon each of cheese and onion down center of each tortilla. Roll up tortillas; place, seam side down, in prepared dish. Pour remaining sour cream mixture over enchiladas. Bake at 400° for 25 minutes or until thoroughly heat-ed. Sprinkle with remaining 1¼ cups cheese; bake 3 to 5 minutes or until cheese melts. Serve with chilled tomato mixture. Yield: 6 servings.

SPICY THAI LOBSTER SOUP

2 fresh or frozen lobster tails,
   thawed
1 tablespoon ground ginger
½ teaspoon ground red pepper
1 tablespoon peanut oil
5 cups chicken broth
1 tablespoon grated lime rind
½ cup long-grain rice, uncooked

½ cup chopped onion
6 large fresh mushrooms, sliced
1 cup unsweetened coconut milk
1 tablespoon chopped fresh
   cilantro
2 tablespoons lime juice
Garnishes: sliced green onions,
   fresh cilantro sprigs

Carefully remove lobster meat from shells; cut meat crosswise into ¼-inch-thick slices. Set aside.

Cook ginger and pepper in hot oil in a large saucepan over medium heat 1 minute; add broth and lime rind. Bring to a boil; stir in rice and chopped onion. Cover, reduce heat, and simmer 15 minutes.

Add lobster meat, mushrooms, coconut milk, and chopped cilantro; cook 5 minutes, stirring occasionally. Remove from heat, and stir in lime juice. Ladle soup into bowls, and garnish, if desired. Yield: 2 quarts.

CHINESE SWEET-AND-SOUR SHRIMP

1 pound unpeeled large fresh
   shrimp
½ cup all-purpose flour
⅓ cup plus 1 tablespoon water
¼ cup cornstarch
1 teaspoon vegetable oil

½ teaspoon salt
½ teaspoon baking powder
1 large egg, lightly beaten
Vegetable oil
Sweet-and-Sour Sauce
Hot cooked rice

Peel shrimp; devein, if desired. Combine flour and next 6 ingredients.

Pour oil to depth of 3 inches into a Dutch oven; heat to 375°. Dip shrimp into batter; fry, a few at a time, in hot oil until golden. Drain on paper towels. Arrange shrimp on a baking sheet; place in a 200° oven to keep warm while frying remaining shrimp. Combine shrimp and Sweet-and-Sour Sauce; serve immediately over rice. Yield: 6 servings.

Sweet-and-Sour Sauce

½ cup sliced carrot
½ cup coarsely chopped green
   pepper
¾ cup sugar
⅓ cup ketchup
1 tablespoon soy sauce

¼ teaspoon salt
1 (15¼-ounce) can pineapple
   chunks, undrained
3½ tablespoons cornstarch
⅓ cup water
½ cup white vinegar

Cook carrot in a small amount of boiling water 2 minutes. Add green pepper; cook 1 minute. Drain; rinse with cold water. Drain; set aside.

Combine sugar and next 3 ingredients in a medium saucepan; stir well. Drain pineapple, reserving juice; stir pineapple juice into sugar mixture. Bring to a boil. Combine cornstarch and water, stirring until smooth; add cornstarch mixture and vinegar to juice mixture. Cook over medium heat, stirring constantly, until mixture is thickened and bubbly. Stir in vegetables and pineapple chunks. Yield: about 4 cups.

Wow your guests with this elegant but easy-to-make meal featuring shrimp. Sweet-and-sour describes a balanced blend of sweet with sour or pungent flavors.

MONGOLIAN BEEF

From the northernmost part of China comes Mongolian Beef. Because this is a cold region, fresh vegetables aren't plentiful, so cooks liven up the cuisine with sweet bean sauce, green onions, and soy sauce.

1 tablespoon cornstarch
1½ teaspoons sugar
¾ teaspoon baking soda
¼ cup soy sauce
2 tablespoons dark sesame oil
1 tablespoon rice wine
2 pounds sirloin steak, cut into thin strips

¼ cup vegetable oil, divided
1 tablespoon cornstarch
1½ cups water, divided
3 tablespoons hoisin sauce
3 tablespoons sweet bean sauce
3 bunches green onions, cut into 1½-inch pieces
Hot cooked rice

Combine first 6 ingredients; stir until smooth. Add steak, stirring to coat.

Pour 2 tablespoons oil around top of preheated wok or large skillet; heat at medium-high (375°) for 2 minutes. Add steak, and stir-fry 8 minutes or until no longer pink. Remove from wok; set aside.

Combine 1 tablespoon cornstarch and 2 tablespoons water; stir until smooth. Stir in remaining water, hoisin sauce, and bean sauce. Set aside.

Pour remaining 2 tablespoons vegetable oil around top of wok, coating sides; heat 2 minutes. Add green onions, and stir-fry 5 minutes or until tender; push up sides of wok. Pour hoisin sauce mixture into center of wok; bring to a boil. Push green onions back down into center of wok, and return steak to wok. Stir-fry 2 minutes or until thoroughly heated. Serve immediately over rice. Yield: 4 servings.

SUKIYAKI

If you're cooking regular rice to serve with Sukiyaki, start the rice, and then begin the stir-fry procedure. Regular rice takes 20 minutes to cook and will be ready just in time to serve with the rest of the meal.

½ cup soy sauce
¼ cup beef broth
1 tablespoon sugar
½ teaspoon salt
2 tablespoons vegetable oil
1 pound sirloin steak, cut into thin strips
1 medium onion, thinly sliced
6 green onions, cut into 1-inch pieces
3 stalks celery, thinly sliced

½ pound fresh mushrooms, sliced
1 (8-ounce) can bamboo shoots, drained
4 ounces firm tofu, cut into ½-inch cubes
½ head Chinese cabbage, sliced
2 tablespoons cornstarch
2 tablespoons water
Hot cooked rice

Combine first 4 ingredients in a small bowl; stir well, and set aside. Pour oil around top of preheated wok or large skillet; heat at medium-high

(375°) for 2 minutes. Add steak, and stir-fry 4 to 5 minutes or until no longer pink; push steak up sides of wok.

Add sliced onion to wok, and stir-fry 2 minutes. Add green onions, celery, and mushrooms; stir-fry 2 minutes or until vegetables are crisp-tender. Push vegetable mixture up sides of wok.

Add bamboo shoots to wok, and stir-fry 1 minute. Add tofu, cabbage, and soy sauce mixture; stir-fry 1 to 2 minutes or until mixture is thoroughly heated. Push mixture up sides of wok.

Combine cornstarch and water, stirring until smooth. Pour cornstarch mixture into center of wok; bring to a boil. Push steak and vegetable mixture back down into center of wok. Stir-fry 1 to 2 minutes or until mixture is thoroughly heated. Serve immediately over rice. Yield: 6 servings.

CHICKEN CHOW MEIN

3 tablespoons cornstarch
3 cups chicken broth, divided
¼ cup dry sherry
¼ cup soy sauce
¼ teaspoon pepper
2 tablespoons vegetable oil
4 skinned, boned chicken breast
    halves, cut into thin strips
1 cup diagonally sliced celery
1 cup chopped green pepper
2 cups sliced fresh mushrooms
1 cup sliced green onions
1 (16-ounce) can bean sprouts,
    drained
1 (8-ounce) can bamboo shoots,
    drained
½ cup sliced water chestnuts
Chow mein noodles

Combine cornstarch and ¼ cup broth; stir until smooth. Combine cornstarch mixture, remaining 2¾ cups broth, sherry, soy sauce, and pepper in a medium bowl; stir well, and set aside.

Pour oil around top of preheated wok or large skillet; heat at medium-high (375°) for 2 minutes. Add chicken strips, and stir-fry 4 to 5 minutes or until lightly browned. Remove chicken from wok, and drain well on paper towels.

Add celery and green pepper to wok; stir-fry 2 minutes. Add mushrooms and green onions; stir-fry 2 to 3 minutes or until vegetables are crisp-tender. Add cornstarch mixture, chicken, bean sprouts, bamboo shoots, and water chestnuts; stir-fry 3 minutes or until mixture is thickened and thoroughly heated. Serve immediately over chow mein noodles. Yield: 6 servings.

Foods prepared quickly in a wok, such as Chicken Chow Mein and the other recipes on this page, retain their nutrition, taste, color, and crispness. Created in China a thousand years ago, a wok is the perfect cooking vessel for health-conscious cooks.

A vinaigrette made of white wine vinegar, olive oil, and lots of garlic is the perfect accompaniment for Salade Niçoise.

SALADE NIÇOISE

2 tablespoons lemon juice
1 tablespoon capers
¼ teaspoon salt
¼ teaspoon pepper
2 (12-ounce) cans solid white tuna packed in water, drained and separated into chunks
½ pound fresh baby green beans
1 pound small round red potatoes, unpeeled

1 pound plum tomatoes, quartered
4 hard-cooked eggs, quartered
2 small purple onions, sliced and separated into rings
¾ cup Niçoise olives or other small black olives
Leaf lettuce leaves
Niçoise Dressing (facing page)

Combine first 4 ingredients; drizzle over tuna. Cover and chill.

Wash beans; remove ends. Set aside. Cook potatoes in boiling water to cover 15 minutes. Add beans; cook 5 minutes or until crisp-tender. Drain vegetables; plunge into ice water, and drain. Quarter potatoes.

Arrange beans, potato, tomato, egg, onion, and olives on a large lettuce-lined serving platter; mound tuna mixture in center. Drizzle Niçoise Dressing over salad. Yield: 6 servings.

Niçoise Dressing

⅔ cup olive oil
⅔ cup white wine vinegar
⅓ cup mayonnaise
1 teaspoon salt

1 teaspoon pepper
1 teaspoon dried oregano
1 teaspoon dried basil
2 cloves garlic, pressed

Combine all ingredients in a jar. Cover tightly, and shake vigorously. Yield: 1½ cups.

PASTICCIO

1 (8-ounce) package elbow
   macaroni, uncooked
1 pound ground lamb or
   ground chuck
1 large onion, chopped
2 (8-ounce) cans tomato sauce
¾ teaspoon salt
¼ teaspoon ground allspice

¼ teaspoon ground cinnamon
¼ teaspoon ground cloves
3 tablespoons butter or
   margarine
3 tablespoons all-purpose flour
2 cups milk
¼ teaspoon salt
2 large eggs, lightly beaten

Cook macaroni according to package directions; drain and set aside.

Cook ground lamb and onion in a large skillet over medium-high heat until meat is browned and onion is tender, stirring until meat crumbles. Drain; stir in tomato sauce and next 4 ingredients. Bring to a boil; reduce heat, and simmer, uncovered, 5 minutes, stirring occasionally.

Spoon half of macaroni into a lightly greased 2½-quart casserole; top with meat mixture. Spoon remaining macaroni over meat mixture.

Melt butter in a saucepan over medium heat; add flour, stirring until smooth. Cook, stirring constantly, 1 minute. Gradually add milk; cook, stirring constantly, until thickened and bubbly. Stir in ¼ teaspoon salt.

Gradually stir about one-fourth of hot mixture into eggs; add to remaining hot mixture, stirring constantly. Cook, stirring constantly, 1 minute; pour over macaroni. Bake, uncovered, at 350° for 45 minutes. Broil 5½ inches from heat (with electric oven door partially opened) 3 minutes or until browned. Let stand 5 minutes. Yield: 8 servings.

Derived from the French *pastiche*, pasticcio literally means hodgepodge or potpourri. That's the perfect description for this Greek casserole featuring savory onions and tomato sauce combined with the sweetness of allspice, cinnamon, and cloves.

HUNGARIAN GOULASH

2 pounds beef stew meat, cut into 1-inch pieces
½ cup all-purpose flour
1½ teaspoons salt
¾ teaspoon pepper
¼ cup vegetable oil
2 medium onions, coarsely chopped
1 large clove garlic, pressed
1 large green pepper, seeded and coarsely chopped
1½ cups tomato juice
1½ cups beef broth
1½ tablespoons Hungarian paprika
½ teaspoon caraway seeds
Hot cooked, buttered noodles
Sour cream (optional)

Combine first 4 ingredients in a zip-top plastic bag. Seal bag; shake until meat is coated. Remove meat from bag; reserve remaining flour mixture.

Brown meat in hot oil in a Dutch oven over medium-high heat. Add onion and garlic; cook, stirring constantly, until onion is tender. Add remaining flour mixture, green pepper, and next 4 ingredients. Bring to a boil; cover, reduce heat, and simmer 1½ hours, stirring frequently. Uncover and simmer 10 minutes, stirring frequently. Serve over noodles with a dollop of sour cream, if desired. Yield: 8 servings.

CHICKEN PAPRIKASH

1 (3-pound) broiler-fryer, cut up
¼ cup butter or margarine, melted
½ cup chopped onion
¼ cup all-purpose flour
2 tablespoons Hungarian paprika
2 cups chicken broth
½ teaspoon salt
¼ teaspoon pepper
1 (8-ounce) carton sour cream
Hot cooked noodles

Brown chicken in butter in a Dutch oven over medium heat. Remove chicken, reserving drippings in Dutch oven; drain on paper towels.

Add onion to drippings; cook over medium heat, stirring constantly, until tender. Add flour and paprika; cook, stirring constantly, 1 minute. Gradually add chicken broth; cook, stirring constantly, until thickened and bubbly. Stir in salt and pepper. Add chicken; cover, reduce heat, and simmer 1 hour or until chicken is tender.

Stir in sour cream; cook, stirring constantly, just until thoroughly heated (do not boil). Serve over noodles. Yield: 4 servings.

MIXED FRUIT TZIMMES WITH BRISKET

1 (12-ounce) package pitted
  prunes
1 (8-ounce) package dried
  apples
1 (6-ounce) package dried
  apricots
1 (3-pound) beef brisket
2 tablespoons vegetable oil
2 teaspoons salt

¼ teaspoon pepper
3 carrots, scraped and cut into
  2-inch pieces
½ lime, cut into ¼-inch slices
2 cups water
2 cups orange juice
¼ cup honey
Garnishes: lime wedge, orange
  wedge, fresh sage sprig

Combine first 3 ingredients in a large bowl; add water to cover. Let stand 1 hour; drain and set aside.

Brown brisket in hot oil in an ovenproof Dutch oven; sprinkle with salt and pepper. Arrange fruit, carrot, and lime slices around brisket.

Combine 2 cups water, orange juice, and honey; pour over brisket. Bring to a boil; remove from heat. Cover and bake at 350° for 3 hours. Transfer brisket, fruit mixture, and carrot to a serving platter; remove and discard lime slices. Garnish, if desired. Yield: 8 servings.

You'll find tzimmes, a stew of brisket, fruits, and vegetables, to be among the dishes served during the Jewish celebration of Rosh Hashanah. The beef brisket in our version comes out tender and juicy, and the lime adds unexpected zip.

Orange juice and fresh lime slices make Mixed Fruit Tzimmes with Brisket melt-in-your-mouth tender.

Indian Kheema

1 pound ground chuck
1¼ cups chopped onion
2 cups water, divided
2 teaspoons curry powder
¾ teaspoon salt
¾ teaspoon ground turmeric
½ teaspoon garlic powder
½ teaspoon ground red pepper
¼ teaspoon ground ginger
¼ teaspoon black pepper
1 large potato, peeled and cut
    into ¾-inch cubes
1 medium tomato, peeled and
    chopped
1 (17-ounce) can English peas,
    drained
Hot cooked rice

Cook ground chuck and onion in a large skillet over medium-high heat until meat is browned and onion is tender, stirring until meat crumbles. Drain; return mixture to skillet.

Combine 1 cup water, curry powder, and next 6 ingredients; add to meat mixture, stirring well. Stir in potato, tomato, peas, and remaining 1 cup water. Bring to a boil; cover, reduce heat, and simmer 20 to 25 minutes or until potato is tender. Serve over rice. Yield: 4 servings.

Chicken Curry

6 skinned chicken breast halves
4 black peppercorns
2 bay leaves
2 cloves garlic
1 teaspoon salt
1 medium apple, peeled, cored,
    and chopped
1 medium onion, sliced
⅔ cup sliced carrot
½ cup chopped celery
3 tablespoons butter or
    margarine, melted
1½ tablespoons curry powder
½ teaspoon chili powder
3 tablespoons all-purpose flour
¼ teaspoon salt
¼ teaspoon ground mace
¼ teaspoon ground allspice
¼ teaspoon ground nutmeg
¼ teaspoon ground cinnamon
¼ teaspoon ground cloves
Hot cooked rice
Assorted condiments: flaked
    coconut, chopped peanuts,
    commercial chutney, raisins,
    chopped green onions,
    cooked and crumbled bacon

Combine first 5 ingredients in a Dutch oven; add water to cover. Bring to a boil; cover, reduce heat, and simmer 35 to 40 minutes or until chicken is tender. Remove chicken from broth, reserving broth. Remove and discard peppercorns, bay leaves, and garlic cloves. Let chicken cool. Bone chicken, and cut meat into bite-size pieces. Skim fat from broth; set aside 1¾ cups broth; reserve any remaining broth for another use, if desired.

Cook apple, onion, carrot, and celery in butter in Dutch oven over medium-low heat 15 to 20 minutes or until tender. Add curry powder and chili powder; cook 5 minutes, stirring occasionally. Stir in ¾ cup broth.

Place apple mixture in container of an electric blender; cover and process until smooth, stopping once to scrape down sides. Add flour, and process until blended. Return mixture to Dutch oven; add remaining 1 cup reserved broth. Cook over medium heat, stirring constantly, 5 minutes. Add chopped chicken, ¼ teaspoon salt, and next 5 ingredients; cook, stirring constantly, until mixture is thoroughly heated. Serve over rice with assorted condiments. Yield: 6 servings.

SHISH KABOBS WITH BROWN RICE

3 pounds lean boneless lamb,
    cut into 1-inch cubes
⅓ cup lemon juice
¼ cup vegetable oil
2 tablespoons grated onion
2 teaspoons salt
2 teaspoons curry powder
1 teaspoon ground ginger
½ teaspoon ground red pepper

1 clove garlic, crushed
16 fresh mushroom caps
16 large cherry tomatoes
4 medium onions, quartered
2 large green peppers, seeded
    and cut into 1-inch pieces
1 (15¼-ounce) can pineapple
    chunks, drained
Hot cooked brown rice

Brown rice has a nuttier flavor and chewier texture than its white counterpart. This is due to the bran coating left on the grain. The bran coating also gives brown rice its characteristic light tan color.

Place lamb in a large heavy-duty, zip-top plastic bag. Combine lemon juice and next 7 ingredients; pour over lamb. Seal bag; marinate in refrigerator 8 hours, turning bag occasionally.

Remove lamb from marinade, reserving marinade. Place marinade in a small saucepan. Bring to a boil; set aside.

Alternately thread lamb, vegetables, and pineapple on 16 (10-inch) skewers; brush with marinade. Grill, covered, over medium coals (300° to 350°) 10 to 12 minutes, turning occasionally and basting with marinade. Serve kabobs with brown rice. Yield: 8 servings.

Cooktop Cuisine

■ The possibilities are endless for cooktop meals. ■ You can turn out a stir-fry in just minutes in a wok, opt for the longer simmering of comfort foods in a Dutch oven, or quickly transform ingredients from simple to spectacular in a skillet. ■ Put your wok to work and stir up some mealtime excitement with Scallop Stir-Fry and Chicken-in-a-Garden. ■ When you have more time, the slower cooking involved with a Dutch oven brings out the rich flavor of recipes like Pepper Steak and Favorite Pot Roast. ■ And don't forget the always-popular skillet used in many of our favorites—Herbed Shrimp and Pasta, Beef Burgundy Stroganoff, and Hurry Curry, to name a few. ■ You're sure to find a few cooktop favorites of your own.

Favorite Pot Roast (page 125)

SALMON FETTUCCINE

8 ounces fettuccine, uncooked
1½ tablespoons butter or
   margarine
1½ tablespoons all-purpose
   flour
2 cups half-and-half
1 cup freshly grated Parmesan
   cheese
1½ teaspoons dry sherry

¼ teaspoon salt
¼ teaspoon ground white
   pepper
1 clove garlic, minced
2 tablespoons butter or
   margarine, melted
1 pound salmon fillet, cut into
   1-inch pieces

Cook fettuccine according to package directions; drain and set aside.

Melt 1½ tablespoons butter in a heavy saucepan over low heat; add flour, stirring until smooth. Cook, stirring constantly, 1 minute. Gradually add half-and-half; cook over medium heat, stirring constantly, until slightly thickened and bubbly. Stir in cheese and next 3 ingredients. Set aside, and keep warm.

Cook garlic in 2 tablespoons butter in a large skillet over medium-high heat, stirring constantly, 2 minutes. Add salmon pieces, and cook 4 to 5 minutes or until fish flakes easily when tested with a fork. Add fettuccine and cheese sauce, tossing gently; cook over low heat just until thoroughly heated. Serve immediately. Yield: 4 servings.

CRAWFISH ÉTOUFFÉE

2 pounds fresh or frozen peeled
   crawfish tails, thawed
½ teaspoon hot sauce
½ teaspoon ground red pepper
1 cup vegetable oil
1 cup all-purpose flour
4 stalks celery, chopped
4 large onions, chopped
4 large green peppers, seeded
   and chopped

1 bunch green onions, chopped
1 cup water
2 teaspoons salt
1 teaspoon black pepper
½ teaspoon ground red pepper
¾ cup chopped fresh parsley
Hot cooked rice

Sprinkle crawfish with hot sauce and ½ teaspoon red pepper; set aside.

Combine oil and flour in a Dutch oven; cook over medium heat, stirring constantly, until roux is chocolate colored (about 20 minutes).

Stir in celery and next 3 ingredients; cook, stirring constantly, until vegetables are tender. Add crawfish tails and water; cook, uncovered, over low heat, 15 minutes, stirring occasionally. Stir in salt, black pepper, and ½ teaspoon red pepper. Simmer, uncovered, 5 minutes; stir in parsley. Serve over rice. Yield: 8 servings.

SCALLOP STIR-FRY

1 tablespoon peanut oil
1 tablespoon sesame oil
1 pound fresh bay scallops
1 (8-ounce) can sliced water
  chestnuts, drained
½ pound fresh mushrooms,
  sliced
2 small carrots, scraped and
  diagonally sliced
2 green onions, sliced
1 medium-size sweet red
  pepper, seeded and cut into
  strips

2 tablespoons cornstarch
½ cup chicken broth, divided
3 tablespoons dry sherry
3 tablespoons soy sauce
1 to 2 tablespoons grated fresh
  ginger
2 cloves garlic, pressed
1 (6-ounce) package frozen
  snow pea pods, thawed and
  drained
Hot cooked rice

Bay scallops, which are called for in Scallop Stir-Fry, are about ½ inch in diameter. Bay scallops are more tender and more expensive than their larger cousins, sea scallops, which average 1½ inches in diameter. Sea scallops may be substituted for bay scallops—simply quarter them before cooking.

Pour peanut and sesame oils around the top of preheated wok or large skillet, coating sides; heat at medium-high (375°) for 2 minutes. Add scallops, and stir-fry 3 minutes.

Add water chestnuts and next 4 ingredients to wok; stir-fry 3 to 4 minutes or until vegetables are tender.

Combine cornstarch and ¼ cup chicken broth; stir until smooth. Stir in remaining ¼ cup chicken broth, sherry, and next 3 ingredients. Add cornstarch mixture and snow peas to scallop mixture; stir-fry 1 to 2 minutes or until mixture is thickened and thoroughly heated. Serve over rice. Yield: 4 servings.

Warm up hungry friends at a cold-weather supper party with generous helpings of robust Shrimp Creole.

SHRIMP CREOLE

$\frac{1}{4}$ cup vegetable oil
$\frac{1}{4}$ cup all-purpose flour
$1\frac{1}{2}$ cups chopped onion
1 cup chopped green onions
1 cup chopped celery
1 cup chopped green pepper
2 cloves garlic, minced
1 (16-ounce) can chopped
 tomatoes, undrained
1 (8-ounce) can tomato sauce
1 (6-ounce) can tomato paste
$1\frac{1}{2}$ cups water
1 tablespoon lemon juice

$1\frac{1}{2}$ teaspoons salt
1 teaspoon black pepper
1 teaspoon Worcestershire
 sauce
$\frac{1}{2}$ teaspoon ground red pepper
$\frac{1}{8}$ teaspoon hot sauce
2 or 3 bay leaves
5 pounds unpeeled large fresh
 shrimp
2 (10-ounce) packages saffron
 yellow rice mix
$\frac{1}{2}$ cup finely chopped fresh
 parsley

Combine oil and flour in a Dutch oven; cook over medium heat, stirring constantly, until roux is chocolate colored (about 15 minutes). Stir in

1½ cups chopped onion and next 4 ingredients; cook 15 minutes or until vegetables are tender, stirring frequently. Stir in tomato and next 10 ingredients. Bring to a boil; cover, reduce heat, and simmer 1 hour, stirring occasionally.

Peel shrimp, and devein, if desired. Add shrimp to tomato mixture. Bring to a boil; cover, reduce heat, and simmer 10 minutes or until shrimp turn pink. Remove and discard bay leaves.

Prepare rice mix according to package directions. Serve shrimp mixture over rice; sprinkle with chopped parsley. Yield: 10 servings.

QUICK CREOLE JAMBALAYA

1½ pounds unpeeled medium-
    size fresh shrimp
¾ cup chopped onion
½ cup chopped celery
¼ cup chopped green pepper
1 tablespoon minced fresh
    parsley
1 clove garlic, minced
2 tablespoons butter or
    margarine, melted
1 (28-ounce) can whole
    tomatoes, undrained and
    chopped

1 (10½-ounce) can condensed
    beef broth, undiluted
2 cups cubed cooked ham
1¼ cups water
½ teaspoon dried thyme
½ teaspoon chili powder
¼ teaspoon pepper
1 cup long-grain rice, uncooked

Quick Creole Jambalaya, Shrimp Creole (facing page), and Creole Pork Chops (page 130) all contain the "holy trinity" of Creole and Cajun cooking—chopped onion, celery, and green pepper.

Peel shrimp, and devein, if desired. Set aside.

Cook onion and next 4 ingredients in butter in a Dutch oven over medium-high heat, stirring constantly, until vegetables are tender. Stir in tomato and next 6 ingredients. Bring to a boil; stir in rice. Cover, reduce heat, and simmer 20 minutes.

Add shrimp to rice mixture. Bring to a boil; cover, reduce heat, and simmer 10 minutes or until shrimp turn pink. Yield: 6 servings.

HERBED SHRIMP AND PASTA

1 pound unpeeled medium-size
  fresh shrimp
2 cloves garlic, minced
½ cup butter or margarine,
  melted
1 cup half-and-half
¼ cup chopped fresh parsley

1 teaspoon chopped fresh
  dillweed or ½ teaspoon
  dried dillweed
¼ teaspoon salt
⅛ teaspoon pepper
Hot cooked angel hair pasta

Peel shrimp, and devein, if desired. Cook shrimp and garlic in butter in a large skillet over medium-high heat, stirring constantly, 3 to 5 minutes or until shrimp turn pink. Remove shrimp, reserving garlic and butter in skillet. Set shrimp aside.

Add half-and-half to skillet. Bring to a boil, stirring constantly. Reduce heat to low, and simmer 20 minutes or until thickened, stirring occasionally. Stir in shrimp, parsley, and next 3 ingredients; cook until mixture is thoroughly heated, stirring occasionally. Serve over angel hair pasta. Yield: 3 servings.

SHRIMP MARINARA

Expect to get 21–30 shrimp in a pound of unpeeled large fresh shrimp. If you'd rather have a greater number of shrimp for this recipe, you can count on getting 31–35 medium or 36–45 small shrimp in a pound.

1 pound unpeeled large fresh
  shrimp
1 medium onion, chopped
1 medium-size green pepper,
  seeded and chopped
1 carrot, scraped and finely
  chopped
2 cloves garlic, pressed
1 cup sliced fresh mushrooms
2 tablespoons olive oil

1 cup water
½ cup dry red wine
⅓ cup frozen English peas
1½ teaspoons dried basil
1 teaspoon dried oregano
¼ to ½ teaspoon pepper
1 (6-ounce) can tomato paste
Hot cooked linguine
Grated Romano cheese
  (optional)

Peel shrimp, and devein, if desired. Set aside.

Cook onion and next 4 ingredients in hot oil in a large skillet over medium heat, stirring constantly, until tender. Stir in water and next 6 ingredients. Bring to a boil; reduce heat, and simmer, uncovered, 5 minutes.

Stir in shrimp. Bring to a boil; reduce heat, and simmer, uncovered, 3 to 5 minutes or until shrimp turn pink. Serve over linguine; sprinkle with Romano cheese, if desired. Yield: 4 servings.

FAVORITE POT ROAST

¼ cup all-purpose flour
½ teaspoon salt
½ teaspoon pepper
1 (3- to 3½-pound) boneless
　chuck roast
2 tablespoons vegetable oil
1 large onion, thinly sliced
1 (10½-ounce) can beef
　consommé, undiluted
½ cup water
½ teaspoon salt

½ teaspoon dried oregano
½ teaspoon liquid smoke
¼ teaspoon garlic powder
¼ teaspoon pepper
1 bay leaf
6 small round red potatoes,
　peeled
6 carrots, scraped and cut into
　2-inch pieces
3 stalks celery, cut into 2-inch
　pieces

Combine first 3 ingredients; dredge roast in flour mixture. Brown roast in hot oil in a large Dutch oven; drain off drippings. Scatter onion over roast. Combine consommé and next 7 ingredients; pour over roast. Bring to a boil; cover, reduce heat, and simmer 2½ hours.

Add potato, carrot, and celery; cover and simmer 30 minutes or until vegetables are tender. Remove and discard bay leaf. Yield: 6 servings.

PEPPER STEAK

1½ pounds boneless top round
　steak
2 tablespoons vegetable oil
2 medium tomatoes, peeled and
　coarsely chopped
2 medium-size green peppers,
　seeded and cut into strips
1 small onion, sliced
1 cup water
¼ cup soy sauce

½ teaspoon beef-flavored
　bouillon granules
½ teaspoon pepper
¼ teaspoon salt
¼ teaspoon garlic powder
¼ teaspoon ground ginger
2 tablespoons cornstarch
2 tablespoons water
Hot cooked rice

Flatten steak to ¼-inch thickness with a meat mallet or rolling pin; slice across grain into thin strips. Brown steak in hot oil in a Dutch oven; drain. Add tomato and next 9 ingredients; cover and simmer 1 hour.

Combine cornstarch and 2 tablespoons water; add to steak mixture. Cook, stirring constantly, 2 minutes or until thickened. Serve over rice. Yield: 4 servings.

The visual impact of the colorful vegetable mixture against white cellophane noodles gives Stir-Fry Beef and Snow Peas dramatic flair.

STIR-FRY BEEF AND SNOW PEAS

1 pound boneless sirloin steak
2 teaspoons cornstarch
1 tablespoon soy sauce
½ cup peanut or vegetable oil
2 ounces cellophane noodles, uncooked
1 (6-ounce) package frozen snow pea pods, thawed and drained
2 tablespoons peanut or vegetable oil
2 (1-inch) slices fresh ginger

1 tablespoon peanut or vegetable oil
2 carrots, scraped and cut into ⅛-inch slices
1 (15-ounce) can baby corn, drained
1 (15-ounce) can straw mushrooms, drained
1 teaspoon cornstarch
2 tablespoons soy sauce
2 tablespoons rice wine

Partially freeze steak; slice diagonally across grain into thin strips. Combine 2 teaspoons cornstarch and 1 tablespoon soy sauce in a medium bowl, stirring until smooth; stir in steak. Cover and marinate in refrigerator 1 to 4 hours, stirring occasionally.

Pour ½ cup oil around top of preheated wok or large skillet, coating sides; heat at medium-high (375°) for 2 minutes. Add noodles, a small amount at a time, and stir-fry 2 to 3 seconds or until noodles expand and turn white. Remove noodles, and drain on paper towels; arrange in a ring on a serving platter.

Drain excess oil from wok. Add snow peas to wok; stir-fry 2 minutes. Remove from wok, and arrange around edge of noodles.

Pour 2 tablespoons oil around top of preheated wok, coating sides; heat for 2 minutes. Add steak and ginger; stir-fry 4 to 5 minutes or until steak is no longer pink. Remove from wok, and set aside.

Pour 1 tablespoon oil around top of preheated wok, coating sides; heat for 2 minutes. Add carrot, corn, and mushrooms; stir-fry 3 minutes.

Combine 1 teaspoon cornstarch, 2 tablespoons soy sauce, and wine; stir until smooth. Add cornstarch mixture to carrot mixture; stir-fry 1 minute or until thickened. Add steak mixture; stir-fry until thoroughly heated. Spoon steak mixture into center of platter. Yield: 4 servings.

BEEF BURGUNDY STROGANOFF

¼ cup chopped onion
½ pound fresh mushrooms, sliced
1 clove garlic, minced
3 tablespoons butter or margarine, melted
1 pound boneless sirloin steak, cut into thin strips
3 tablespoons all-purpose flour

3 tablespoons lemon juice
3 tablespoons Burgundy or other dry red wine
¼ teaspoon pepper
1 (10½-ounce) can beef consommé, undiluted
1 (8-ounce) carton sour cream
Hot cooked medium egg noodles

Stir sour cream into Beef Burgundy Stroganoff just before serving, and cook over low heat just until the mixture is heated through. If you let the sour cream mixture boil, it will curdle.

Cook first 3 ingredients in butter in a large skillet over medium-high heat, stirring constantly, until tender. Add steak; cook, stirring constantly, until steak is no longer pink. Stir in flour and next 4 ingredients. Bring to a boil; reduce heat, and simmer, uncovered, 15 minutes, stirring occasionally.

Stir in sour cream; cook just until mixture is thoroughly heated (do not boil). Serve over noodles. Yield: 4 servings.

SWEDISH MEATBALLS

■■■■■■■■■■
To prevent the meat
mixture from sticking to
your hands as you form
these meatballs, dampen
your hands with cold
water. Or use a small ice
cream scoop to help form
the meatballs instead.

3 slices white bread
¼ cup milk
¼ cup minced onion
1 tablespoon butter or
    margarine, melted
½ pound ground chuck
½ pound ground veal
1 large egg, lightly beaten
2 tablespoons chopped fresh
    parsley
¾ teaspoon salt
¼ teaspoon ground nutmeg
⅛ teaspoon ground allspice

3 to 4 tablespoons butter or
    margarine, melted and
    divided
¼ cup all-purpose flour
2 cups beef broth
1 (8-ounce) carton sour cream
2 teaspoons chopped fresh
    dillweed
¼ teaspoon salt
¼ teaspoon freshly ground
    pepper
Hot cooked noodles

Place bread in a shallow dish; add milk. Let stand until milk is absorbed. Tear bread into bite-size pieces; set aside.

Cook onion in 1 tablespoon butter in a large skillet over medium-high heat, stirring constantly, until tender. Combine cooked onion, bread, ground chuck, and next 6 ingredients in a large bowl; stir well. Shape meat mixture into 20 (1½-inch) meatballs. Brown meatballs in 1 tablespoon butter in skillet over medium-high heat. Remove meatballs from skillet, reserving drippings. Drain meatballs on paper towels; set aside, and keep warm.

Pour drippings into a 1-cup glass measuring cup; add enough remaining butter to equal ¼ cup. Return drippings mixture to skillet, and heat over low heat. Add flour, stirring until smooth. Cook, stirring constantly, 1 minute. Gradually add broth; cook over medium heat, stirring constantly, until mixture is thickened and bubbly. Stir in sour cream and next 3 ingredients. Add meatballs, and cook just until mixture is thoroughly heated (do not boil). Serve over noodles. Yield: 4 servings.

Brown rice adds nutty flavor and chewy texture to Hearty Lamb Pilaf.

HEARTY LAMB PILAF

1 pound ground lamb
2 medium onions, chopped
2 cloves garlic, minced
2 teaspoons dried oregano
2 cups brown rice, uncooked
½ cup butter or margarine
2 (28-ounce) cans whole
   tomatoes, undrained and
   chopped

2 cups beef broth
½ teaspoon salt
½ teaspoon pepper
1 (10-ounce) package frozen
   English peas, thawed
1 (4-ounce) jar diced pimiento,
   drained
½ cup raisins
Garnish: fresh oregano sprigs

■■■■■■■■■■
**If your family prefers
beef, ground chuck can be
substituted for the ground
lamb in Hearty
Lamb Pilaf.**

Cook first 4 ingredients in a Dutch oven over medium-high heat until meat is browned and onion is tender, stirring to crumble meat. Drain; set aside.

Combine rice and butter in Dutch oven; cook over medium-high heat, stirring constantly, until rice is lightly browned. Add meat mixture, tomato, and next 3 ingredients. Bring to a boil; cover, reduce heat, and simmer 1 hour. Add peas, pimiento, and raisins; cover and cook 10 minutes or until rice is done. Garnish, if desired. Yield: 8 servings.

CREOLE PORK CHOPS

¼ cup all-purpose flour
¾ teaspoon salt
¼ teaspoon pepper
¼ teaspoon dried rosemary,
   crushed
6 (¾-inch-thick) pork chops
2 tablespoons vegetable oil
¾ cup chopped onion
¾ cup chopped green pepper
2 stalks celery, thinly sliced
2 cloves garlic, minced

2 tablespoons butter or
   margarine, melted
2 cups beef broth
1 tablespoon chopped fresh
   parsley
½ pound small fresh
   mushrooms, halved
4 tomatoes, peeled and quartered
1 (6-ounce) can tomato paste
1 bay leaf
Hot cooked rice

Combine first 4 ingredients; dredge chops in flour mixture. Brown chops in hot oil in a large skillet. Remove chops from skillet; drain on paper towels. Discard drippings; wipe skillet with a paper towel.

Cook onion and next 3 ingredients in butter in skillet over medium-high heat, stirring constantly, until tender. Stir in beef broth and next 5 ingredients. Bring to a boil; reduce heat, and simmer, uncovered, 20 minutes, stirring occasionally. Add chops; cover and cook 45 minutes, spooning tomato mixture over chops. Uncover and cook 15 minutes. Remove and discard bay leaf. Serve over rice. Yield: 6 servings.

HURRY CURRY

The crystallized ginger in this curry recipe is simply chunks of fresh ginger that have been cooked in a sugar syrup and coated with coarse sugar. You might also see it called candied ginger.

1½ pounds boneless pork, cut
   into ¾-inch pieces
¼ cup butter or margarine,
   melted and divided
½ cup chopped onion
1 clove garlic, pressed
1 cup chopped cooking apple
2 teaspoons curry powder
1 tablespoon all-purpose flour
1 teaspoon chopped crystallized
   ginger

¼ teaspoon salt
¼ teaspoon ground cardamom
⅛ teaspoon pepper
1 (10½-ounce) can condensed
   chicken broth, undiluted
1 teaspoon lemon juice
¼ cup chutney
Hot cooked rice

Brown pork in 2 tablespoons butter in a large skillet over medium-high heat; drain on paper towels. Set aside.

Cook onion and garlic in remaining 2 tablespoons butter in skillet over medium heat until tender. Add apple and curry powder; cook, stirring constantly, until apple is crisp-tender. Stir in flour and next 4 ingredients. Gradually stir in chicken broth and lemon juice. Bring to a boil; reduce heat, and simmer, uncovered, 5 minutes, stirring occasionally. Stir in pork and chutney. Bring to a boil; cover, reduce heat, and simmer 10 minutes. Serve over rice. Yield: 4 servings.

SWEET-AND-SOUR PORK

½ cup all-purpose flour
¼ cup cornstarch
½ teaspoon salt
½ cup water
1 large egg, lightly beaten
1½ pounds boneless pork, cut into ¾-inch pieces
Vegetable oil
1 (20-ounce) can pineapple chunks, undrained
½ cup firmly packed brown sugar
½ cup white vinegar

1 tablespoon soy sauce
2 tablespoons cornstarch
2 tablespoons water
2 tablespoons vegetable oil
2 medium carrots, scraped and thinly sliced
1 medium-size green pepper, seeded and cut into ¾-inch pieces
1 small onion, cut into thin wedges
1 clove garlic, minced
Hot cooked rice

Combine first 5 ingredients in a medium bowl; stir with a wire whisk until well blended. Add pork, stirring well.

Pour oil to depth of 2 inches into a large heavy saucepan; heat to 375°. Carefully drop pork into hot oil; fry 5 minutes or until golden. Drain on paper towels. Arrange pork in a single layer on a baking sheet; place in a 200° oven to keep warm while frying remaining pork.

Drain pineapple, reserving juice. Set pineapple aside. Add enough water to juice to make 1 cup. Combine juice, brown sugar, vinegar, and soy sauce; stir until sugar dissolves. Set aside. Combine 2 tablespoons cornstarch and 2 tablespoons water, stirring until smooth; set aside.

Pour 2 tablespoons oil around top of preheated wok or large skillet, coating sides; heat at medium-high (375°) for 2 minutes. Add carrot and next 3 ingredients; stir-fry 3 to 5 minutes or until crisp-tender. Stir in juice mixture. Bring to a boil; boil 1 minute. Stir in cornstarch mixture; cook, stirring constantly, until thickened. Add pork and pineapple; stir-fry until thoroughly heated. Serve over rice. Yield: 6 servings.

All that's needed for a romantic Italian dinner is Tortellini Carbonara and a glass of Chianti.

TORTELLINI CARBONARA

1 (9-ounce) package fresh
　cheese-filled tortellini,
　uncooked
1 small clove garlic, minced
1 ½ teaspoons olive oil
½ teaspoon white vinegar
3 slices bacon, cooked and
　crumbled

⅓ cup grated Parmesan cheese
¼ cup whipping cream
1 tablespoon minced fresh
　parsley
¼ teaspoon freshly ground
　pepper
Garnish: fresh parsley sprigs

Cook tortellini according to package directions; drain and place in a medium bowl.

　Cook garlic in hot oil in a small saucepan over medium-high heat, stirring constantly, 30 seconds; stir in vinegar. Add garlic mixture, bacon, and next 4 ingredients to tortellini; toss gently to combine. Garnish, if desired. Serve immediately. Yield: 2 servings.

HOPPING JOHN

1 cup sliced celery
⅔ cup chopped onion
1 clove garlic, minced
1 tablespoon vegetable oil
1 (16-ounce) package frozen
   black-eyed peas

¾ pound cubed cooked ham
2½ cups chicken broth
¼ teaspoon dried crushed red
   pepper
1 bay leaf
1 cup long-grain rice, uncooked

Cook first 3 ingredients in hot oil in a Dutch oven over medium-high heat, stirring constantly, until tender. Stir in peas and next 4 ingredients. Bring to a boil; cover, reduce heat, and simmer 30 minutes. Stir in rice; cover and cook 20 to 25 minutes or until rice is tender and liquid is absorbed. Remove and discard bay leaf. Yield: 4 servings.

Tradition dictates that eating Hopping John, a combination of black-eyed peas, rice, and ham, on New Year's Day will bring good luck for the coming year.

CHEESY SHELLS AND HAM

1 (7-ounce) package shell
   macaroni, uncooked
2 cups milk
1 teaspoon chicken-flavored
   bouillon granules
1 teaspoon Worcestershire
   sauce
½ teaspoon dry mustard
¼ teaspoon salt
¼ teaspoon pepper
1 small onion, chopped
½ small green pepper, seeded
   and chopped

¼ cup butter or margarine,
   melted
¼ cup all-purpose flour
2 cups chopped cooked ham
1 cup (4 ounces) shredded
   Cheddar cheese
1 (6-ounce) jar sliced
   mushrooms, drained
Grated Parmesan cheese
   (optional)

Cook macaroni according to package directions; drain. Set aside.

Combine milk and next 5 ingredients; stir well, and set aside. Cook onion and green pepper in butter in a Dutch oven over medium-high heat, stirring constantly, until tender. Add flour; cook, stirring constantly, 1 minute. Gradually add milk mixture; cook over medium heat, stirring constantly, until mixture is thickened and bubbly.

Stir in macaroni, ham, Cheddar cheese, and mushrooms; cook, stirring gently, until cheese melts and mixture is thoroughly heated. Serve with Parmesan cheese, if desired. Yield: 6 servings.

CHEESY CHICKEN SPAGHETTI

If a large hen isn't available for Cheesy Chicken Spaghetti, substitute two 3- to 3¼-pound broiler-fryers instead.

1 (6- to 6½-pound) hen
3 quarts water
1 (12-ounce) package spaghetti, uncooked and broken in half
1½ cups chopped onion
1 cup chopped green pepper
1 cup chopped celery
1 (16-ounce) loaf process American cheese, shredded
1 (6-ounce) jar sliced mushrooms, drained
1 (4-ounce) jar diced pimiento, drained
½ teaspoon salt
½ teaspoon pepper

Combine hen and water in a large Dutch oven. Bring to a boil; cover, reduce heat, and simmer 1½ hours or until hen is tender. (If substituting 2 broiler-fryers for hen, reduce cooking time to 1 hour.) Remove hen from broth, reserving broth. Let hen cool. Skin, bone, and chop chicken. Skim fat from broth. Reserve 7 cups broth. Reserve remaining broth for another use, if desired.

Bring 5 cups reserved broth to a boil in Dutch oven; add spaghetti and next 3 ingredients. Cook, uncovered, 10 minutes or until spaghetti is tender; drain. Combine spaghetti mixture, remaining 2 cups broth, chopped chicken, cheese, and remaining ingredients in Dutch oven; cook over low heat, stirring constantly, until cheese melts and mixture is thoroughly heated. Yield: 8 servings.

COUNTRY-STYLE CHICKEN AND DUMPLINGS

This recipe features rolled or slick dumplings. For drop dumplings, increase the reserved broth to one cup. Combine the flour mixture and broth, stirring with a fork just until the dry ingredients are moistened. Drop the dough by tablespoonfuls into the boiling broth, and cook as directed.

1 (3½- to 4-pound) broiler-fryer
2 quarts water
1 carrot, halved
1 stalk celery, halved
1 medium onion, quartered
1½ teaspoons salt
½ teaspoon pepper
2 cups all-purpose flour
2 teaspoons baking powder
¾ teaspoon salt
⅓ cup shortening

Combine first 7 ingredients in a Dutch oven. Bring to a boil; cover, reduce heat, and simmer 1 hour or until chicken is tender. Remove chicken from broth, reserving broth in Dutch oven. Let chicken cool. Skin, bone, and coarsely chop chicken; set aside. Remove vegetables from broth, and discard. Skim fat from broth, if desired. Reserve and set aside ⅔ cup broth. Return chopped chicken to broth in Dutch oven.

Combine flour, baking powder, and ¾ teaspoon salt; cut in shortening with a pastry blender until mixture is crumbly. Add reserved ⅔ cup broth, stirring with a fork just until dry ingredients are moistened. Turn dough out onto a lightly floured surface, and knead lightly 30 seconds. Roll dough to ⅛-inch thickness; cut dough into ¾- x 2-inch strips or 2-inch squares.

Bring broth mixture in Dutch oven to a boil; drop dumplings, one at a time, into boiling broth. Cover, reduce heat, and simmer 10 minutes. Yield: 4 servings.

Whether you like your dumplings thin and slick or puffy and cakelike, Country-Style Chicken and Dumplings is sure to satisfy.

CHICKEN CACCIATORE

Sweet vermouth is a reddish-brown fortified wine flavored with herbs and spices. You can substitute water for the sweet vermouth in Chicken Cacciatore, but expect the tomato mixture to be slightly less flavorful.

¼ cup all-purpose flour
½ teaspoon salt
½ teaspoon pepper
8 chicken breast halves, skinned
¼ cup olive oil
1 large onion, chopped
3 or 4 cloves garlic, minced
½ pound fresh mushrooms, sliced
2 (16-ounce) cans whole tomatoes, undrained and quartered
1 (4-ounce) jar whole pimientos, undrained and sliced
3 bay leaves
½ cup sweet vermouth
1 teaspoon dried thyme
1 teaspoon dried oregano
½ teaspoon salt
¼ teaspoon pepper
2 medium-size green peppers, seeded and cut into strips
Hot cooked spaghetti
Garnish: fresh thyme sprigs

Combine first 3 ingredients; dredge chicken in flour mixture. Brown chicken in hot oil in a Dutch oven over medium-high heat. Remove chicken, reserving drippings; drain on paper towels.

Cook onion and garlic in drippings in Dutch oven over medium heat 5 minutes. Stir in mushrooms and next 8 ingredients. Add chicken to mixture in Dutch oven. Bring to a boil; reduce heat, and simmer, uncovered, 30 minutes, stirring occasionally. Stir in green pepper; cook, uncovered, 30 minutes, stirring occasionally. Remove and discard bay leaves. Serve over spaghetti; garnish, if desired. Yield: 8 servings.

CASHEW CHICKEN

1 pound skinned, boned chicken breast halves, cut into 1-inch pieces
1 tablespoon vegetable oil
2 cups sliced fresh mushrooms
½ cup sliced green onions
1 small green pepper, seeded and cut into 1-inch pieces
1 (8-ounce) can sliced water chestnuts, drained
2 teaspoons chicken-flavored bouillon granules
1 cup hot water
1 tablespoon cornstarch
2 tablespoons soy sauce
2 teaspoons brown sugar
½ teaspoon ground ginger
½ cup cashews, toasted
Hot cooked rice

Brown chicken in hot oil in a large skillet over medium-high heat. Remove chicken, reserving drippings; drain on paper towels.

Cook mushrooms and next 3 ingredients in drippings over medium-high heat, stirring constantly, until tender.

Dissolve bouillon granules in hot water. Combine cornstarch and soy sauce; stir until smooth. Combine bouillon mixture, cornstarch mixture, brown sugar, and ginger. Add bouillon mixture and chicken to vegetable mixture; cook over medium heat, stirring constantly, 2 minutes or until thickened. Stir in cashews. Serve over rice. Yield: 4 servings.

CHICKEN-IN-A-GARDEN

6 skinned, boned chicken breast halves, cut into 1-inch pieces
3 tablespoons cornstarch, divided
2 tablespoons soy sauce, divided
1 tablespoon peanut or vegetable oil
¾ cup water
¾ teaspoon chicken-flavored bouillon granules
½ teaspoon garlic powder
¼ teaspoon salt
¼ teaspoon pepper
⅛ teaspoon ground ginger
2 tablespoons peanut or vegetable oil

3 medium-size green peppers, seeded and cut into 1-inch pieces
8 green onions, cut into ½-inch pieces
1 (6-ounce) package frozen snow pea pods, thawed and drained
1 cup diagonally sliced celery (1-inch pieces)
3 medium tomatoes, cut into eighths
Hot cooked rice
Cracked black pepper (optional)

Combine chicken, 1½ teaspoons cornstarch, 1 tablespoon soy sauce, and 1 tablespoon oil; let stand 20 minutes. Combine remaining 2½ tablespoons cornstarch and remaining 1 tablespoon soy sauce; stir until smooth. Stir in water and next 5 ingredients; set aside.

Pour 2 tablespoons oil around top of preheated wok or large skillet, coating sides; heat at medium-high (375°) for 2 minutes. Add green pepper, and stir-fry 4 minutes. Add green onions, snow peas, and celery; stir-fry 2 minutes. Remove vegetable mixture from wok, and set aside.

Add chicken mixture to wok, and stir-fry 3 minutes. Add bouillon mixture, vegetable mixture, and tomato to wok; stir-fry over low heat (325°) for 3 minutes or until mixture is thickened and bubbly. Serve chicken mixture over rice; sprinkle with cracked black pepper, if desired. Yield: 6 servings.

Crown Pasta-Chicken Potpourri with freshly grated Parmesan cheese.

PASTA-CHICKEN POTPOURRI

4 ounces penne, uncooked
1 teaspoon sesame oil
1½ tablespoons olive oil
1½ tablespoons sesame oil
2 medium carrots, scraped and
   diagonally sliced
1 small purple onion, chopped
2 medium zucchini, halved
   lengthwise and sliced

2 cloves garlic, pressed
1½ teaspoons grated fresh
   ginger
½ teaspoon dried crushed red
   pepper
2 cups chopped cooked chicken
2 tablespoons soy sauce
2 teaspoons rice wine vinegar
Freshly grated Parmesan cheese

Cook pasta according to package directions; drain and toss with 1 teaspoon sesame oil. Set aside.

Pour olive oil and 1½ tablespoons sesame oil around top of preheated wok or large skillet, coating sides; heat at medium-high (375°) for 2 minutes. Add carrot and onion; stir-fry 3 minutes. Add zucchini and next 3 ingredients; stir-fry 1 minute. Stir in pasta, chicken, soy sauce, and vinegar; stir-fry 1 minute or until thoroughly heated. Transfer to a serving dish; sprinkle with Parmesan cheese. Yield: 4 servings.

TURKEY CUTLETS WITH MUSHROOM SAUCE

1 pound turkey cutlets
2 tablespoons vegetable oil
1 pound fresh mushrooms,
 sliced
2 large green onions, sliced
2 (3-ounce) packages cream
 cheese, cubed

⅓ cup milk
1 teaspoon salt
½ teaspoon pepper
Hot cooked rice or noodles

Brown turkey in hot oil in a large nonstick skillet over medium heat. Remove from skillet; set aside, and keep warm.

Add mushrooms and green onions to skillet; cook until green onions are tender. Add cream cheese and next 3 ingredients, stirring until cream cheese melts. To serve, place turkey over rice or noodles, and top with mushroom mixture. Yield: 4 servings.

TURKEY SPAGHETTI SAUCE

¾ cup chopped onion
1 clove garlic, minced
2 tablespoons olive oil or
 vegetable oil
1½ pounds ground turkey
1 (28-ounce) can whole
 tomatoes, undrained and
 chopped
2 (6-ounce) cans tomato paste
1 cup water

1½ teaspoons sugar
1½ teaspoons dried oregano
¾ teaspoon salt
¼ teaspoon pepper
¼ teaspoon dried basil
1 bay leaf
½ pound fresh mushrooms,
 sliced
Hot cooked spaghetti
Grated Parmesan cheese

Cook onion and garlic in hot oil in a Dutch oven over medium-high heat, stirring constantly, until tender. Add turkey; cook until meat is browned, stirring until it crumbles. Drain; add tomato and next 8 ingredients. Bring to a boil; reduce heat, and simmer, uncovered, 1 hour, stirring occasionally.

Stir in mushrooms; simmer, uncovered, 30 minutes or until mushrooms are tender, stirring occasionally. Remove and discard bay leaf. Serve over spaghetti; sprinkle with Parmesan cheese. Yield: 8 cups.

Oven-Baked Bounty

■ Clever cooks repeatedly turn to one-dish meals from the oven for the ultimate in ease and convenience. ■ Many of our recipes take mere minutes to prepare, and most need no attention once you put them in to bake. ■ These selections aren't limited to the tuna and ground beef dishes our mothers used to make. ■ Yes, we've included the best of those favorites, but we've also tossed in some surprises that transcend the usual "casserole" category. ■ Marinated Shrimp Kabobs, Beef Burgundy, and Turkey Parmigiana—to name a few—will have your family begging for seconds.

Stuffed Flank Steak with Noodles (page 149)

TUNA-NOODLE CASSEROLE

1 (5-ounce) package wide egg
    noodles, uncooked
1 (10¾-ounce) can cream of
    celery soup, undiluted
1 (6½-ounce) can tuna packed
    in water, drained and flaked
1 (2-ounce) jar diced pimiento,
    drained
1 cup chopped celery

1 cup (4 ounces) shredded sharp
    Cheddar cheese
1 cup milk
½ cup chopped onion
½ cup mayonnaise
¼ cup chopped green pepper
1 teaspoon salt
½ cup slivered almonds, toasted

Cook noodles according to package directions; drain. Combine noodles and next 10 ingredients; spoon into a greased 2-quart casserole. Sprinkle with almonds. Bake, uncovered, at 350° for 30 minutes. Yield: 4 servings.

SEAFOOD BROCHETTES

Seafood Brochettes may be grilled rather than broiled. Grill them, uncovered, over medium-hot coals (350° to 400°) 8 to 10 minutes or until the shrimp turn pink and the fish flakes easily, turning the brochettes occasionally and basting them with Sunshine Sauce.

1 pound unpeeled large fresh
    shrimp
1 pound grouper fillets, cut into
    1-inch pieces
½ pound sea scallops
4 slices bacon, quartered

8 medium-size fresh mushroom
    caps
1 large green pepper, seeded
    and cut into 1-inch pieces
Sunshine Sauce
Hot cooked rice

Peel shrimp, and devein, if desired. Alternately thread shrimp and next 5 ingredients on 8 (12-inch) skewers. Place skewers, in batches, on a lightly greased rack of a broiler pan. Broil 5½ inches from heat (with electric oven door partially opened) 12 to 15 minutes or until shrimp turn pink and fish flakes easily, turning and basting with Sunshine Sauce. Serve over rice. Yield: 4 servings.

Sunshine Sauce

½ cup butter or margarine,
    melted
½ cup pineapple juice
2 tablespoons lemon juice

2 tablespoons Dijon mustard
1 teaspoon ground ginger
Freshly ground pepper to taste

Combine all ingredients; stir well. Yield: 1¼ cups.

SHRIMP AND CHICKEN CASSEROLE

1 (2½- to 3-pound) broiler-fryer
1 teaspoon salt
4 cups water
1 pound unpeeled medium-size
    fresh shrimp
2 (16-ounce) packages frozen
    broccoli cuts, thawed and
    drained
1 (10¾-ounce) can cream of
    chicken soup, undiluted
1 (10¾-ounce) can cream of
    celery soup, undiluted

1 cup mayonnaise
2 tablespoons lemon juice
¼ teaspoon ground white
    pepper
1 cup (4 ounces) shredded
    Cheddar cheese
½ cup soft breadcrumbs
1 tablespoon butter or
    margarine, melted
Paprika
Garnishes: cooked shrimp, fresh
    parsley sprigs

Combine chicken and salt in a Dutch oven; add enough water to cover. Bring to a boil; cover, reduce heat, and simmer 45 minutes or until chicken is tender. Remove chicken from broth; reserve broth for another use, if desired. Let chicken cool; skin, bone, and cut chicken into bite-size pieces. Set aside.

Bring 4 cups water to a boil; add shrimp, and cook 3 to 5 minutes or until shrimp turn pink. Drain well; rinse with cold water. Chill. Peel shrimp, and devein, if desired. Set 3 shrimp aside for garnish, if desired.

Spread broccoli evenly in a lightly greased 13- x 9- x 2-inch baking dish. Combine cream of chicken soup and next 4 ingredients; spread about one-third of soup mixture over broccoli. Sprinkle chicken and shrimp evenly over soup mixture in dish. Spread remaining soup mixture over chicken and shrimp.

Cover and bake at 350° for 30 minutes. Uncover and sprinkle with cheese. Combine breadcrumbs and butter; sprinkle over cheese. Bake, uncovered, 15 minutes or until thoroughly heated and bubbly. Sprinkle with paprika, and garnish, if desired. Yield: 8 servings.

If you'd rather use chicken breasts than a broiler-fryer in Shrimp and Chicken Casserole, you'll need about 1½ pounds of uncooked skinned, boned chicken breast halves to yield the same amount of chopped cooked chicken— about three cups.

The tangy marinade in Marinated Shrimp Kabobs is accented by the sweetness of pineapple and ginger.

MARINATED SHRIMP KABOBS

Marinated Shrimp Kabobs may be grilled, if you prefer. Grill them, uncovered, over medium-hot coals (350° to 400°) 8 to 10 minutes or until the shrimp turn pink, turning the kabobs occasionally and basting them with the reserved boiled marinade.

1 pound unpeeled large fresh shrimp
½ (8-ounce) can pineapple chunks, undrained
2 tablespoons dark sesame oil
2 tablespoons soy sauce
¼ teaspoon ground white pepper
⅛ teaspoon garlic powder

⅛ teaspoon ground ginger
16 pearl onions, peeled
16 cherry tomatoes
1 large green pepper, seeded and cut into 1-inch pieces
Hot cooked rice
Chopped fresh parsley (optional)

Peel shrimp, and devein, if desired. Place shrimp in a large heavy-duty, zip-top plastic bag. Drain pineapple, reserving juice; set pineapple aside. Combine pineapple juice, oil, and next 4 ingredients in a small bowl; stir well, and pour over shrimp. Seal bag, and marinate in refrigerator 2 hours, turning bag occasionally.

Cook onions in boiling water 3 to 4 minutes or until crisp-tender; drain.

Remove shrimp from marinade, reserving marinade. Place marinade in a small saucepan; bring to a boil. Remove from heat, and set aside.

Alternately thread shrimp, pineapple, onions, tomatoes, and green pepper on 8 (10-inch) skewers. Place skewers, in batches, on a lightly greased rack of a broiler pan. Broil 5½ inches from heat (with electric oven door partially opened) 6 to 8 minutes or until shrimp turn pink, turning and basting with marinade. Spoon rice onto a platter; sprinkle with parsley, if desired. Serve kabobs over rice. Yield: 4 servings.

SHRIMP AND ASPARAGUS EN PAPILLOTE

2 pounds unpeeled medium-size
    fresh shrimp
1½ pounds fresh asparagus
¼ cup butter or margarine,
    softened
2 tablespoons minced fresh
    ginger
2 teaspoons grated lemon rind
1½ tablespoons fresh lemon
    juice
¼ teaspoon salt
1 large clove garlic, crushed
Vegetable oil
6 lemon slices

Peel shrimp, and devein, if desired. Set aside.

Snap off tough ends of asparagus, making stalks 7 inches in length. Remove scales from stalks with a knife or vegetable peeler, if desired. Cook asparagus, covered, in a small amount of boiling water 3 minutes; drain and rinse with cold water. Drain and set aside.

Combine butter and next 5 ingredients, stirring well. Set aside.

Cut 6 (15- x 12-inch) pieces of parchment paper; fold each piece in half lengthwise, and trim into a large heart shape. Place parchment hearts on a large baking sheet, and open out flat. Lightly brush one side of each heart with oil. Arrange asparagus evenly on greased sides of parchment hearts near the crease. Arrange shrimp evenly over asparagus; dot evenly with butter mixture, and top with lemon slices.

Fold over remaining halves of hearts. Fold edges over to seal securely. Starting with rounded edges, pleat and crimp edges together to make an airtight seal. Bake at 400° for 15 minutes or until puffed and lightly browned. Place packets on individual plates; cut an opening in the top of each, and fold paper back. Serve immediately. Yield: 6 servings.

■ ■ ■ ■ ■ ■ ■ ■ □
Cooking food en papillote means baking it in a parchment bag, which allows the food to cook in its own juices. Parchment paper is available in most supermarkets and kitchen shops. Aluminum foil can be substituted.

SHEPHERD'S PIE

2 pounds top sirloin steak, cut
    into ½-inch pieces
3 cups water
3 large carrots, scraped and
    chopped
1 medium onion, chopped
2 (¾-ounce) packages beef-
    flavored gravy mix
1 beef-flavored bouillon cube

1½ pounds round red potatoes,
    peeled and sliced (about
    4 large)
¼ cup milk
3 tablespoons butter or
    margarine
1 cup (4 ounces) shredded
    Cheddar cheese
Paprika

Combine steak and water in a saucepan. Bring to a boil; cover, reduce heat, and simmer 15 minutes. Remove meat from broth, reserving broth. Set meat aside. Add carrot and onion to broth. Bring to a boil; cover, reduce heat, and simmer 12 minutes or until vegetables are tender. Drain, reserving 2 cups broth. (Add enough water to broth to measure 2 cups, if necessary.) Set vegetable mixture aside.

Combine broth, gravy mix, and bouillon cube in pan. Bring to a boil, stirring constantly; reduce heat, and simmer 1 minute. Stir in meat and vegetable mixture; spoon into a greased 13- x 9- x 2-inch baking dish.

Cook potato in boiling water to cover 12 minutes or until tender; drain and mash. Stir in milk and butter. Spread potato mixture evenly over meat mixture; sprinkle with cheese and paprika. Bake, uncovered, at 350° for 20 to 25 minutes or until bubbly. Yield: 8 servings.

BEEF AND VEGETABLE KABOBS

Some vegetables take less time to broil or grill than others. This recipe suggests you cook each vegetable on separate skewers to allow each to be broiled or grilled to the ideal degree of doneness.

½ cup butter or margarine
¼ cup lemon juice
3 tablespoons chopped fresh
    chives
1 tablespoon Worcestershire
    sauce
1 teaspoon prepared mustard
½ teaspoon salt
Dash of pepper

2 medium-size green peppers,
    seeded and cut into 1½-inch
    pieces
6 small boiling onions
12 fresh mushrooms
12 cherry tomatoes
2 pounds (1-inch-thick) sirloin
    steak, cut into 1-inch pieces
Hot cooked rice

Combine first 7 ingredients in a saucepan. Bring to a boil; reduce heat, and simmer 5 minutes, stirring occasionally. Set aside ½ cup butter mixture;

use remaining butter mixture for basting. Thread each type of vegetable on a separate 14-inch skewer. Thread steak on 3 (14-inch) skewers, and brush all kabobs with a portion of basting mixture.

Place green pepper kabob on a lightly greased rack of a broiler pan; broil 5½ inches from heat (with electric oven door partially opened) 3 minutes. Add onion kabob and beef kabobs; broil 10 minutes, turning all kabobs occasionally, and basting beef kabobs with remaining basting mixture. Add mushroom kabob; broil 2 minutes. Add tomato kabob; broil 3 minutes or until beef kabobs reach desired degree of doneness. Remove vegetables and beef from skewers; serve over rice with reserved ½ cup butter mixture. Yield: 6 servings.

Note: Beef and Vegetable Kabobs may be grilled, if desired. Grill green pepper kabob, uncovered, over medium-hot coals (350° to 400°) 3 minutes. Add onion and beef kabobs; grill 10 minutes, turning all kabobs occasionally and basting beef kabobs with butter mixture. Add mushroom kabob; grill 2 minutes. Add tomato kabob; grill 3 minutes or until beef kabobs reach desired degree of doneness.

SWISS STEAK WITH VEGETABLES

¼ cup all-purpose flour
½ teaspoon salt
½ teaspoon pepper
1 pound boneless top round
  steak, cut into serving-size
  pieces
2 tablespoons vegetable oil
3 large carrots, scraped and
  sliced
2 stalks celery, sliced

1 large onion, sliced
1½ teaspoons beef-flavored
  bouillon granules
1 cup hot water
2 (8-ounce) cans tomato sauce
1 tablespoon butter or
  margarine, melted
2 teaspoons browning-and-
  seasoning sauce
Hot cooked noodles or rice

Combine flour, salt, and pepper; dredge steak in flour mixture. Lightly flatten floured steak using a meat mallet or rolling pin. Brown steak in hot oil in a large skillet over medium-high heat; transfer to a 2-quart casserole. Top with carrot, celery, and onion.

Dissolve bouillon granules in hot water. Stir in tomato sauce, butter, and browning-and-seasoning sauce; pour mixture over vegetables. Cover and bake at 350° for 1 hour and 15 minutes or to desired degree of doneness. Serve over noodles or rice. Yield: 4 servings.

Long, slow cooking in a rich wine sauce makes the meat in Beef Burgundy melt-in-your-mouth tender.

BEEF BURGUNDY

When choosing a Burgundy to use in this recipe, remember not to cook with a wine you wouldn't drink. You may be tempted to buy the least expensive wine on the shelf to keep on hand for cooking, but the cooking process will bring out the worst in inferior wine.

1½ pounds boneless top round steak, cut into 1-inch pieces
1 tablespoon vegetable oil
⅔ cup chopped onion
2 cloves garlic, minced
1 cup water
1 cup Burgundy
1 tablespoon beef-flavored bouillon granules
1 teaspoon dried thyme

1 small bay leaf
4 medium carrots, scraped and cut into ½-inch slices
3 tablespoons all-purpose flour
½ cup water
¼ pound fresh mushrooms, quartered
6 small boiling onions
¼ teaspoon pepper
Hot cooked noodles or rice

Brown steak in hot oil in a skillet over medium-high heat; transfer to a lightly greased 2-quart casserole, reserving drippings in skillet. Cook onion and garlic in drippings, stirring constantly, 2 minutes. Add 1 cup water and next 4 ingredients. Bring to a boil; pour over steak. Cover and bake at 350° for 1½ hours. Stir in carrot; cover and bake 20 minutes.

Combine flour and ½ cup water; add to steak. Stir in mushrooms, onions, and pepper. Cover and bake 30 minutes or until onions are tender. Remove and discard bay leaf. Serve over noodles. Yield: 4 servings.

STUFFED FLANK STEAK WITH NOODLES

1 cup chopped fresh spinach
1 cup sliced green onions
½ cup freshly grated Parmesan
    cheese
½ cup frozen artichoke hearts,
    thawed, drained, and
    chopped
¼ cup soft breadcrumbs
½ teaspoon salt
½ teaspoon freshly ground
    pepper
2 (1-pound) cubed flank steaks
2 cloves garlic, crushed
2 tablespoons Worcestershire
    sauce

2 tablespoons vegetable oil
¼ pound fresh mushrooms,
    sliced
1 small onion, thinly sliced
1 teaspoon chicken-flavored
    bouillon granules
½ cup hot water
2 fresh parsley sprigs
1 bay leaf
1 tablespoon cornstarch
2 tablespoons water
Hot cooked fettuccine

■ ■ ■ ■ ■ ■ ■ ■ □
If you don't find cubed flank steaks in the meat case at your supermarket, ask the butcher to run regular flank steaks through the meat tenderizer twice.

Combine first 5 ingredients; set aside.

Sprinkle salt and pepper over steaks. Overlap narrow ends of steaks by 1 inch, and press together to form 1 long piece. Spread spinach mixture down center of steak to within 1 inch of edges. Roll up jellyroll fashion, starting with long side; tie steak roll with heavy string at 2-inch intervals. Rub garlic over steak roll, and drizzle with Worcestershire sauce.

Brown steak roll in hot oil in a large skillet over medium-high heat. Remove steak roll from skillet, reserving drippings in skillet; place in a 13- x 9- x 2-inch pan. Add mushrooms and onion to drippings; cook over medium-high heat, stirring constantly, until crisp-tender. Spoon mushroom mixture into pan with steak roll, reserving drippings in skillet.

Dissolve bouillon granules in ½ cup hot water; pour mixture around steak roll. Add parsley sprigs and bay leaf to bouillon mixture. Cover and bake at 300° for 40 to 50 minutes or until steak roll reaches desired degree of doneness.

Transfer steak roll to a serving platter; let stand 15 minutes before slicing. Remove and discard parsley sprigs and bay leaf from mushroom mixture. Combine cornstarch and 2 tablespoons water, stirring until smooth. Add cornstarch mixture and mushroom mixture to drippings in skillet. Bring to a boil; boil, stirring constantly, 1 minute. Slice steak roll, and arrange slices over fettuccine. Spoon mushroom mixture over steak slices. Yield: 6 servings.

MATADOR MANIA

■■■■■■■■■■■
You may use a ground
beef with a fat content
lower than ground chuck
(such as ground round,
ground sirloin, or low-fat
ground beef) in Matador
Mania or Fiesta Enchiladas
(below), but the dish may
be less flavorful.

1 pound ground chuck
1 medium onion, chopped
½ cup water
3 tablespoons chili powder
1 teaspoon salt
1 teaspoon ground cumin
¼ teaspoon pepper
1 (16-ounce) can refried beans

2 (8-ounce) jars picante sauce,
   divided
6 (6-inch) corn tortillas, divided
1 (8-ounce) carton sour cream
2 cups (8 ounces) shredded
   sharp Cheddar cheese,
   divided

Cook ground chuck and onion in a large skillet over medium-high heat until meat is browned and onion is tender, stirring until meat crumbles; drain. Stir in water and next 4 ingredients. Bring to a boil; reduce heat, and simmer, uncovered, 5 minutes, stirring occasionally. Remove from heat; stir in beans, and set aside.

Spread ½ cup picante sauce in a lightly greased 11- x 7- x 1½-inch baking dish; place 2 tortillas on top of sauce. Spread half of meat mixture, sour cream, and ½ cup picante sauce over tortillas; top with 2 additional tortillas. Spread ½ cup picante sauce and remaining meat mixture over tortillas; sprinkle with ½ cup cheese. Top with remaining 2 tortillas; spread with remaining picante sauce.

Cover and bake at 350° for 35 minutes or until thoroughly heated. Sprinkle with remaining 1½ cups cheese; bake 5 additional minutes or until cheese melts. Let stand 5 minutes before serving. Yield: 6 servings.

FIESTA ENCHILADAS

8 (8-inch) flour tortillas
1½ cups tomato juice
1 tablespoon vegetable oil
1 (1.25-ounce) envelope taco
   seasoning mix
½ pound ground chuck
1 (16-ounce) can refried beans
3 cups (12 ounces) shredded
   Cheddar cheese, divided

1½ cups shredded iceberg
   lettuce
1 cup seeded, chopped tomato
1 small avocado, peeled, seeded,
   and cubed
Sour cream

Wrap tortillas tightly in aluminum foil; bake at 350° for 15 minutes or until thoroughly heated.

Combine tomato juice, oil, and seasoning mix; stir well. Brown ground chuck in a large skillet, stirring until it crumbles; drain. Stir in ½ cup tomato juice mixture and beans. Bring to a boil; cover, reduce heat, and simmer 5 minutes or until mixture is thoroughly heated, stirring occasionally. Remove from heat.

Place about ¼ cup meat mixture and 2½ tablespoons cheese down center of each tortilla. Roll up tortillas, and place, seam side down, in a lightly greased 13- x 9- x 2-inch baking dish. Pour remaining tomato juice mixture over casserole. Cover and bake at 350° for 35 minutes or until thoroughly heated. Uncover and sprinkle with remaining cheese; bake 5 additional minutes or until cheese melts.

Sprinkle lettuce, tomato, and avocado over enchiladas; serve with sour cream. Yield: 4 servings.

Toppings of lettuce, tomato, avocado, and sour cream offer a cool contrast to the spiciness of Fiesta Enchiladas.

Pizza Casserole

1 pound ground chuck
1 cup chopped onion
1 cup chopped green pepper
1 (14-ounce) jar pizza sauce
½ teaspoon garlic salt
¼ teaspoon pepper
¼ teaspoon dried oregano
¼ teaspoon dried basil
1 (8-ounce) package macaroni, uncooked
1 (3½-ounce) package sliced pepperoni
1 cup (4 ounces) shredded mozzarella cheese

Cook first 3 ingredients in a large Dutch oven over medium-high heat until meat is browned and vegetables are tender, stirring until meat crumbles; drain. Stir in pizza sauce and next 4 ingredients. Bring to a boil; cover, reduce heat, and simmer 15 minutes, stirring occasionally.

Cook macaroni according to package directions, omitting salt; drain. Add macaroni to meat mixture, stirring well; spoon into a lightly greased 11- x 7- x 1½-inch baking dish; top with pepperoni. Cover and bake at 350° for 25 minutes or until thoroughly heated. Sprinkle with cheese; bake 5 additional minutes or until cheese melts. Yield: 6 servings.

Ground Beef and Sausage Casserole

8 ounces spaghetti, uncooked
2 cups (8 ounces) shredded Cheddar cheese, divided
1 pound ground chuck
1 pound ground hot pork sausage
¼ cup chopped onion
1 clove garlic, crushed
1 (15-ounce) can tomato sauce
½ cup ketchup
3 tablespoons Worcestershire sauce
1 teaspoon dried basil
¼ teaspoon salt

Cook spaghetti according to package directions; drain, and place in a lightly greased 11- x 7- x 1½-inch baking dish. Sprinkle with 1 cup cheese.

Cook ground chuck, sausage, onion, and garlic in a large skillet over medium-high heat until meat is browned and vegetables are tender, stirring until meat crumbles; drain. Stir in tomato sauce and remaining ingredients. Bring to a boil; reduce heat, and simmer, uncovered, 5 minutes, stirring occasionally. Spoon mixture over cheese in baking dish.

Bake, uncovered, at 350° for 25 minutes or until thoroughly heated. Sprinkle with remaining 1 cup cheese; bake 5 additional minutes or until cheese melts. Yield: 6 servings.

Deep-Dish Taco Squares

2 cups biscuit and baking mix
½ cup cold water
1 pound ground chuck
¾ cup chopped green pepper
2 tablespoons chopped onion
1 (8-ounce) can tomato sauce
1 (8-ounce) carton sour cream
1 cup (4 ounces) shredded sharp
    Cheddar cheese
⅓ cup mayonnaise
Paprika

Combine baking mix and water, stirring with a fork until blended. Press mixture in bottom of a lightly greased 11- x 7- x 1½-inch baking dish. Bake at 375° for 9 minutes.

Cook ground chuck, green pepper, and onion in a large skillet over medium-high heat until meat is browned and vegetables are tender, stirring until meat crumbles; drain. Stir in tomato sauce. Spoon meat mixture over crust.

Combine sour cream, cheese, and mayonnaise; spoon over meat mixture. Sprinkle with paprika. Bake, uncovered, at 375° for 25 minutes or until thoroughly heated and crust is lightly browned. Let stand 5 minutes; cut into squares to serve. Yield: 4 servings.

Reuben Casserole

1 (32-ounce) jar sauerkraut,
    drained
1 medium onion, finely chopped
1¼ cups sour cream
¼ teaspoon garlic powder
4 (2.5-ounce) packages thinly
    sliced corned beef, cut into
    thin strips
2½ cups (10 ounces) shredded
    Swiss cheese
8 slices rye bread
2 tablespoons butter or
    margarine, melted

If you love a Reuben sandwich, then this casserole is for you. It contains all the ingredients and flavors of a traditional Reuben.

Press sauerkraut between paper towels to remove excess moisture. Combine sauerkraut, onion, sour cream, and garlic powder; stir well. Spoon mixture into a lightly greased 13- x 9- x 2-inch baking dish. Sprinkle corned beef evenly over sauerkraut mixture; top with cheese.

Remove crusts from bread; cut each slice in half diagonally. Arrange bread triangles over cheese, completely covering top of casserole; brush with melted butter. Bake, uncovered, at 350° for 35 minutes or until bread is lightly browned. Yield: 8 servings.

VEAL AND WILD RICE CASSEROLE

1 (8-ounce) carton sour cream
1 tablespoon all-purpose flour
1 (10¾-ounce) can cream of
    mushroom soup, undiluted
1 (6-ounce) package wild rice,
    uncooked
1½ cups chicken broth
½ cup dry sherry
1 teaspoon Worcestershire
    sauce

¾ teaspoon salt
¼ teaspoon pepper
2 pounds boneless veal, cut into
    ¾-inch pieces
1 large stalk celery, chopped
1 medium onion, chopped
1 cup sliced fresh mushrooms
2 tablespoons butter or
    margarine, melted
½ cup grated Romano cheese

Combine sour cream and flour in a large bowl; stir well. Add soup and next 6 ingredients; stir well. Set aside.

Brown veal in a large nonstick skillet over medium-high heat. Remove veal from skillet, discarding drippings. Drain veal on paper towels. Wipe skillet with a paper towel. Cook celery, onion, and mushrooms in butter in skillet over medium-high heat, stirring constantly, until crisp-tender.

Add vegetable mixture and veal to sour cream mixture; stir well. Spoon mixture into a lightly greased 13- x 9- x 2-inch baking dish. Bake, uncovered, at 350° for 1½ hours or until veal and rice are tender. Sprinkle with cheese; bake 5 additional minutes or until cheese melts. Yield: 8 servings.

LAMB PIE

2½ pounds lean boneless lamb,
    cut into ¾-inch pieces
6 cups water
1 teaspoon salt
½ teaspoon pepper
1 cup pearl onions, peeled
½ cup water
⅓ cup vegetable oil
⅓ cup all-purpose flour

½ teaspoon salt
½ teaspoon pepper
1 (10-ounce) package frozen
    English peas, thawed
1 teaspoon browning-and-
    seasoning sauce
Pastry for 9-inch pie
¼ to ½ teaspoon poppy seeds

Combine first 4 ingredients in a Dutch oven. Bring to a boil; cover, reduce heat, and simmer 45 minutes or until lamb is tender. Drain, reserving 3 cups broth. Set meat and reserved broth aside.

Combine pearl onions and ½ cup water in a small saucepan. Bring to a boil; cover, reduce heat, and simmer 10 to 15 minutes or until onions are tender. Drain.

Heat oil in a large heavy saucepan over medium heat; add flour, ½ teaspoon salt, and ½ teaspoon pepper. Cook, stirring constantly, 1 minute. Gradually add reserved broth; cook, stirring constantly, until mixture is thickened and bubbly. Add lamb, pearl onions, peas, and browning-and-seasoning sauce; stir well. Spoon mixture into a lightly greased 2-quart casserole.

Roll pastry to a 9-inch circle; sprinkle evenly with poppy seeds. Roll pastry until poppy seeds are pressed into pastry. Transfer pastry to top of pie; fold edges under, and crimp. Cut an **X** in center of pastry. Starting with 4 points in center, roll flaps of pastry toward outer edges, exposing lamb filling.

Bake at 400° for 30 minutes or until filling in center is bubbly. (Cover edges of pastry with strips of aluminum foil to prevent excessive browning, if necessary.) Yield: 4 servings.

Savory Lamb Pie is crowned with a flaky poppy seed-studded pastry.

PORK CHOP CASSEROLE

■■■■■■■■■■
You'll notice that we didn't add salt to Pork Chop Casserole as we did in the other pork chop recipes featured. That's because our staff felt that the long-grain-and-wild rice mix contains enough sodium for this dish.

1 (6-ounce) package long-grain-and-wild rice mix
2 cups hot water
6 (½-inch-thick) bone-in pork chops
¼ teaspoon pepper
1 (10¾-ounce) can cream of celery soup, undiluted
½ cup milk

Combine rice, seasoning packet from rice mix, and hot water; pour mixture into a lightly greased 13- x 9- x 2-inch baking dish.

Sprinkle chops with pepper; arrange chops over rice mixture. Cover and bake at 350° for 1 hour.

Combine soup and milk; pour evenly over chops. Bake, uncovered, 15 minutes or until chops are tender and mixture is thoroughly heated. Yield: 6 servings.

PEPPERED PORK CHOP CASSEROLE

6 (½- to ¾-inch-thick) bone-in pork chops
¼ teaspoon salt
¼ teaspoon pepper
2 tablespoons vegetable oil
2 medium-size green peppers
1 (15-ounce) can tomato sauce
1 (14½-ounce) can Italian-style stewed tomatoes, undrained and chopped
1 cup water
½ cup chopped onion
¾ teaspoon salt
¼ teaspoon pepper
1 clove garlic, minced
1½ cups long-grain rice, uncooked

Sprinkle chops with ¼ teaspoon salt and ¼ teaspoon pepper. Brown chops in hot oil in a large skillet over medium-high heat. Remove chops from skillet; drain and set aside.

Cut top off 1 green pepper; remove seeds. Cut 6 (¼-inch-thick) rings from green pepper; set pepper rings aside. Seed and chop all remaining green pepper. Combine chopped green pepper, tomato sauce, and next 6 ingredients; stir well.

Spread rice evenly in a lightly greased 13- x 9- x 2-inch baking dish; pour tomato mixture over rice. Arrange chops over rice mixture; top each chop with a pepper ring. Cover and bake at 350° for 1 hour or until chops and rice are tender. Yield: 6 servings.

PORK CHOPS AND SCALLOPED POTATOES

1 pound round red potatoes,
    sliced (about 4 medium)
1 medium onion, thinly sliced
    and separated into rings
1½ teaspoons salt, divided
½ teaspoon pepper, divided

¼ cup all-purpose flour
4 (¾-inch-thick) boneless pork
    chops
2 tablespoons vegetable oil
1 tablespoon all-purpose flour
1 cup milk

Layer potato and onion in a lightly greased 11- x 7- x 1½-inch baking dish. Sprinkle with 1 teaspoon salt and ¼ teaspoon pepper; set aside.

Combine ¼ cup flour, remaining ½ teaspoon salt, and remaining ¼ teaspoon pepper; dredge chops in flour mixture. Brown chops in hot oil in a large skillet over medium-high heat. Remove chops from skillet, reserving drippings in skillet. Drain chops, and set aside.

Add 1 tablespoon flour to drippings, stirring until smooth. Cook over low heat, stirring constantly, 1 minute. Gradually add milk; cook over medium heat, stirring constantly, until mixture is slightly thickened. Pour mixture over potato and onion; top with chops. Cover and bake at 350° for 1 hour or until chops and potato are tender. Yield: 4 servings.

SPAGHETTI-HAM PIE

6 ounces spaghetti, uncooked
2 tablespoons finely chopped
    green onions
4 cloves garlic, minced
2½ tablespoons olive oil
¼ cup all-purpose flour
¼ teaspoon salt

⅛ teaspoon freshly ground
    pepper
1½ cups milk
¾ cup half-and-half
¾ cup chopped cooked ham
¼ cup grated Parmesan cheese,
    divided

Cook spaghetti according to package directions; drain. Set aside.

Cook green onions and garlic in hot oil in a Dutch oven over medium heat, stirring constantly, 5 minutes. Stir in flour, salt, and pepper; cook, stirring constantly, 1 minute. Gradually add milk and half-and-half; cook, stirring constantly, until thickened and bubbly. Stir in spaghetti.

Spoon half of spaghetti mixture into a lightly greased 9-inch pieplate; sprinkle with ham and 2 tablespoons cheese. Top with remaining spaghetti mixture; sprinkle with remaining 2 tablespoons cheese. Bake, uncovered at 425° for 15 minutes or until lightly browned. Yield: 6 servings.

BROCCOLI-HAM AU GRATIN

1 medium onion, chopped
1 tablespoon butter or
    margarine, melted
1 (10¾-ounce) can Cheddar
    cheese soup, undiluted
1 (6-ounce) roll sharp process
    cheese spread, sliced
½ teaspoon garlic powder
3 cups cooked long-grain rice
2 cups diced cooked ham

1 (10-ounce) package frozen
    chopped broccoli, thawed
    and drained
1 (8-ounce) can sliced
    mushrooms, drained
1 (2-ounce) jar diced pimiento,
    drained
1 (2.8-ounce) can French fried
    onions

Cook chopped onion in butter in a Dutch oven over medium-high heat, stirring constantly, until tender. Add soup, cheese, and garlic powder, stirring until cheese melts. Stir in rice and next 4 ingredients.

Spoon mixture into a lightly greased 2½-quart casserole. Cover and bake at 350° for 40 minutes or until bubbly. Sprinkle with fried onions; bake 3 to 5 minutes or until onions begin to brown. Yield: 6 servings.

No-fuss Broccoli-Ham au Gratin makes an ideal entrée when time is short and company's coming for dinner.

SPICY CABBAGE ROLLS

16 large cabbage leaves
2 medium onions, chopped
2 stalks celery, chopped
2 tablespoons butter or
    margarine, melted
1 pound hot ground pork
    sausage
1½ cups cooked long-grain rice
1 tablespoon salt

¼ teaspoon pepper
2 tablespoons butter or
    margarine
2 tablespoons all-purpose flour
1 (28-ounce) can whole
    tomatoes, undrained and
    chopped
1 teaspoon ground nutmeg
½ teaspoon sugar

Cook cabbage leaves in boiling water 3 to 5 minutes or just until tender; drain and set aside.

Cook onion and celery in 2 tablespoons melted butter in a large skillet over medium-high heat, stirring constantly, until tender. Stir in sausage and next 3 ingredients.

For each cabbage roll, place about ½ cup meat mixture in center of 1 cabbage leaf. Fold left and right sides of leaf over meat mixture, and roll up, beginning at bottom. Place cabbage rolls, seam side down, in a lightly greased 13- x 9- x 2-inch baking dish.

Melt 2 tablespoons butter in a saucepan over low heat; add flour, stirring until smooth. Gradually add tomato; cook over medium heat, stirring constantly, until thickened and bubbly. Stir in nutmeg and sugar; pour mixture over cabbage rolls. Cover and bake at 350° for 45 minutes. Uncover and bake 15 additional minutes. Yield: 8 servings.

Trying to remove whole leaves from a head of cabbage? Immerse the cored head in a pot of boiling water; reduce the heat, and simmer one minute. Drain the cabbage head, and pat it dry with paper towels. Carefully peel away the slightly softened outer leaves. When the leaves no longer separate easily, repeat the blanching process.

SAUSAGE CASSEROLE

1 pound ground pork sausage
1 large onion, finely chopped
4½ cups water
½ cup long-grain rice, uncooked

1 (4.5-ounce) package chicken
    noodle soup mix
¾ cup slivered almonds
    (optional)

Cook sausage and onion in a large skillet over medium-high heat until meat is browned and onion is tender, stirring until meat crumbles; drain. Add water, rice, and soup mix; stir well. Bring to a boil; reduce heat, and simmer, uncovered, 7 minutes. Spoon mixture into a lightly greased 2½-quart casserole. Bake, uncovered, at 400° for 15 minutes. Sprinkle with almonds, if desired, and bake 15 additional minutes. Yield: 6 servings.

CHICKEN DIVAN

4 skinned chicken breast halves
1 large fresh rosemary sprig
½ teaspoon salt
¼ teaspoon pepper
2 tablespoons butter or
    margarine
¼ cup all-purpose flour
1 cup milk
1 egg yolk, lightly beaten
1 (8-ounce) carton sour cream
½ cup mayonnaise
½ teaspoon grated lemon rind
1½ tablespoons lemon juice
½ teaspoon salt
½ teaspoon curry powder
2 (10-ounce) packages frozen
    broccoli spears, thawed
    and drained
⅓ cup grated Parmesan cheese
Paprika

Combine first 4 ingredients in a large saucepan; add water to cover. Bring to a boil; cover, reduce heat, and simmer 30 minutes or until chicken is tender. Remove chicken from broth, reserving ½ cup broth; reserve remaining broth for another use, if desired. Remove and discard rosemary sprig. Let chicken cool; bone and chop chicken. Set aside.

Melt butter in a heavy saucepan over low heat; add flour, stirring until smooth. Cook, stirring constantly, 1 minute. Gradually add reserved ½ cup chicken broth and milk; cook over medium heat, stirring constantly, until mixture is thickened and bubbly.

Gradually stir about one-fourth of hot mixture into egg yolk; add to remaining hot mixture, stirring constantly. Cook, stirring constantly, 1 minute. Remove from heat; add sour cream and next 5 ingredients, stirring well.

Layer half each of broccoli, chicken, and sauce in a lightly greased 2-quart casserole. Repeat layers; sprinkle with cheese. Bake, uncovered, at 350° for 30 to 35 minutes or until bubbly. Sprinkle with paprika. Yield: 6 servings.

DELUXE CHICKEN POT PIE

6 skinned, boned chicken breast
    halves, cut into 1-inch pieces
1 medium onion, chopped
2 tablespoons butter or
    margarine, melted
1 stalk celery, chopped
1½ cups frozen English peas
    and carrots, thawed and
    drained
1 cup sliced fresh mushrooms
1 cup peeled, chopped potato
1 cup chicken broth
¼ cup dry white wine

½ teaspoon dried parsley flakes
¼ teaspoon pepper
1 bay leaf
2 tablespoons cornstarch
2 tablespoons water
1 (10¾-ounce) can cream of
    mushroom soup, undiluted
1 cup (4 ounces) shredded
    Cheddar cheese
¼ cup sour cream
Pot Pie Pastry
1 egg yolk, lightly beaten
1 tablespoon milk

Cook chicken and onion in butter in a large saucepan over medium-high heat, stirring constantly, until chicken is browned and onion is tender. Stir in celery and next 8 ingredients. Bring to a boil; cover, reduce heat, and simmer 15 minutes or until vegetables are tender. Remove and discard bay leaf.

Combine cornstarch and water, stirring until smooth; add cornstarch mixture to chicken mixture. Cook over medium heat, stirring constantly, until mixture comes to a boil. Remove from heat; stir in soup, cheese, and sour cream.

Roll half of Pot Pie Pastry to ⅛-inch thickness on a lightly floured surface; fit pastry into an ungreased 2-quart casserole. Spoon chicken mixture into casserole. Roll remaining pastry to ⅛-inch thickness, and place over chicken mixture. Trim, seal, and flute edges. Cut slits in pastry. Combine egg yolk and milk; brush over pastry. Bake at 400° for 35 to 40 minutes or until golden. Yield: 6 servings.

Pot Pie Pastry

3 cups all-purpose flour
1 teaspoon salt

1 cup shortening
4 to 6 tablespoons cold water

Combine flour and salt; cut in shortening with a pastry blender until mixture is crumbly. Sprinkle cold water (1 tablespoon at a time) evenly over surface; stir with a fork until dry ingredients are moistened. Shape into a ball; chill. Yield: pastry for one double-crust pie.

Cornstarch helps to thicken the vegetable-rich sauce of Deluxe Chicken Pot Pie. To prevent cornstarch from forming lumps when it's added to a hot mixture, combine the cornstarch with a small amount of cold water, and stir until the cornstarch dissolves. Then stir constantly when adding the dissolved cornstarch mixture to a hot liquid.

TIPSY CHICKEN AND DRESSING

8 skinned, boned chicken breast
   halves
2 tablespoons butter or
   margarine, melted
3 slices bread, crumbled
2 large eggs, lightly beaten
1 stalk celery, finely chopped
1 small onion, finely chopped
1 (14½-ounce) can condensed
   chicken broth, undiluted
1 (8-ounce) package cornbread
   stuffing mix

1 (14-ounce) can artichoke
   hearts, drained and
   quartered
1 (10¾-ounce) can cream of
   celery soup, undiluted
1 cup dry white wine
½ teaspoon dried basil
4 fresh mushrooms, sliced
8 slices Swiss cheese
¼ cup grated Parmesan cheese
2 tablespoons minced fresh
   parsley

Brown chicken in butter in a skillet over medium heat. Drain; set aside.

Combine bread and next 5 ingredients; spoon evenly into 8 greased 2-cup baking dishes. Arrange artichoke quarters evenly over dressing mixture in each dish; top evenly with chicken. Combine soup, wine, and basil; pour evenly over chicken. Top evenly with mushroom slices.

Cover and bake at 350° for 40 minutes. Cut each Swiss cheese slice into 4 strips. Uncover dishes, and arrange cheese strips evenly over casseroles; sprinkle evenly with Parmesan cheese and parsley. Bake, uncovered, 10 additional minutes. Yield: 8 servings.

CHICKEN RAGOÛT WITH CHEDDAR PINWHEELS

2 cups diagonally sliced carrot
1 medium-size sweet red
   pepper, seeded and cut
   into strips
3 tablespoons butter or
   margarine
¼ cup all-purpose flour
1 (14½-ounce) can condensed
   chicken broth, undiluted
1 cup milk

1 tablespoon lemon juice
½ teaspoon salt
½ teaspoon pepper
3 cups chopped cooked chicken
1 cup frozen English peas,
   thawed and drained
2 cups biscuit and baking mix
⅔ cup milk
¾ cup (3 ounces) shredded
   sharp Cheddar cheese

Arrange carrot and pepper strips in a steamer basket over boiling water. Cover and steam 8 minutes or until crisp-tender; set aside.

Melt butter in a large heavy saucepan over low heat; add flour, stirring until smooth. Cook, stirring constantly, 1 minute. Gradually add chicken broth and 1 cup milk; cook over medium heat, stirring constantly, until mixture is thickened and bubbly. Remove from heat; stir in lemon juice, salt, and ½ teaspoon pepper. Add carrot mixture, chicken, and peas, stirring gently. Spoon mixture into a lightly greased 11- x 7- x 1½-inch baking dish; set aside.

Combine biscuit mix and ⅔ cup milk in a small bowl; stir vigorously 30 seconds. Turn dough out onto a lightly floured surface, and knead 4 or 5 times.

Roll dough to a 12- x 9-inch rectangle; sprinkle with cheese to within ½ inch of edges. Roll up jellyroll fashion starting with long side; cut into 1-inch-thick slices. Arrange slices, cut side down, over chicken mixture. Bake at 375° for 35 minutes or until thoroughly heated. (Cover loosely with aluminum foil during the last 5 minutes of baking to prevent excessive browning, if necessary.) Yield: 6 servings.

The cheesy spiral biscuits sitting atop Chicken Ragoût with Cheddar Pinwheels give this casserole a fun look.

TURKEY PARMIGIANA

1 medium onion, chopped
3 cloves garlic, minced
3 tablespoons olive oil, divided
1 (28-ounce) can whole
    tomatoes, undrained and
    chopped
1 (8-ounce) can tomato sauce
¼ teaspoon dried thyme
¼ teaspoon pepper

½ cup fine, dry breadcrumbs
¼ cup grated Parmesan cheese
1 large egg, lightly beaten
1 tablespoon water
1 pound turkey cutlets
2 cups (8 ounces) shredded
    mozzarella cheese
⅔ cup grated Parmesan cheese
Hot cooked spaghetti

Cook onion and garlic in 1 tablespoon hot oil in a medium saucepan over medium-high heat, stirring constantly, until tender. Remove from heat; stir in chopped tomato and next 3 ingredients. Set aside.

Combine breadcrumbs and ¼ cup Parmesan cheese in a shallow bowl. Combine egg and water in another shallow bowl. Dip turkey in egg mixture; dredge in breadcrumb mixture. Brown half of turkey in 1 tablespoon hot oil in a large skillet over medium heat. Repeat procedure with remaining half of turkey and remaining 1 tablespoon oil.

Place turkey in a lightly greased 13- x 9- x 2-inch baking dish; pour tomato mixture evenly over turkey. Bake, uncovered, at 350° for 25 to 30 minutes or until sauce is thickened. Sprinkle with mozzarella cheese and ⅔ cup Parmesan cheese. Bake, uncovered, 5 additional minutes or until cheese melts. Serve over spaghetti. Yield: 6 servings.

LATTICE-TOPPED TURKEY PIE

■■■■■■■■■■
The crescent roll strips topping the pie pictured on the facing page are woven. For an easier version of our lattice crust, lay half of the crescent roll strips in one direction across the turkey mixture. Lay the remaining strips perpendicular to the first half.

½ cup mayonnaise
2 tablespoons all-purpose flour
1 cup milk
1 teaspoon chicken-flavored
    bouillon granules
1 (10-ounce) package frozen
    mixed vegetables, thawed
    and drained

2 cups chopped cooked turkey
⅛ teaspoon pepper
1 (4-ounce) can refrigerated
    crescent rolls

Combine mayonnaise and flour in a medium saucepan; stir well with a wire whisk. Add milk and bouillon granules, stirring well. Cook over medium heat, stirring constantly, until mixture is thickened and bubbly.

Although Lattice-Topped Turkey Pie looks as if it might be difficult to prepare, it's really quite simple.

Stir in vegetables, turkey, and pepper; cook until thoroughly heated, stirring occasionally. Spoon mixture into an ungreased 9-inch pieplate.

Unroll crescent rolls, and place rectangular pieces side by side on a lightly floured surface. Press perforations together to seal. Roll dough to a 10-inch square; cut into 1-inch strips. Arrange strips in a lattice design over turkey mixture. Bake at 375° for 15 to 20 minutes or until lightly browned. Let stand 5 minutes before serving. Yield: 4 servings.

No Time To Cook

■ Electric slow cookers, microwave ovens, and pressure cookers come in handy when you need to get dinner on the table
fast. ■ With an electric slow cooker, you can safely cook a
meal while you're away from home. ■ A microwave oven will
help you fix supper in minutes without heating up your kitchen.

■ And using a pressure cooker can cut recipe preparation time
by two-thirds. ■ No one will guess you didn't spend hours
preparing dinner when you serve Tangy Short Ribs and
Vegetables, Ginger-Nut Chicken, or Black-Eyed Pea Jambalaya—
just a few of our favorites made with these timesaving appliances.

Ginger-Nut Chicken (page 180)

BEEF RAGOÛT

Liquids don't boil away in electric slow cookers as in conventional cooking. Be sure to use the amount of liquid called for in slow cooker recipes, especially for a thick stew like Beef Ragoût.

3 pounds beef stew meat, cut into 1-inch pieces
2 tablespoons vegetable oil
2 stalks celery, chopped
2 cloves garlic, minced
1 medium onion, chopped
2 teaspoons salt, divided
½ teaspoon pepper
¾ cup all-purpose flour
2 cups water, divided

1 cup dry red wine
1 cup chopped fresh tomato
1 tablespoon chopped fresh parsley
¼ teaspoon ground thyme
2 bay leaves
5 small onions, quartered
5 carrots, scraped and halved
5 small round red potatoes, halved

Brown meat in hot oil in a large Dutch oven; drain. Add celery, garlic, chopped onion, 1 teaspoon salt, and pepper. Cook over medium heat, stirring constantly, until vegetables are tender. Combine flour and 1 cup water, stirring until smooth; add to meat mixture, stirring well. Spoon meat mixture into a 4-quart electric slow cooker.

Combine remaining 1 teaspoon salt, remaining 1 cup water, wine, and next 4 ingredients; pour over meat mixture. Place onion quarters, carrot, and potato over meat mixture (do not stir). Cover and cook on high setting 4 to 4½ hours or until meat and vegetables are tender. Remove and discard bay leaves. Yield: 10 servings.

COUNTRY STEW

After preparing Country Stew or other electric slow cooker recipes, allow the insert to cool completely before washing it. Running cold water over the insert to cool it may cause it to crack. Never immerse the electric unit in water; unplug it, and wipe it clean with a damp cloth.

2 pounds beef stew meat, cut into ¾-inch pieces
1 large baking potato, cubed
2 medium onions, sliced
1 cup thinly sliced carrot
1 cup frozen English peas, thawed

1 (10¾-ounce) can tomato soup, undiluted
1⅓ cups water
1 teaspoon salt
¼ teaspoon pepper
1 bay leaf

Layer first 5 ingredients in a 4-quart electric slow cooker.

Combine soup and remaining ingredients; pour over layered ingredients. Cover and cook on high setting 4½ to 5 hours or until meat and vegetables are tender. Remove and discard bay leaf. Yield: 2 quarts.

Tangy Short Ribs and Vegetables cook for several hours in an electric slow cooker, leaving you free time for other activities.

TANGY SHORT RIBS AND VEGETABLES

3 pounds lean beef short ribs
3 tablespoons vegetable oil
4 medium baking potatoes, unpeeled and quartered
4 carrots, scraped and cut into 2-inch pieces
1 medium onion, sliced
1 cup beef broth
2 tablespoons white vinegar

2 tablespoons ketchup
1 tablespoon prepared horseradish
1 tablespoon prepared mustard
1 teaspoon salt
1/4 teaspoon pepper
1/4 cup all-purpose flour
1/4 cup water

Brown ribs in hot oil in a large skillet; drain. Place potato, carrot, and onion in a 4-quart electric slow cooker; arrange ribs over vegetables.

Combine broth and next 6 ingredients; pour over ribs. Cover and cook on high setting 3 to 3½ hours or until ribs are tender. Remove ribs and vegetables from slow cooker; set aside, and keep warm.

Combine flour and water, stirring until smooth; add to liquid in slow cooker. Cook, uncovered, 10 to 15 minutes or until mixture is thickened. Serve gravy mixture with ribs and vegetables. Yield: 4 servings.

■■■■■■■■■■
Tangy Short Ribs and Vegetables are perfect for the electric slow cooker because beef short ribs are tough and need slow, moist-heat cooking to tenderize them. Leaving the peel on the potatoes helps them to retain nutrients and keep their shape.

SAVORY POT ROAST

1 (3-pound) boneless chuck
  roast
¼ teaspoon salt
1 tablespoon vegetable oil
¼ cup ketchup
¼ cup red wine vinegar
¼ cup dry red wine
2 tablespoons soy sauce

2 tablespoons Worcestershire
  sauce
1 teaspoon dried rosemary
½ teaspoon garlic powder
½ teaspoon dry mustard
1 tablespoon all-purpose flour
2 tablespoons water
Hot cooked noodles or rice

Trim any excess fat from roast; cut into bite-size pieces. Sprinkle roast with salt; brown in hot oil in a large skillet. Place roast in a 4-quart electric slow cooker. Combine ketchup and next 7 ingredients; pour over roast. Cover and cook on high setting 3 to 3½ hours or until roast is tender.

Combine flour and water, stirring until smooth; add to meat mixture. Cook, uncovered, 10 to 15 minutes or until mixture is thickened. Serve over noodles or rice. Yield: 8 servings.

PORK CHOP DINNER

You won't have to pay much attention to Pork Chop Dinner while it cooks. And after the meal, you have only one utensil to clean.

4 (½-inch-thick) boneless pork
  chops
1 tablespoon vegetable oil
4 medium baking potatoes,
  quartered
4 large carrots, scraped and cut
  into 1-inch-thick slices
¼ cup chopped onion

¼ cup chopped celery
1 teaspoon chicken-flavored
  bouillon granules
1 cup hot water
¾ teaspoon salt
¼ teaspoon pepper
2 tablespoons all-purpose flour
1 cup water

Cook chops in hot oil in an electric skillet set at 300° for 15 minutes, turning twice; drain. Top chops with potato and next 3 ingredients.

Dissolve bouillon granules in hot water; pour over vegetables. Sprinkle evenly with salt and pepper. Reduce heat to 200°; cover and cook 40 minutes or until chops and vegetables are tender. Remove chops and vegetables to a serving platter, reserving drippings in skillet.

Increase skillet temperature to 225°. Combine flour and 1 cup water, stirring until smooth. Gradually add flour mixture to drippings in skillet; cook, stirring constantly, until mixture is thickened and bubbly. Serve sauce with meat and vegetables. Yield: 4 servings.

LOUISIANA OYSTER-AND-ARTICHOKE SOUP

2 (12-ounce) containers fresh
    Standard oysters
3 tablespoons butter or
    margarine
½ cup finely chopped shallots
¼ teaspoon ground red pepper
¼ teaspoon dried thyme
1 bay leaf
3 tablespoons all-purpose flour
1 (14½-ounce) can ready-to-
    serve chicken broth

1 (14-ounce) can artichoke
    hearts, drained and cut
    into eighths
1 tablespoon chopped fresh
    parsley
2 tablespoons dry sherry
½ teaspoon salt
¼ teaspoon hot sauce
½ cup whipping cream
Freshly grated Parmesan cheese

Even though this recipe yields only 1½ quarts, using a 3-quart casserole allows room for stirring and simmering.

Drain oysters, reserving liquid. Add water to oyster liquid to equal 1 cup. Quarter oysters, and set aside.

Place butter in a 3-quart casserole; microwave at HIGH 50 seconds or until melted. Add shallots and next 3 ingredients. Cover with heavy-duty plastic wrap; fold back a small edge to allow steam to escape. Microwave at HIGH 3 minutes, stirring after 2 minutes. Stir in flour. Gradually stir in oyster liquid and broth. Cover and microwave at HIGH 9 to 10 minutes, stirring after 5 minutes. Remove and discard bay leaf.

Add oysters, artichoke hearts, and next 4 ingredients; cover and microwave at HIGH 5 to 8 minutes, stirring after 4 minutes. Stir in whipping cream. Serve with Parmesan cheese. Yield: 1½ quarts.

FISH AND VEGETABLE DINNER

4 (6-ounce) orange roughy fillets
½ teaspoon salt
¼ teaspoon pepper
½ cup commercial buttermilk
    salad dressing

2 cups broccoli flowerets
1 medium-size sweet red
    pepper, seeded and cut
    into strips
1 small onion, cut into strips

Place fish in an 11- x 7- x 1½-inch baking dish; sprinkle with salt and pepper. Spread 2 tablespoons salad dressing over each fillet. Arrange broccoli, pepper strips, and onion over fish.

Cover with heavy-duty plastic wrap; fold back a small corner to allow steam to escape. Microwave at HIGH 13 to 15 minutes or until fish flakes easily, giving dish a half-turn after 7 minutes. Yield: 4 servings.

Microwave Ocean Papillote for an impressive dish to serve company.

Ocean Papillote

2¼ cups water
¾ pound unpeeled medium-size
   fresh shrimp
4 flounder fillets (about 1½
   pounds)
2 tablespoons brandy
1 tablespoon lemon juice
3 tablespoons butter or
   margarine

1½ cups sliced fresh
   mushrooms
1 cup sweet red pepper strips
1 small onion, thinly sliced and
   separated into rings
¼ cup chopped green onions
¼ teaspoon salt
Dash of ground white pepper
Paprika

Bring water to a boil; add shrimp, and cook 3 minutes. Drain shrimp well, and rinse with cold water. Chill. Peel shrimp, and devein, if desired. Set aside.

Cut 4 (15-inch) squares of parchment paper; fold in half diagonally, forming triangles. Crease firmly. Place 1 fillet on half of each square near the crease; sprinkle evenly with brandy and lemon juice. Set aside.

Place butter in a 2-quart casserole; microwave at HIGH 50 seconds or until melted. Add mushrooms and pepper strips. Cover tightly with heavy-duty plastic wrap; fold back a small edge of wrap to allow steam to escape. Microwave at HIGH 2 to 3 minutes or until vegetables are tender, stirring after 1 minute.

Arrange mushroom mixture, shrimp, and onion rings evenly over fillets. Sprinkle with green onions and remaining ingredients. Fold over free halves of squares; fold paper edges over to seal. Starting at one end of each triangle, pleat and crimp edges of parchment to make an airtight seal. Fold pointed ends under. Arrange pouches on a large glass platter. Microwave at HIGH 7 to 8 minutes or until fish flakes easily when tested with a fork. Cut an opening in the top of each packet, and fold paper back. Serve immediately. Yield: 4 servings.

BEEFY NOODLE CASSEROLE

4 ounces medium egg noodles, uncooked
1 (8-ounce) package cream cheese, cubed
1 cup cream-style cottage cheese
½ cup sour cream
1 pound ground chuck
1 (14-ounce) jar spaghetti sauce
½ cup grated Parmesan cheese

Cook noodles according to package directions; drain. Place noodles in a lightly greased 11- x 7- x 1½-inch baking dish. Set aside.

Place cream cheese in a 1-quart glass measure; microwave at HIGH 45 to 60 seconds or until softened. Add cottage cheese and sour cream; stir well. Spread mixture over noodles.

Crumble ground chuck into a 2-quart casserole; cover with wax paper. Microwave at HIGH 5 to 7 minutes or until meat is no longer pink, stirring at 2-minute intervals to crumble meat; drain.

Combine meat and spaghetti sauce; spoon over cream cheese mixture. Sprinkle with Parmesan cheese. Cover and microwave at HIGH 8 to 10 minutes or until mixture is thoroughly heated, giving dish a half-turn after 5 minutes. Yield: 4 servings.

CHEESE-TOPPED CHILI

1 pound ground chuck
½ cup finely chopped onion
½ cup finely chopped green
  pepper
1 clove garlic, minced
1 (16-ounce) can kidney beans,
  drained
1 (16-ounce) can whole
  tomatoes, undrained and
  chopped

1 (8-ounce) can tomato sauce
½ cup beef broth
2 teaspoons chili powder
½ teaspoon ground cumin
¼ teaspoon salt
¼ teaspoon dried oregano
⅛ teaspoon pepper
⅛ teaspoon hot sauce
¾ cup (3 ounces) shredded
  sharp Cheddar cheese

Combine first 4 ingredients in a 2-quart casserole. Cover with wax paper, and microwave at HIGH 5 to 7 minutes or until meat is no longer pink, stirring at 2-minute intervals to crumble meat; drain.

Stir in beans and next 9 ingredients. Cover and microwave at HIGH 15 to 20 minutes or until mixture is thoroughly heated, stirring at 5-minute intervals. Spoon chili into bowls, and sprinkle evenly with cheese. Yield: 5 cups.

EASY SPAGHETTI

Resist the temptation to increase the amount of seasonings in Easy Spaghetti. Because microwave oven recipes usually call for less liquid, it's easy for seasonings to become overpowering. You can adjust the seasonings at the end of the cooking time.

1 (8-ounce) package spaghetti,
  uncooked
1 pound ground chuck
1 small onion, chopped
1 (15-ounce) can tomato sauce
1 (6-ounce) can tomato paste
⅓ cup dry red wine
1 teaspoon Worcestershire
  sauce

½ teaspoon salt
½ teaspoon dried oregano
½ teaspoon dried basil
¼ teaspoon dried thyme
¼ teaspoon garlic powder
¼ teaspoon pepper
Grated Parmesan cheese

Cook spaghetti according to package directions; drain. Set aside.

Combine ground chuck and onion in a 2-quart casserole. Cover with wax paper, and microwave at HIGH 5 to 7 minutes or until meat is no longer pink, stirring at 2-minute intervals to crumble meat; drain.

Stir in tomato sauce and next 9 ingredients. Cover and microwave at HIGH 12 minutes or until thoroughly heated, stirring after 6 minutes. Serve over spaghetti; sprinkle with Parmesan cheese. Yield: 4 servings.

MEXI CASSEROLE

1 pound ground chuck
¾ cup chopped onion
½ cup chopped celery
1 (16-ounce) can kidney beans, drained
1 (11-ounce) can whole kernel corn, drained
1 (8-ounce) can tomato sauce
½ cup sliced ripe olives
2 teaspoons chili powder
¾ teaspoon seasoned salt
½ teaspoon pepper
1 cup (4 ounces) shredded sharp Cheddar cheese
1 cup crushed corn chips
Additional sliced ripe olives

Combine ground chuck, onion, and celery in a 2½-quart casserole. Cover with wax paper. Microwave at HIGH 5 to 7 minutes or until meat is no longer pink, stirring at 2-minute intervals to crumble meat; drain.

Stir in beans and next 6 ingredients. Cover and microwave at HIGH 5 to 7 minutes or until thoroughly heated, giving dish a half-turn after 3 minutes. Sprinkle with cheese and corn chips. Reduce to MEDIUM HIGH (70% power); microwave, uncovered, 1 minute or until cheese melts. Sprinkle with additional sliced ripe olives. Yield: 6 servings.

Put Mexi Casserole on the table in less than 20 minutes with the help of your microwave oven.

MICRO MACARONI AND CHEESE WITH HAM

■■■■■■■■■■■
Omit the ham in this
recipe for a creamy
macaroni and cheese
side dish.

1 (8-ounce) package elbow
　　macaroni, uncooked
¼ cup butter or margarine
½ cup chopped green pepper
¼ cup all-purpose flour
2 cups milk

2 cups (8 ounces) shredded
　　Cheddar cheese
½ to ¾ teaspoon salt
¼ teaspoon pepper
1½ cups chopped cooked ham

Cook macaroni according to package directions; drain. Place macaroni in a lightly greased 2½-quart casserole; set aside.

Place butter in a 1-quart glass measure; microwave at HIGH 55 seconds or until melted. Add green pepper. Cover tightly with heavy-duty plastic wrap; fold back a small edge of wrap to allow steam to escape. Microwave at HIGH 1½ minutes or until green pepper is crisp-tender, stirring after 1 minute. Add flour; stir until blended. Gradually stir in milk; microwave at HIGH 5 to 7 minutes or until mixture is thickened, stirring at 2-minute intervals.

Add cheese, salt, and pepper; stir until cheese melts. Pour over macaroni; add ham, and stir well. Cover with wax paper; microwave at MEDIUM HIGH (70% power) 8 to 10 minutes or until thoroughly heated, stirring after 4 minutes. Let stand 2 minutes. Yield: 5 servings.

HAM TETRAZZINI

1 (12-ounce) package spaghetti,
　　uncooked
½ cup sliced almonds
¼ cup butter or margarine
¾ cup chopped green pepper
1 clove garlic, minced
1 tablespoon all-purpose flour
1 cup milk
3 cups (12 ounces) shredded
　　process American cheese,
　　divided

1½ cups diced cooked ham
⅓ cup grated Parmesan cheese
¼ cup dry sherry
1 (10¾-ounce) can cream of
　　mushroom soup, undiluted
1 (4-ounce) jar sliced
　　mushrooms, drained
1 (2-ounce) jar diced pimiento,
　　undrained

Cook spaghetti according to package directions; drain and set aside.

Spread sliced almonds on a glass plate. Microwave at HIGH 2 to 4 minutes or until lightly toasted, stirring once. Set aside.

Place butter in a 2-quart casserole; microwave at HIGH 55 seconds or until melted. Add green pepper and garlic. Cover tightly with heavy-duty plastic wrap; fold back a small edge of wrap to allow steam to escape. Microwave at HIGH 2 minutes or until crisp-tender. Add flour; stir until blended. Gradually add milk, stirring well. Cover and microwave at HIGH 3 to 4 minutes or until mixture is thickened and bubbly, stirring after 2 minutes and then at 1-minute intervals.

Stir in 2 cups American cheese, ham, and remaining ingredients. Cover and microwave at HIGH 4 minutes or until cheese melts, stirring after 2 minutes. Combine spaghetti and ham mixture.

Spoon spaghetti mixture into a lightly greased 2½ quart casserole. Sprinkle with remaining 1 cup American cheese and toasted almonds. Reduce to MEDIUM HIGH (70% power); cover and microwave 8 to 10 minutes or until mixture is thoroughly heated, giving dish a half-turn after 4 minutes. Serve immediately. Yield: 6 servings.

CHEESY HAM TOWERS

4 commercial frozen puff pastry patty shells
3 tablespoons butter or margarine
3 tablespoons all-purpose flour
1½ cups milk
1½ cups cubed cooked ham
¾ cup (3 ounces) shredded Cheddar cheese
3 tablespoons sliced ripe olives
1½ tablespoons minced fresh parsley
1½ tablespoons diced pimiento
¾ teaspoon chicken-flavored bouillon granules
¾ teaspoon prepared mustard
¾ teaspoon Worcestershire sauce

Bake patty shells according to package directions. Set aside; keep warm.

Place butter in a 1-quart glass measure; microwave at HIGH 50 seconds or until melted. Add flour, stirring until smooth. Gradually add milk, stirring well. Microwave at HIGH 3 to 4 minutes or until mixture is thickened and bubbly, stirring after 2 minutes.

Stir in ham and remaining ingredients. Microwave at HIGH 1 to 1½ minutes or until mixture is thoroughly heated. Spoon ham mixture evenly into patty shells. Yield: 4 servings.

Making a white sauce in the microwave oven for recipes such as Cheesy Ham Towers is quicker and easier than the conventional method. Just be sure to start with a container large enough to prevent the sauce from bubbling over and to allow room for adding other ingredients.

Both cream-style and whole kernel corn are used in quick-to-fix Sausage-Corn Chowder, sure to please on a blustery day.

SAUSAGE-CORN CHOWDER

½ pound ground pork sausage
½ cup chopped onion
½ cup chopped green pepper
3 cups milk, divided
⅓ cup all-purpose flour
1 tablespoon chopped fresh
    parsley

1 teaspoon onion salt
¼ teaspoon pepper
1 (17-ounce) can cream-style corn
1 (16½-ounce) can whole kernel
    corn, drained
¼ cup diced pimiento, drained
Garnish: fresh parsley sprigs

Combine first 3 ingredients in a 3-quart casserole. Cover with wax paper, and microwave at HIGH 4 to 6 minutes or until meat is no longer pink, stirring at 2-minute intervals to crumble meat; drain. Return mixture to casserole.

Combine 1 cup milk and flour, stirring well; stir into sausage mixture. Add chopped parsley, onion salt, and ¼ teaspoon pepper; cover and microwave at HIGH 2 to 3 minutes or until thickened, stirring at 1-minute intervals. Stir in remaining 2 cups milk, cream-style corn, whole kernel corn, and pimiento; cover and microwave at HIGH 7 to 9 minutes or just until slightly thickened, stirring after 4 minutes. Ladle soup into individual bowls, and garnish, if desired. Yield: 7 cups.

EASY CHICKEN

2 tablespoons butter or
   margarine
¼ cup sliced green onions
2 tablespoons dry white wine
2 tablespoons lemon juice
2 tablespoons olive oil
½ teaspoon salt
½ teaspoon dried marjoram

½ teaspoon paprika
¼ teaspoon pepper
2 cloves garlic, minced
6 skinned chicken breast halves
1½ tablespoons browning-and-
   seasoning sauce
Hot cooked rice

Browning-and-seasoning sauce gives Easy Chicken its dark, rich color. You'd never guess that this recipe was prepared in a microwave oven.

Place butter in a 2-cup glass measure; microwave at HIGH 45 seconds or until melted. Add green onions and next 8 ingredients; stir well, and set aside.

Brush chicken on each side with browning-and-seasoning sauce; place chicken, bone side up, in an 8-inch square baking dish, overlapping slightly. Cover tightly with heavy-duty plastic wrap; fold back a small corner of wrap to allow steam to escape. Microwave at HIGH 15 minutes. Turn chicken; spoon sauce over chicken. Reduce to MEDIUM (50% power); cover and microwave 13 to 15 minutes. Let stand, covered, 5 minutes. Serve with rice. Yield: 6 servings.

GINGER-NUT CHICKEN

■■■■■■■■■■
Cut the meat for
Ginger-Nut Chicken into
uniform pieces to
promote even cooking.

1 tablespoon butter or
  margarine
2 skinned, boned chicken breast
  halves, cut into bite-size
  pieces
4 green onions, cut into 1-inch
  pieces
1 stalk celery, cut into 1-inch
  pieces
1½ cups broccoli flowerets

1 teaspoon minced fresh ginger
2 tablespoons cornstarch
½ cup water, divided
1 tablespoon soy sauce
¼ teaspoon lemon-pepper
  seasoning
⅛ teaspoon garlic salt
⅓ cup dry-roasted peanuts
Hot cooked rice

Place butter in a 1½-quart casserole; microwave at HIGH 35 seconds or until melted. Add chicken to casserole, and toss with butter. Cover with wax paper, and microwave at HIGH 4 minutes, stirring after 2 minutes. Add green onions, celery, broccoli, and ginger. Cover and microwave at HIGH 2 minutes.

Combine cornstarch and ¼ cup water in a small bowl; stir until smooth. Add remaining ¼ cup water, soy sauce, lemon-pepper seasoning, and garlic salt; stir well. Pour cornstarch mixture over chicken and vegetables. Cover and microwave at HIGH 2 to 3 minutes or until sauce is slightly thickened, stirring after 2 minutes. Stir in peanuts; serve over rice. Yield: 2 servings.

PRESSURE COOKER ROAST

■■■■■■■■■■
Because pressure cookers
quickly tenderize tougher
cuts of meat, Pressure
Cooker Roast is ready in
an hour. The amount of
food in the pressure
cooker doesn't affect
cooking time.

1 (3- to 3½-pound) boneless
  chuck roast or sirloin tip
  roast
2 tablespoons vegetable oil
2 cups water
1 teaspoon dried oregano or
  dried rosemary
1 teaspoon salt
¼ teaspoon pepper
⅛ teaspoon hot sauce

4 carrots, scraped and cut into
  1-inch pieces
4 stalks celery with leaves, cut
  into 1-inch pieces
2 small onions, cut into eighths
2 bay leaves
1 clove garlic, minced
2 tablespoons cornstarch
2 tablespoons water

Brown roast in hot oil in a 6-quart pressure cooker. Add 2 cups water and next 9 ingredients. Close lid securely. According to manufacturer's directions, bring to high pressure over high heat (about 10 to 12 minutes). Reduce heat to medium or level needed to maintain high pressure; cook 45 minutes. Remove from heat; run cold water over cooker to reduce pressure rapidly. Remove lid so that steam escapes away from you.

Remove roast and vegetables from cooker, reserving drippings. Remove and discard bay leaves. Transfer roast and vegetables to a serving platter; set aside, and keep warm. Skim fat from drippings. Add enough water to drippings to measure 2 cups. Place drippings mixture in a medium saucepan.

Combine cornstarch and 2 tablespoons water, stirring until smooth; add to drippings mixture. Cook over medium heat, stirring constantly, until mixture is thickened and bubbly. Serve gravy mixture with roast. Yield: 6 servings.

QUICK BEEF STEW

2 pounds beef stew meat, cut
    into 1-inch pieces
¼ cup all-purpose flour
2 tablespoons vegetable oil
1½ cups beef broth
1 cup beer
¼ cup chopped fresh parsley
¾ teaspoon salt
½ teaspoon dried thyme
½ teaspoon pepper

1¾ pounds round red potatoes,
    cut into 1-inch cubes
1 pound carrots, scraped and
    cut into 1-inch pieces
2 medium onions, sliced
3 cloves garlic, minced
1 (10-ounce) package frozen
    English peas
1 tablespoon red wine vinegar

Combine meat and flour in a large heavy-duty, zip-top plastic bag; seal bag, and shake well. Brown meat in hot oil in a 6-quart pressure cooker over medium-high heat. Add beef broth and next 9 ingredients. Close lid securely. According to manufacturer's directions, bring to high pressure over high heat (about 10 to 12 minutes). Reduce heat to medium or level needed to maintain high pressure; cook 15 minutes. Remove from heat; run cold water over cooker to reduce pressure rapidly. Remove lid so that steam escapes away from you.

Stir in peas and vinegar. Bring to a boil; reduce heat, and simmer, uncovered, 15 minutes. Yield: about 3½ quarts.

With a pressure cooker to speed up the cooking time, Black-Eyed Pea Jambalaya is ready in less than 45 minutes.

BLACK-EYED PEA JAMBALAYA

Follow the manufacturer's instructions when preparing this and other recipes with your pressure cooker. Wash the cooker after each use, making certain the vent isn't clogged. To store, turn the lid upside down and place on top of the cooker; don't lock the lid to the pan.

1½ cups dried black-eyed peas
4 (10½-ounce) cans condensed chicken broth, undiluted
2 medium tomatoes, chopped
2 cloves garlic, minced
1 medium-size green pepper, seeded and chopped
1 small onion, chopped
1 stalk celery, chopped

1 bay leaf
1 cup cubed cooked ham
½ teaspoon salt
¼ teaspoon dried thyme
⅛ teaspoon ground cloves
1½ cups long-grain rice, uncooked
½ cup sliced green onions
1½ teaspoons hot sauce

Sort and wash peas; place in a 6-quart pressure cooker. Add water to chicken broth to make 5 cups. Add broth, tomato, and next 9 ingredients to peas; stir well. Close lid securely. According to manufacturer's directions, bring to high pressure over high heat (about 10 to 12 minutes). Reduce heat to medium or level needed to maintain high pressure; cook 15 minutes. Remove from heat; run cold water over cooker to reduce pressure rapidly. Remove lid so that steam escapes away from you.

Drain pea mixture, reserving 3 cups liquid. Remove and discard bay leaf. Remove pea mixture from cooker; set aside, and keep warm.

Add rice and reserved liquid to cooker; stir gently. Close lid securely; bring to high pressure over high heat (about 5 minutes). Reduce heat to medium or level needed to maintain high pressure; cook 5 minutes. Remove from heat; run cold water over cooker to reduce pressure rapidly. Remove lid so that steam escapes away from you. Stir in pea mixture, green onions, and hot sauce. Yield: 6 servings.

CHICKEN MARENGO

Vegetable cooking spray
1 (3- to 3½-pound) broiler-
  fryer, skinned and cut up
1 (16-ounce) can whole
  tomatoes, undrained and
  chopped
⅓ cup chopped onion
¼ cup dry sherry
½ teaspoon salt

½ teaspoon dried thyme
¼ teaspoon pepper
1 clove garlic, minced
1 bay leaf
1½ cups sliced fresh
  mushrooms
2 tablespoons cornstarch
Hot cooked rice

Coat a 6-quart pressure cooker with cooking spray; add chicken and next 8 ingredients. Close lid securely. According to manufacturer's directions, bring to high pressure over high heat (about 10 to 12 minutes). Reduce heat to medium or level needed to maintain high pressure; cook 9 minutes. Remove from heat; run cold water over cooker to reduce pressure rapidly. Remove lid so that steam escapes away from you.

Transfer chicken to a serving platter; keep warm. Remove ¼ cup liquid; set aside. Add mushrooms to cooker; close lid securely. Bring to high pressure over high heat (about 5 minutes). Reduce heat to medium or level needed to maintain high pressure; cook 5 minutes. Remove from heat; run cold water over cooker to reduce pressure rapidly. Remove lid so that steam escapes away from you.

Combine cornstarch and reserved liquid; stir into mushroom mixture. Bring to a boil; cook, stirring constantly, 1 minute. Remove and discard bay leaf. Pour sauce over chicken; serve with rice. Yield: 4 servings.

Minus the Meat

■ Many of you have let us know that you're eating more meat-less meals than ever. ■ If that's the case at your house, then this chapter's for you. ■ We've selected our best bean, cheese, and pasta entrées for you to enjoy. ■ From Bean Chalupas to Eggplant Parmesan to Mediterranean Ravioli, we've got the recipes to prove that eating meatless meals doesn't mean set-tling for less taste or less nutrition. ■ Each recipe in this chap-ter contains at least 10 grams of protein per serving, enough for a complete meal.

Grilled Polenta with Black Bean Salsa (page 186)

BLACK BEAN SPAGHETTI

1 large onion, sliced
1 small sweet red pepper,
    seeded and cut into strips
1 small sweet yellow pepper,
    seeded and cut into strips
½ pound fresh mushrooms,
    sliced
2 tablespoons olive oil
1 (16-ounce) can whole
    tomatoes, undrained and
    chopped
1 (15-ounce) can black beans,
    drained and rinsed

1 (15-ounce) can kidney beans,
    undrained
¼ cup sliced ripe olives
2 tablespoons capers
¼ teaspoon dried rosemary
¼ teaspoon dried basil
¼ teaspoon pepper
Hot cooked spaghetti
Freshly grated Parmesan cheese
Garnish: fresh basil sprigs

Cook first 4 ingredients in hot oil in a large skillet over medium-high heat, stirring constantly, until tender. Add tomato and next 7 ingredients. Bring to a boil; cover, reduce heat, and simmer 30 minutes, stirring occasionally.

Serve bean mixture over spaghetti, and sprinkle with Parmesan cheese. Garnish, if desired. Yield: 6 servings.

GRILLED POLENTA WITH BLACK BEAN SALSA

Made from a slow-cooked cornmeal mush, traditional Italian polenta is equally delicious served straight from the saucepan with a pat of butter or shaped and sliced, as in our version here. Slices or wedges of polenta are usually pan-fried or grilled for extra flavor.

3 cups chicken broth
1 cup yellow cornmeal
Vegetable cooking spray

Black Bean Salsa
Garnishes: fresh cilantro sprigs,
    jalapeño peppers

Bring chicken broth to a boil in a large heavy saucepan. Add cornmeal in a slow, steady stream, stirring constantly. Reduce heat; cook over medium heat, stirring constantly, 20 minutes or until mixture pulls away from sides of pan.

Spread cornmeal mixture in a 9-inch square pan coated with cooking spray; cover and chill until firm. Cut polenta into 4 squares; cut each square in half diagonally, forming 8 triangles.

Coat grill rack with cooking spray. Grill polenta triangles, covered, over hot coals (400° to 500°) 5 minutes on each side or until polenta begins to brown. Place 2 polenta triangles on each of 4 serving plates; top evenly with Black Bean Salsa. Garnish, if desired. Yield: 4 servings.

Black Bean Salsa

1 (15-ounce) can black beans,
   rinsed and drained
2 tomatoes, chopped
4 green onions, sliced
1 clove garlic, crushed
3 tablespoons chopped fresh
   cilantro

2½ tablespoons vegetable oil
2 tablespoons fresh lime juice
½ teaspoon ground cumin
¼ teaspoon salt
¼ teaspoon pepper

Combine all ingredients; cover and chill at least 8 hours. Drain before serving. Yield: 3 cups.

MEXICAN BEAN CASSEROLE

2 cups (8 ounces) shredded
   Monterey Jack cheese
1 cup small-curd cottage cheese
¼ cup chopped green onions
2 tablespoons chopped green
   chiles
¼ teaspoon salt
1 (8-ounce) carton sour cream
¼ cup chopped onion
2 tablespoons chopped green
   pepper
1 clove garlic, minced
1 tablespoon vegetable oil

2 (15-ounce) cans kidney beans,
   drained
1 (14½-ounce) can whole
   tomatoes, undrained and
   chopped
1 (8-ounce) can tomato sauce
1 tablespoon chili powder
1 (2¼-ounce) can sliced ripe
   olives, drained
2 cups coarsely crushed corn
   chips, divided
1 cup (4 ounces) shredded sharp
   Cheddar cheese

Combine first 6 ingredients; stir well, and set aside.

Cook ¼ cup onion, green pepper, and garlic in hot oil in a large saucepan over medium-high heat, stirring constantly, until tender. Stir in beans and next 3 ingredients. Bring to a boil; reduce heat, and simmer, uncovered, 5 minutes. Stir in olives.

Sprinkle ½ cup corn chips in bottom of a greased 2½-quart casserole. Layer half of cheese and bean mixtures over corn chips. Sprinkle ¾ cup corn chips over bean layer. Top with remaining cheese and bean mixtures.

Bake, uncovered, at 350° for 30 minutes or until bubbly. Sprinkle casserole with remaining ¾ cup corn chips and Cheddar cheese; bake 5 additional minutes or until cheese melts. Yield: 6 servings.

A Bean Chalupa sits atop a bed of cool, crisp iceberg lettuce, the ideal accompaniment for this main dish.

BEAN CHALUPAS

The taco salad shells called for in Bean Chalupas are perfect for holding the ingredients—*chalupa* is Spanish for "boat."

2 cups dried pinto beans
5 cups water
½ cup chopped onion
2 cloves garlic, minced
1 (4.5-ounce) can chopped green chiles, drained
2 tablespoons chili powder
2 teaspoons ground cumin
1½ teaspoons salt
1 teaspoon dried oregano
1 (6.5-ounce) package taco salad shells

Shredded iceberg lettuce
¾ cup (3 ounces) shredded Monterey Jack cheese
¾ cup (3 ounces) shredded sharp Cheddar cheese
1 (2¼-ounce) can sliced ripe olives, drained
½ cup sour cream
2 tomatoes, cut into wedges

Sort and wash beans; place in a Dutch oven. Cover with water 2 inches above beans; let soak 8 hours.

Drain beans, and return to Dutch oven; add 5 cups water, onion, and garlic. Bring to a boil; cover, reduce heat, and simmer 1 hour. Stir in chiles and next 4 ingredients. Cover and simmer 30 minutes.

Remove 1 cup of bean mixture; place in container of an electric blender. Cover and process until smooth, stopping once to scrape down sides. Stir pureed mixture into remaining bean mixture. Cook, uncovered, over medium-low heat 1 hour or until thickened, stirring frequently.

Bake shells according to package directions. Divide lettuce evenly among 8 individual plates; place shells on lettuce. Spoon bean mixture evenly into shells; sprinkle evenly with cheeses. Top evenly with sour cream and olives. Arrange tomato wedges around chalupas. Yield: 8 servings.

MEATLESS ENCHILADAS

1 large onion, chopped
3 cloves garlic, minced
1 tablespoon olive oil
1 (15-ounce) can tomato sauce
1 (14½-ounce) can diced tomatoes, undrained
1½ tablespoons chili powder
½ teaspoon dried oregano
½ teaspoon ground cumin
1 (15-ounce) can pinto beans, drained

1 (11-ounce) can whole kernel corn, drained
1 (2¼-ounce) can sliced ripe olives, drained
1 (4.5-ounce) can chopped green chiles, drained
1 cup small-curd cottage cheese
2 cups (8 ounces) shredded Cheddar cheese, divided
10 (6-inch) corn tortillas

Cook onion and garlic in hot oil in a saucepan over medium-high heat, stirring constantly, until tender. Stir in tomato sauce and next 4 ingredients. Bring to a boil; reduce heat, and simmer, uncovered, 20 minutes. Spoon 1 cup sauce mixture into a greased 13- x 9- x 2-inch baking dish. Add beans, corn, and olives to remaining sauce mixture; stir well.

Combine green chiles, cottage cheese, and ¾ cup Cheddar cheese; stir well, and set aside.

Wrap tortillas tightly in aluminum foil; bake at 350° for 15 minutes or until heated. For each enchilada, spoon about 2 tablespoons cottage cheese mixture down center of tortilla; roll up and place, seam side down, in dish. Spoon remaining sauce mixture over enchiladas.

Cover and bake at 350° for 20 minutes. Uncover; sprinkle with remaining 1¼ cups Cheddar cheese, and bake 5 additional minutes or until cheese melts. Yield: 10 enchiladas.

LENTIL SPAGHETTI

¾ cup chopped onion
2 cloves garlic, minced
1 tablespoon butter or
    margarine, melted
4 cups vegetable broth
1½ cups dried lentils, uncooked
1 teaspoon dried crushed red
    pepper
1 (14½-ounce) can whole
    tomatoes, undrained and
    chopped

1 (6-ounce) can tomato paste
1 tablespoon white vinegar
¾ teaspoon salt
½ teaspoon black pepper
½ teaspoon dried basil
½ teaspoon dried oregano
Hot cooked spaghetti
Grated Parmesan cheese

Cook onion and garlic in butter in a Dutch oven over medium-high heat, stirring constantly, until tender. Add broth, lentils, and red pepper. Bring to a boil; cover, reduce heat, and simmer 40 to 45 minutes or until lentils are tender.

Stir in tomato and next 6 ingredients. Bring to a boil; reduce heat, and simmer, uncovered, 15 minutes or to desired thickness, stirring frequently. Serve lentil mixture over spaghetti; sprinkle with Parmesan cheese. Yield: 6 servings.

SOUR CREAM ENCHILADAS

Don't be tempted to substitute regular tomato sauce for the no-salt-added variety called for in this recipe. Our staff feels the enchilada sauce mix and abundance of cheeses provide all the salt this dish needs.

1½ cups water
1 (8-ounce) can no-salt-added
    tomato sauce
1 (1.5-ounce) package enchilada
    sauce mix
1 (16-ounce) carton sour cream
2½ cups (10 ounces) shredded
    Longhorn cheese, divided

1 cup (4 ounces) shredded
    Monterey Jack cheese with
    jalapeño peppers, divided
1 cup chopped green onions
½ teaspoon ground cumin
12 (6-inch) corn tortillas
Chopped green onions
    (optional)

Combine first 3 ingredients in a small saucepan; stir well. Bring to a boil; reduce heat, and simmer, uncovered, 10 minutes.

Combine sour cream, ½ cup of each cheese, 1 cup chopped green onions, and cumin; stir well, and set aside.

Wrap tortillas tightly in aluminum foil; bake at 350° for 15 minutes or until thoroughly heated. For each enchilada, spread 2 tablespoons sour cream mixture over tortilla. Roll up tortilla, and place, seam side down, in a lightly greased 13- x 9- x 2-inch baking dish; pour enchilada sauce over top of all enchiladas.

Bake, uncovered, at 375° for 20 minutes. Sprinkle with remaining amounts of both cheeses; bake 5 additional minutes. Sprinkle with additional chopped green onions, if desired. Yield: 12 enchiladas.

EGGPLANT PARMESAN

1 cup chopped onion
1 clove garlic, minced
1 tablespoon vegetable oil
1 (14½-ounce) can whole
    tomatoes, undrained and
    chopped
1 (8-ounce) can tomato sauce
½ teaspoon salt
½ teaspoon dried basil
½ teaspoon dried oregano

1 cup toasted wheat germ
⅔ cup fine, dry breadcrumbs
½ teaspoon salt
1 large eggplant, peeled and cut
    into ½-inch-thick slices
2 large eggs, lightly beaten
Vegetable oil
2 cups (8 ounces) shredded
    mozzarella cheese
½ cup grated Parmesan cheese

If your eggplant is past its peak, it might taste bitter. To improve the flavor, simply salt the cut surfaces of each eggplant slice, and let stand 20 minutes. Then rinse the salt from the eggplant, and pat the slices dry.

Cook onion and garlic in hot oil in a medium saucepan over medium-high heat, stirring constantly, until tender. Stir in tomato and next 4 ingredients. Bring to a boil; cover, reduce heat, and simmer 20 minutes, stirring occasionally.

Combine wheat germ, breadcrumbs, and ½ teaspoon salt, stirring well. Dip eggplant slices in beaten egg, and dredge in wheat germ mixture. Pour oil to depth of ¼ inch into a large heavy skillet. Fry eggplant slices in hot oil over medium-high heat until browned on both sides. Drain on paper towels.

Spoon half of tomato mixture into a 13- x 9- x 2-inch baking dish. Arrange eggplant over tomato mixture; sprinkle with mozzarella cheese, and top with remaining half of tomato mixture. Sprinkle with Parmesan cheese. Bake at 400° for 12 to 14 minutes or until bubbly. Yield: 6 servings.

SPINACH-CHEESE PUFF

■■■■■■■■■■
Spinach-Cheese Puff
is simply a strata that is
refrigerated overnight in
order for the bread to
absorb the milk mixture.
Be sure to remove as
much moisture as possible
from the spinach so that
the puff will not be soggy.

12 slices white bread
2 cups (8 ounces) shredded
  Cheddar cheese
1 (10-ounce) package frozen
  chopped spinach, thawed
1 (4½-ounce) jar sliced
  mushrooms, drained
4 large eggs, lightly beaten
2½ cups milk
1 tablespoon grated onion
1 teaspoon seasoned salt
½ teaspoon prepared mustard
¼ teaspoon salt
Dash of ground red pepper
Dash of black pepper

Trim crusts from bread. Arrange 6 bread slices in bottom of a lightly greased 13- x 9- x 2-inch baking dish; sprinkle evenly with cheese.

Drain spinach; press between layers of paper towels to remove excess moisture. Sprinkle spinach and mushrooms over cheese; top with remaining 6 bread slices.

Combine eggs and remaining ingredients; stir with a wire whisk or fork until blended. Pour mixture over bread; cover and chill 8 hours.

Remove from refrigerator; let stand, covered, 30 minutes. Uncover and bake at 325° for 1 hour. Serve immediately. Yield: 6 servings.

GARDEN SANDWICHES

1 (10-ounce) package frozen
  chopped spinach, thawed
½ cup minced green onions
⅓ cup mayonnaise or salad
  dressing
1 tablespoon minced green
  pepper
1 tablespoon lemon juice
¼ teaspoon salt
½ pound fresh mushrooms,
  sliced
1 tablespoon butter or
  margarine, melted
2 tablespoons butter or
  margarine, softened
12 slices pumpernickel bread
¾ cup fresh alfalfa sprouts
2 tablespoons salted sunflower
  kernels
6 slices provolone cheese
6 slices Cheddar cheese
6 slices Swiss cheese
Garnish: fresh mushroom slices

Drain spinach; press between paper towels to remove excess moisture. Combine spinach, green onions, and next 4 ingredients in a medium bowl; stir well, and set aside.

Cook ½ pound mushrooms in melted butter in a skillet over medium-high heat, stirring constantly, until tender; set aside.

Spread ½ teaspoon softened butter on one side of each bread slice. Lightly brown 6 bread slices, buttered side down, on a hot griddle; remove from heat. Spread spinach mixture evenly on unbuttered sides of toasted bread; sprinkle evenly with cooked mushrooms, alfalfa sprouts, and sunflower kernels. Set aside.

Layer 1 slice each of provolone, Cheddar, and Swiss cheese on unbuttered side of remaining 6 bread slices. Place bread, buttered side down, on hot griddle; cook just until cheeses soften and bread begins to brown.

To serve, put cheese-topped bread slices and spinach-topped bread slices together. Cut sandwiches in half diagonally. If desired, skewer a fresh mushroom slice on each of 12 wooden picks; secure each sandwich half with a prepared wooden pick. Yield: 6 sandwiches.

You'll find it hard to resist tasty Garden Sandwiches, layered with lots of vegetables and cheese.

VEGETABLE-CHEESE SOUP

■■■■■■■■■■■

If you're looking for the perfect wintertime soup, this is it. Vegetable Cheese Soup combines the goodness of chunky vegetable soup with the creamy richness of Cheddar cheese soup. It's sure to be a family pleaser.

1 cup chopped onion
2 tablespoons butter or margarine, melted
2 cups vegetable broth
2 cups shredded cabbage
1 cup cubed potato
1 cup sliced carrot
1 (10-ounce) package frozen baby limas, thawed

3 tablespoons butter or margarine
3 tablespoons all-purpose flour
3 cups milk
1½ cups (6 ounces) shredded Cheddar cheese
¼ teaspoon paprika
¼ teaspoon pepper

Cook onion in 2 tablespoons melted butter in a Dutch oven over medium-high heat, stirring constantly, until tender. Add broth and next 4 ingredients. Bring to a boil; cover, reduce heat, and simmer 20 minutes.

Melt 3 tablespoons butter in a saucepan over medium heat. Add flour; stir until smooth. Cook, stirring constantly, 1 minute. Gradually add milk; cook, stirring constantly, until thickened. Add cheese, paprika, and pepper; stir until cheese melts. Gradually stir cheese mixture into vegetable mixture; cook, stirring constantly, just until heated. Yield: 1½ quarts.

DEEP-DISH VEGETARIAN PIZZA

1 (10¾-ounce) can tomato puree
1 clove garlic, crushed
2 tablespoons thinly sliced green onions
1 tablespoon chopped fresh parsley
½ teaspoon dried oregano
¼ teaspoon dried basil
⅛ teaspoon pepper
½ pound fresh mushrooms, sliced

1 medium-size green pepper, seeded and cut into strips
1 cup broccoli flowerets
1 tablespoon butter or margarine, melted
Pizza Crust
2 tablespoons sliced pimiento-stuffed olives
2 tablespoons sliced ripe olives
¼ cup grated Parmesan cheese
2 cups (8 ounces) shredded mozzarella cheese

Combine first 7 ingredients in a saucepan. Bring to a boil; reduce heat, and simmer, uncovered, 15 minutes, stirring occasionally. Let stand 30 minutes.

Cook mushrooms, green pepper, and broccoli in butter in a large skillet over medium-high heat, stirring constantly, until crisp-tender.

Indulge your pizza craving with mouth-watering Deep-Dish Vegetarian Pizza.

Spread tomato mixture over Pizza Crust. Arrange vegetables and olives over tomato mixture; sprinkle with Parmesan cheese. Bake at 425° for 10 minutes. Sprinkle with mozzarella cheese, and bake 5 minutes or until cheese melts. Let stand 10 minutes. Yield: one 10-inch pizza.

Pizza Crust

1 package active dry yeast
¼ cup warm water (105° to
   115°)
2 cups all-purpose flour

½ cup milk
1 tablespoon vegetable oil
1 teaspoon sugar
1 teaspoon salt

Combine yeast and warm water in a 1-cup liquid measuring cup; let stand 5 minutes. Combine yeast mixture, flour, and remaining ingredients in a large bowl; stir well. Cover and let rise 15 minutes.

Turn dough out onto a floured surface; knead 8 times. Pat dough into bottom and up sides of a greased 10¼-inch cast-iron skillet. Line crust with aluminum foil; place pie weights or dried beans evenly over foil. Bake at 425° for 8 minutes. Remove foil and pie weights; bake 5 minutes. Yield: one 10-inch pizza crust.

MUSHROOMS AND EGGS IN PATTY SHELLS

1 (10-ounce) package
   frozen puff pastry
   patty shells
½ pound fresh mushrooms,
   sliced
2 tablespoons chopped onion
2 tablespoons butter or
   margarine, melted
¼ cup butter or margarine
3 tablespoons all-purpose flour

1½ cups milk
3 tablespoons dry white wine
¾ teaspoon salt
⅛ teaspoon ground red pepper
5 hard-cooked eggs, chopped
1 tablespoon chopped fresh
   parsley
Garnishes: paprika, fresh
   parsley sprigs

Bake patty shells according to package directions. Set aside; keep warm.

Cook mushrooms and onion in 2 tablespoons butter in a large skillet over medium-high heat, stirring constantly, until tender. Remove mushroom mixture from skillet; set aside.

Melt ¼ cup butter in skillet over medium heat. Add flour; stir until smooth. Cook, stirring constantly, 1 minute. Gradually add milk; cook, stirring constantly, until thickened. Stir in wine, salt, and pepper. Add mushroom mixture, eggs, and chopped parsley; stir gently. Spoon mushroom mixture into patty shells; garnish, if desired. Yield: 6 servings.

VEGETARIAN OMELETS

¼ cup shredded carrot
2 tablespoons chopped green
   onions
2 tablespoons chopped green
   pepper
2 tablespoons commercial
   Italian salad dressing
¼ cup peeled, seeded, and
   chopped cucumber
¼ cup seeded and coarsely
   chopped tomato

5 large eggs
2 tablespoons water
½ teaspoon salt
¼ teaspoon pepper
1 tablespoon butter or
   margarine, divided
1 cup (4 ounces) shredded
   Swiss cheese, divided
½ cup alfalfa sprouts, divided
Plain yogurt (optional)
Chopped fresh chives (optional)

Combine first 4 ingredients in a small saucepan. Bring to a boil; reduce heat, and simmer, uncovered, until vegetables are tender, stirring occasionally. Remove from heat; stir in cucumber and tomato. Set aside.

Combine eggs, water, salt, and pepper; stir with a wire whisk or fork until blended.

Heat an 8-inch omelet pan or nonstick skillet over medium heat until hot enough to sizzle a drop of water. Add 1½ teaspoons butter, and tilt pan to coat bottom. Pour half of egg mixture into pan. As mixture starts to cook, gently lift edges of omelet with a spatula, and tilt pan so uncooked portion flows underneath.

Sprinkle half of vegetable mixture over half of omelet; top with half each of cheese and sprouts. Fold omelet in half, and transfer to a serving plate. Repeat procedure with remaining 1½ teaspoons butter, egg mixture, vegetable mixture, cheese, and sprouts. If desired, dollop with yogurt, and sprinkle with chives. Serve immediately. Yield: 2 servings.

CHEDDAR-LEEK QUICHE

1⅓ cups all-purpose flour
½ teaspoon salt
½ cup shortening
3 to 4 tablespoons cold water
4 leeks
2 tablespoons butter or
    margarine, melted
4 large eggs, lightly beaten
2 cups half-and-half

1¼ teaspoons Worcestershire
    sauce
½ teaspoon salt
⅛ teaspoon pepper
2 cups (8 ounces) shredded
    Cheddar cheese
Garnishes: leek strips, tomato
    rose

Leeks are in the onion family, but they have a more subtle flavor that's perfect for dishes where onion or garlic might be overpowering, like this quiche. Split leeks lengthwise, and rinse thoroughly to remove the grit trapped in the layers of the leaves.

Combine flour and ½ teaspoon salt; cut in shortening with a pastry blender until mixture is crumbly. Sprinkle cold water (1 tablespoon at a time) evenly over surface; stir with a fork until dry ingredients are moistened. Shape dough into a ball; chill.

Roll pastry to ⅛-inch thickness on a floured surface. Place in a 10-inch pieplate; trim excess pastry along edges. Fold edges under, and crimp. Prick bottom of pastry with a fork. Bake at 400° for 10 minutes.

Trim white portion of 4 leeks to 3 inches in length, reserving remainder for another use, if desired. Wash leeks, and cut in half; thinly slice. Cook leeks in butter in a small skillet over medium-high heat, stirring constantly, until tender; drain. Spoon leeks into pastry shell.

Combine eggs and next 4 ingredients; stir with a wire whisk or fork until blended. Pour mixture into pastry shell. Bake at 350° for 30 minutes. Sprinkle with cheese; bake 20 to 25 minutes or until set and golden. Let stand 10 minutes. Garnish, if desired. Yield: one 10-inch quiche.

Be careful not to overcook the vegetables in Bow-Tie Pasta Primavera. Keep them crisp-tender for maximum flavor and color.

BOW-TIE PASTA PRIMAVERA

Before adding the dried herbs to Bow-Tie Pasta Primavera, rub them between the palms of your hands or crush them with your fingertips to release more flavor. When substituting fresh herbs, remember that one teaspoon of dried herbs equals one table- spoon of fresh.

8 ounces bow-tie pasta,
   uncooked
2 tablespoons olive oil, divided
3 green onions, cut into 1-inch
   pieces
2 cloves garlic, minced
½ pound fresh asparagus
2 cups fresh broccoli flowerets
1 (10-ounce) package frozen
   English peas, thawed and
   drained
½ pound fresh mushrooms,
   sliced
1 small tomato, finely chopped

1 small sweet red pepper,
   seeded and chopped
1 cup freshly grated Parmesan
   cheese
¼ cup minced fresh parsley
¼ cup white wine vinegar
¼ cup olive oil
½ teaspoon salt
½ teaspoon dried oregano
½ teaspoon dried basil
½ teaspoon dried thyme
¼ teaspoon black pepper
⅛ teaspoon ground red pepper

Cook pasta according to package directions; drain. Place pasta in a large serving bowl; toss with 1 tablespoon olive oil.

Cook green onions and garlic in 1 tablespoon hot olive oil in a large skillet over medium-high heat, stirring constantly, until crisp-tender; add to pasta, tossing gently.

Snap off tough ends of asparagus. Remove scales with a vegetable peeler or knife, if desired. Cut asparagus into 1-inch pieces. Arrange asparagus and broccoli in a vegetable steamer over boiling water; cover and steam 4 minutes or until crisp-tender.

Add asparagus mixture, peas, and remaining ingredients to pasta mixture; toss gently. Cover and chill 3 to 4 hours, tossing occasionally. Yield: 8 servings.

VEGETABLE FETTUCCINE

4 green onions, cut into 1-inch pieces
2 small zucchini, cut into thin strips
2 carrots, scraped and cut into thin strips
1 clove garlic, minced
1 cup sliced fresh mushrooms
¼ cup butter or margarine, melted
1 (15-ounce) can garbanzo beans, drained

½ teaspoon dried basil
½ teaspoon salt
¼ teaspoon pepper
4 ounces fettuccine, uncooked
4 ounces spinach fettuccine, uncooked
1 cup freshly grated Parmesan cheese, divided
2 egg yolks, lightly beaten
1 cup whipping cream

■■■■■■■■■■□

Vegetable Fettuccine contains all of the basic ingredients of fettuccine Alfredo. The addition of garbanzo beans and vegetables boosts the protein level and makes this recipe a hearty meal.

Cook first 5 ingredients in butter in a large skillet over medium-high heat, stirring constantly, until tender. Stir in beans, basil, salt, and pepper; set aside.

Cook fettuccine and spinach fettuccine according to package directions; drain. Combine fettuccine and vegetable mixture in a large Dutch oven; toss gently. Cook over medium heat just until mixture is thoroughly heated, tossing occasionally. Stir in ¾ cup Parmesan cheese.

Combine egg yolks and whipping cream in a small saucepan. Cook until mixture reaches 160°, stirring frequently. Add to fettuccine mixture; toss gently. Cook over medium heat until thoroughly heated, tossing occasionally. Spoon mixture onto a serving platter; sprinkle with remaining ¼ cup Parmesan cheese. Yield: 6 servings.

GARDEN LASAGNA

4 medium zucchini, coarsely chopped
3 cloves garlic, minced
1 large onion, chopped
1 medium-size green pepper, seeded and chopped
1 medium carrot, scraped and diced
½ cup chopped celery
3 tablespoons olive oil
2 (16-ounce) cans stewed tomatoes, undrained
1 (8-ounce) can tomato sauce
1 (6-ounce) can tomato paste
¼ cup chopped fresh parsley
¼ cup dry red wine
2 teaspoons dried Italian seasoning
1 teaspoon dried basil
½ teaspoon salt
¼ teaspoon freshly ground pepper
9 lasagna noodles, uncooked
1 (16-ounce) carton ricotta cheese
2 cups (8 ounces) shredded mozzarella cheese
1 cup grated Parmesan cheese

Cook first 6 ingredients in hot oil in a large Dutch oven over medium heat, stirring constantly, 15 minutes or until tender. Stir in tomato and next 8 ingredients. Bring to a boil; cover, reduce heat, and simmer 30 minutes, stirring occasionally. Uncover and simmer 45 minutes or until sauce is thick, stirring occasionally.

Cook noodles according to package directions; drain.

Spread one-fourth of sauce in a greased 13- x 9- x 2-inch baking dish. Layer 3 noodles, one-third of ricotta cheese, one-fourth of mozzarella cheese, and one-fourth of Parmesan cheese over sauce; repeat layers twice. Top layers with remaining one-fourth each of sauce, mozzarella cheese, and Parmesan cheese. Bake, uncovered, at 350° for 35 to 40 minutes or until thoroughly heated. Let stand 10 minutes. Yield: 8 servings.

OLD-FASHIONED MACARONI AND CHEESE

1 (8-ounce) package elbow macaroni
3 cups (12 ounces) shredded Cheddar cheese, divided
2 large eggs, lightly beaten
1½ cups milk
¾ teaspoon salt
⅛ teaspoon ground white pepper
Paprika

Cook macaroni according to package directions; drain. Layer one-third of macaroni in a lightly greased 2-quart casserole; sprinkle with 1 cup cheese. Repeat layers with remaining two-thirds macaroni and 1 cup cheese, ending with macaroni layer. Reserve remaining 1 cup cheese.

Combine eggs and next 3 ingredients, stirring with a wire whisk or fork until blended. Pour egg mixture over macaroni. Cover and bake at 350° for 45 minutes or until thoroughly heated. Uncover and sprinkle with remaining 1 cup cheese and paprika. Cover and let stand 10 minutes before serving. Yield: 8 servings.

SPINACH-STUFFED MANICOTTI

8 manicotti shells, uncooked
1 (10-ounce) package frozen chopped spinach, thawed
½ (8-ounce) package cream cheese, softened
1 cup ricotta cheese
1 cup (4 ounces) mozzarella cheese
½ cup freshly grated Parmesan cheese
1 teaspoon dried Italian seasoning
¼ teaspoon salt
2 cups commercial pasta sauce
½ cup freshly grated Parmesan cheese

■ ■ ■ ■ ■ ■ ■ ■ ◻
Four kinds of cheese form the base of the thick, rich filling in these manicotti shells.

Cook manicotti according to package directions; drain and set aside.

Drain spinach, pressing between layers of paper towels to remove excess moisture. Combine spinach, cream cheese, and next 5 ingredients, stirring well. Stuff mixture evenly into manicotti shells.

Pour ½ cup pasta sauce into a lightly greased 11- x 7- x 1½-inch baking dish; arrange stuffed shells over sauce. Spoon remaining 1½ cups pasta sauce over shells. Cover and bake at 350° for 30 minutes or until thoroughly heated. Sprinkle with ½ cup Parmesan cheese; bake, uncovered, 5 additional minutes or until cheese melts. Yield: 4 servings.

MEDITERRANEAN RAVIOLI

■■■■■■■■■■■

You can substitute commercial chunky spaghetti sauce for the refrigerated sauce in Mediterranean Ravioli.

2 cups peeled, cubed eggplant
1 cup chopped onion
2 cloves garlic, minced
2 tablespoons olive oil
1 (15-ounce) package
   refrigerated chunky tomato
   sauce
3 tablespoons sliced ripe olives
1 tablespoon balsamic vinegar

1 teaspoon dried thyme
1 (9-ounce) package
   fresh cheese-filled ravioli,
   uncooked
⅔ cup freshly grated Parmesan
   cheese
Garnishes: fresh basil sprigs,
   fresh thyme sprigs

Cook first 3 ingredients in hot oil in a large skillet over medium-high heat, stirring constantly, until tender. Stir in tomato sauce and next 3 ingredients. Remove from heat; set aside.

Cook ravioli according to package directions; drain. Rinse with cold water; drain.

Combine vegetable mixture and ravioli, tossing gently; spoon into a lightly greased shallow 2-quart baking dish. Cover and bake at 350° for 20 minutes. Uncover and sprinkle with cheese; bake, uncovered, 10 minutes or until thoroughly heated. Garnish, if desired. Yield: 4 servings.

PASTA-BEAN SALAD

2 cups cooked rotelle or wagon
    wheel-shaped pasta
1 cup frozen English peas,
    thawed and drained
1 cup diced carrot
1 (15-ounce) can kidney beans,
    rinsed and drained
½ cup mayonnaise or salad
    dressing

¼ cup chopped fresh parsley
¼ cup grated Parmesan cheese
2 tablespoons lemon juice
1 teaspoon dried basil
1 clove garlic, crushed
Leaf lettuce leaves (optional)

Combine first 4 ingredients in a large bowl; toss gently. Combine mayonnaise and next 5 ingredients; add to macaroni mixture, tossing gently to coat. Cover and chill at least 2 hours. Serve on lettuce leaves, if desired. Yield: 4 servings.

SHELLS WITH PEPPERS AND BROCCOLI

1 (7.5-ounce) jar roasted
    peppers, drained and cut
    into strips
⅔ cup pine nuts
½ cup chopped fresh parsley
½ cup olive oil
1 pound fresh broccoli

1 (12-ounce) package small shell
    pasta, uncooked
1 cup freshly grated Parmesan
    cheese
⅛ teaspoon black pepper
⅛ teaspoon ground red pepper

Use kitchen shears to snip the fresh parsley for this quick-to-fix meal. Place the parsley in a measuring cup, and snip until chopped. It's easy to measure, and it's less messy.

Combine first 4 ingredients in a skillet; cook over medium heat until pine nuts are golden, stirring frequently. Set aside.

Remove broccoli leaves, and cut off tough ends of stalks; discard. Wash broccoli, and cut into flowerets. Set aside.

Cook pasta according to package directions, adding broccoli during the last 2 minutes of cooking time; drain. Combine pasta mixture, pepper mixture, cheese, black pepper, and ground red pepper; toss gently. Serve immediately. Yield: 6 servings.

With the addition of a few ingredients, convenient commercial products make Mediterranean Ravioli simple to prepare.

PASTA STUFFED WITH FIVE CHEESES

1 (14½-ounce) can stewed
   tomatoes, undrained
1 (8-ounce) can mushroom
   stems and pieces, drained
1 (8-ounce) can tomato sauce
1 (6-ounce) can tomato paste
½ cup dry white wine
1 teaspoon dried oregano
1 teaspoon dried thyme
1 clove garlic, minced
16 jumbo pasta shells, uncooked
1 (8-ounce) package cream
   cheese, softened

1 large egg, lightly beaten
1 cup (4 ounces) shredded
   mozzarella cheese
1 cup low-fat cottage cheese
¼ cup grated Parmesan and
   Romano cheese blend
2 tablespoons chopped fresh
   parsley
2 teaspoons dried basil
½ teaspoon dried oregano
½ teaspoon dried thyme
⅛ teaspoon grated lemon rind
Pinch of ground nutmeg

Place tomatoes in container of an electric blender or food processor; cover and process until smooth. Pour puree into a Dutch oven; stir in mushroom stems and pieces and next 6 ingredients. Bring to a boil; reduce heat, and simmer, uncovered, 20 minutes or until thickened. Spoon mushroom mixture into a lightly greased 11- x 7- x 1½-inch baking dish.

Cook shells according to package directions; drain. Combine cream cheese and remaining ingredients. Stuff shells evenly with cheese mixture; arrange over mushroom mixture. Cover and bake at 350° for 25 to 30 minutes or until thoroughly heated. Yield: 4 servings.

THREE-CHEESE SPAGHETTI

1 tablespoon butter or
   margarine
1 tablespoon all-purpose flour
1 cup milk
½ cup (2 ounces) shredded
   Swiss cheese
½ cup (2 ounces) shredded
   Gouda cheese
¼ teaspoon salt

1 (4½-ounce) jar sliced
   mushrooms, drained
1 (7-ounce) package spaghetti,
   uncooked
2 tablespoons butter or
   margarine, melted
½ cup grated Parmesan cheese
1 tablespoon dried parsley
   flakes

Melt 1 tablespoon butter in a heavy saucepan over low heat; add flour, stirring until smooth. Cook, stirring constantly, 1 minute. Gradually add milk; cook over medium heat, stirring constantly, until mixture is thickened and bubbly. Remove from heat; add Swiss cheese, Gouda cheese, salt, and mushrooms, stirring until cheeses melt.

Cook spaghetti according to package directions; drain. Combine spaghetti, 2 tablespoons melted butter, Parmesan cheese, and parsley flakes; toss well. Combine cheese sauce and spaghetti mixture, stirring well. Yield: 2 servings.

TORTELLINI-PESTO SALAD

1 (9-ounce) package fresh cheese-filled tortellini
1 small sweet red pepper, seeded and cut into thin strips
¾ cup broccoli flowerets
⅓ cup sliced carrot
⅓ cup sliced pimiento-stuffed olives

½ cup mayonnaise or salad dressing
¼ cup milk
¼ cup commercial pesto sauce
2 tablespoons grated Parmesan cheese
1 tablespoon olive oil
1 teaspoon white vinegar
1 clove garlic, minced

Cook tortellini according to package directions; drain. Rinse tortellini in cold water; drain. Combine tortellini, pepper, broccoli, carrot, and olives in a medium bowl.

Combine mayonnaise and remaining ingredients, stirring well with a wire whisk. Spoon mayonnaise mixture over vegetable mixture; toss gently. Cover and chill thoroughly. Yield: 4 servings.

Added Attractions

More than ever, today's fast-paced lifestyles lend themselves to one-dish meals. But sometimes you may prefer to pad the menu with a little something extra. It may be a pasta side dish to accompany a main-dish green salad, a broccoli or green bean dish to serve with a meaty casserole, or a simple side salad to enhance lasagna or spaghetti. Whatever you choose, this collection will give you lots of options. We've even included a large assortment of quick and easy desserts, many of which can be made ahead and chilled or frozen so that they're ready when you are.

Quick Garlic Rolls (page 211), Easy Spaghetti (page 174), Spinach and
Sun-Dried Tomato Salad (page 220)

CHEESE BISCUITS

■■■■■■■■■■
Handle biscuit dough with a light touch for fluffy biscuits. A good biscuit dough should be slightly sticky to the touch and should be kneaded gently just a few times.

⅓ cup shortening
2 cups self-rising flour
¾ cup milk

½ cup (2 ounces) shredded
    sharp Cheddar cheese

Cut shortening into flour with a pastry blender until mixture is crumbly. Add milk and cheese, stirring with a fork just until dry ingredients are moistened. Turn dough out onto a lightly floured surface, and knead lightly 3 or 4 times.

Roll or pat dough to ½-inch thickness; cut with a 2-inch biscuit cutter. Place biscuits on an ungreased baking sheet. Bake at 450° for 10 minutes or until golden. Yield: 1 dozen.

CLOUD BISCUITS

2½ cups self-rising flour
1 tablespoon sugar
½ cup butter-flavored
    shortening

1 large egg, lightly beaten
⅔ cup milk
1 tablespoon butter or
    margarine, melted

Combine flour and sugar; cut in shortening with a pastry blender until mixture is crumbly.

Combine egg and milk; add to flour mixture, stirring just until dry ingredients are moistened. Turn dough out onto a lightly floured surface, and knead lightly 3 or 4 times.

Roll or pat dough to ½-inch thickness; cut with a 2½-inch biscuit cutter. Place biscuits on an ungreased baking sheet. Bake at 450° for 10 to 12 minutes or until golden. Remove from oven; brush with melted butter. Yield: 1 dozen.

CHEESE-AND-PEPPER MUFFINS

2½ cups all-purpose flour
¼ cup yellow cornmeal
2 tablespoons baking powder
1 teaspoon salt
¼ cup sugar
¼ teaspoon ground red pepper
¾ cup (3 ounces) shredded
    sharp Cheddar cheese

¼ cup finely chopped onion
3 tablespoons finely chopped
    green pepper
1 (2-ounce) jar diced pimiento,
    drained
2 large eggs, lightly beaten
1½ cups milk
¼ cup vegetable oil

Combine first 6 ingredients in a medium bowl; stir well. Stir in cheese, onion, green pepper, and pimiento; make a well in center of mixture. Combine eggs, milk, and oil; add to dry ingredients, stirring just until dry ingredients are moistened.

Spoon batter into greased muffin pans, filling two-thirds full. Bake at 400° for 20 to 25 minutes or until golden. Remove from pans immediately. Yield: 1½ dozen.

SOUTHERN CORNCAKES

1½ cups self-rising cornmeal
1¼ cups buttermilk
1 tablespoon sugar

1 tablespoon vegetable oil
1 large egg, lightly beaten
Vegetable oil

Combine first 5 ingredients in a large bowl, stirring just until dry ingredients are moistened.

Pour oil to depth of ¼ inch into a large heavy skillet. For each corncake, pour ¼ cup batter into skillet. Fry corncakes in hot oil over medium-high heat 3 minutes on each side or until golden. Serve immediately. Yield: 8 corncakes.

For ease and convenience, Southern Corncakes and Mexican Hush Puppies (page 210) are made with self-rising cornmeal. Self-rising products have the baking powder already mixed with the flour.

Add the goodness of crusty cornbread to your menu with Mexican Hush Puppies and Southern Corncakes (page 209).

MEXICAN HUSH PUPPIES

2 cups self-rising cornmeal
1 cup self-rising flour
½ teaspoon salt
3 tablespoons sugar
3 large eggs, lightly beaten
1 (16½-ounce) can cream-style corn

½ cup milk
1½ cups (6 ounces) shredded Cheddar cheese
1 large onion, chopped
2 jalapeño peppers, seeded and chopped
Vegetable oil

Combine first 4 ingredients in a large bowl. Combine eggs, corn, and milk; add to dry ingredients, stirring just until dry ingredients are moistened. Stir in cheese, onion, and pepper (do not overstir batter).

Pour oil to depth of 2 inches into a Dutch oven; heat to 375°. Drop batter by rounded tablespoonfuls into hot oil; fry hush puppies, a few at a time, 3 minutes or until golden, turning once. Drain on paper towels. Yield: 3½ dozen.

EASY BREAD

¼ cup butter or margarine,
   melted
½ teaspoon dried parsley flakes
⅛ teaspoon garlic powder

2 (2½-ounce) French rolls
2 tablespoons grated Parmesan
   cheese
½ teaspoon poppy seeds

Combine first 3 ingredients. Split rolls horizontally; brush butter mixture evenly over cut sides of rolls. Sprinkle evenly with Parmesan cheese and poppy seeds. Place bread on a baking sheet; broil 5½ inches from heat (with electric oven door partially opened) 1 to 2 minutes or until golden. Cut each half into 2 pieces. Yield: 4 servings.

QUICK GARLIC ROLLS

½ (32-ounce) package frozen
   bread dough, thawed (1 loaf)
1 large egg, lightly beaten
¼ cup unsalted butter, melted

1 tablespoon chopped fresh
   parsley
½ teaspoon garlic salt

Divide dough into 20 portions; shape each portion into a ball.

Combine egg and remaining ingredients in a small bowl; stir well. Dip balls of dough in butter mixture; place in a lightly greased 9-inch round cakepan. Cover and let rise in a warm place (85°), free from drafts, 45 minutes or until doubled in bulk. Bake at 350° for 25 to 30 minutes or until golden. Yield: 20 rolls.

What could be easier than using frozen bread dough to make feathery-light dinner rolls like these? Keep the bread dough on hand in the freezer for quick rolls anytime.

CINNAMON-PECAN ROLLS

⅓ cup chopped pecans
⅓ cup firmly packed brown
   sugar
¼ teaspoon ground cinnamon

1 (8-ounce) package refrigerated
   crescent dinner rolls
2 tablespoons butter or
   margarine, melted

Combine first 3 ingredients. Separate rolls at perforations to form triangles. Brush one side of triangles evenly with butter; sprinkle evenly with pecan mixture. Roll up triangles according to package directions, and place on a lightly greased baking sheet. Bake at 400° for 10 to 12 minutes or until golden. Yield: 8 servings.

CURRIED RICE

2½ cups water
2 teaspoons chicken-flavored
    bouillon granules
¼ teaspoon salt
1 cup long-grain rice, uncooked

⅓ cup chopped walnuts
2 tablespoons butter or
    margarine, melted
⅓ cup raisins
2 teaspoons curry powder

Combine first 3 ingredients in a medium saucepan; bring to a boil. Stir in rice; cover, reduce heat, and simmer 20 to 25 minutes or until rice is tender and liquid is absorbed.

Cook walnuts in butter in a small skillet over medium-high heat, stirring constantly, 2 minutes or until toasted. Stir walnuts, raisins, and curry powder into rice. Serve immediately. Yield: 4 servings.

RICE PILAF

1½ cups long-grain rice,
    uncooked
2 tablespoons butter or
    margarine, melted
3¼ cups chicken broth
⅓ cup chopped fresh parsley

⅓ cup chopped celery
⅓ cup chopped carrot
⅓ cup sliced almonds
¼ teaspoon pepper
Garnishes: whole natural
    almonds, fresh parsley sprigs

Cook rice in butter in a large skillet over medium-high heat until rice is lightly browned, stirring frequently. Stir in chicken broth and next 5 ingredients. Bring to a boil, and remove from heat.

Pour rice mixture into a lightly greased 2-quart casserole. Cover and bake at 375° for 30 minutes or until rice is tender and liquid is absorbed. Garnish, if desired. Yield: 8 servings.

SAVANNAH RED RICE

5 slices bacon
1¼ cups chopped onion
½ cup chopped celery
½ cup chopped green pepper
1 (14½-ounce) can whole
  tomatoes, undrained and
  chopped

1 cup long-grain rice, uncooked
¾ cup water
½ teaspoon salt
¼ teaspoon black pepper
¼ teaspoon ground red pepper
⅛ teaspoon hot sauce

Cook bacon in a large skillet until crisp; remove bacon, reserving 2 tablespoons drippings in skillet. Crumble bacon, and set aside.

Cook onion, celery, and green pepper in drippings over medium-high heat, stirring constantly, until tender. Stir in bacon, tomato, and remaining ingredients. Spoon rice mixture into a lightly greased 2-quart casserole. Cover and bake at 350° for 1 hour or until rice is tender and liquid is absorbed. Yield: 6 servings.

PESTO PASTA

½ cup tightly packed chopped
  fresh basil
¼ cup minced fresh parsley
¼ cup grated Parmesan cheese
2 tablespoons pine nuts or
  chopped walnuts
2 tablespoons olive oil

2 tablespoons butter or
  margarine, softened
¼ teaspoon salt
¼ teaspoon pepper
1 clove garlic, halved
6 ounces linguine, uncooked

Combine all ingredients except linguine in container of an electric blender; cover and process until smooth, stopping once to scrape down sides.

Cook linguine according to package directions; drain. Combine pesto mixture and linguine; toss gently. Serve immediately. Yield: 4 servings.

Because pesto is an uncooked sauce, the taste of the fresh basil really comes through in Pesto Pasta. This pesto is made in an electric blender, which ensures that the ingredients are well blended.

FETTUCCINE WITH POPPY SEEDS

6 ounces fettuccine, uncooked
½ cup sour cream
⅓ cup butter or margarine,
  melted
2½ teaspoons chopped fresh
  parsley

¾ teaspoon garlic salt
½ teaspoon poppy seeds
⅛ teaspoon pepper
½ cup freshly grated Parmesan
  cheese
Garnish: fresh parsley sprigs

Cook fettuccine according to package directions; drain.

Combine sour cream and next 5 ingredients; stir well. Combine sour cream mixture and fettuccine; add cheese, and toss until fettuccine is coated. Spoon into a bowl, and garnish, if desired. Serve immediately. Yield: 4 servings.

Delicately flavored Fettuccine with Poppy Seeds is a perfect side dish for Spicy Italian Ham Salad (page 38).

LEMON VERMICELLI

⅓ cup milk
3 tablespoons butter or
   margarine
1 (7-ounce) package vermicelli
¼ teaspoon grated lemon rind

¼ cup fresh lemon juice
½ cup freshly grated Parmesan
   cheese
Garnishes: chopped fresh
   parsley, lemon twists

Combine milk and butter in a saucepan; cook over low heat until butter melts. Set aside, and keep warm.

Cook vermicelli according to package directions; drain. Place vermicelli in a large bowl. Add lemon rind and lemon juice; toss well. Let stand 1 minute. Add cheese and warm milk mixture, tossing well. Garnish, if desired. Yield: 6 servings.

GINGERED PEACH SALAD

1 (29-ounce) can spiced
   peaches, undrained
1 (8-ounce) can crushed
   pineapple, undrained
1 (3-ounce) package orange-
   flavored gelatin
1 (3-ounce) package lemon-
   flavored gelatin
1 cup boiling water
1 tablespoon orange juice

1 tablespoon lemon juice
1 teaspoon ground ginger
½ teaspoon salt
½ cup chopped celery
½ cup chopped pecans
½ cup sour cream
¼ teaspoon ground ginger
Leaf lettuce leaves
Garnish: celery leaves

■ ■ ■ ■ ■ ■ ■ ■ ■ ■ □
Gingered Peach Salad
needs to be made ahead
and chilled, which makes
it an ideal addition
to a menu.

Drain peaches and pineapple into a bowl; stir well. Reserve 1¾ cups juice mixture. Pit and chop peaches; set peaches and pineapple aside.

Combine orange and lemon gelatins and boiling water, stirring 2 minutes or until gelatins dissolve. Add reserved juice mixture, orange juice, and next 3 ingredients to gelatin mixture; stir well. Chill until the consistency of unbeaten egg white.

Fold in chopped peaches, pineapple, chopped celery, and pecans. Pour mixture into a lightly oiled 9-inch square dish. Cover and chill until firm.

Combine sour cream and ¼ teaspoon ginger; stir well. Cut salad into rectangles. Serve on lettuce leaves; dollop with sour cream mixture. Garnish, if desired. Yield: 12 servings.

New Wave Waldorf Salad

1 large Red Delicious apple,
   chopped
1 large Granny Smith apple,
   chopped
1 large pear, chopped
1 tablespoon lemon juice
¼ cup golden raisins
1 stalk celery, diagonally sliced

½ cup mayonnaise or
   plain yogurt
½ cup sour cream
1 tablespoon honey
1 teaspoon grated orange rind
¼ cup slivered almonds, toasted
Garnish: celery leaves

Combine first 4 ingredients in a medium bowl; toss gently. Stir in raisins and sliced celery. Set aside.

Combine mayonnaise and next 3 ingredients; stir ¼ cup mayonnaise mixture into fruit mixture. Transfer salad to a serving bowl, and sprinkle with almonds. Garnish, if desired. Serve with remaining mayonnaise mixture. Yield: 6 servings.

Easy Antipasto

1 large head iceberg lettuce
1 small bunch fresh parsley,
   chopped
2 (6½-ounce) jars marinated
   artichoke hearts, drained
1 (11½-ounce) jar pickled
   cauliflower, drained
1 (9-ounce) jar pickled peppers,
   drained
1 (3-ounce) jar almond-stuffed
   olives, drained

1 bunch green onions, cut into
   3-inch pieces
1½ cups small cherry tomatoes
1 cup radishes
¾ cup pimiento-stuffed olives
¾ cup ripe olives
¾ cup commercial Italian salad
   dressing

Line a large serving platter with outer leaves of lettuce. Tear remaining lettuce into bite-size pieces. Combine torn lettuce and parsley; arrange mixture over lettuce leaves. Arrange artichoke hearts and next 8 ingredients over lettuce mixture. Cover and chill. Pour dressing over salad just before serving. Yield: 10 servings.

Take your tastebuds on a south-of-the-border excursion with Guacamole Salad and a Meat-and-Bean Burrito (page 103).

GUACAMOLE SALAD

2 ripe avocados, peeled, seeded, and coarsely chopped
3 tablespoons picante sauce
¼ teaspoon salt
⅛ teaspoon pepper

1 small tomato, peeled, seeded, and finely chopped
2 tablespoons chopped onion
4 cups finely shredded iceberg lettuce

Position knife blade in food processor bowl; add first 4 ingredients. Process until smooth, stopping once to scrape down sides. Stir in tomato and onion.

Arrange shredded lettuce on a large serving platter or individual plates. Top lettuce evenly with avocado mixture, and serve immediately. Yield: 6 servings.

FRESH BROCCOLI SALAD

4 cups fresh broccoli flowerets
1 cup thinly sliced carrot
½ cup (2 ounces) shredded
  Cheddar cheese
½ cup mayonnaise or salad
  dressing

3 tablespoons sugar
1½ tablespoons red wine
  vinegar
8 slices bacon, cooked and
  crumbled

Cook broccoli in boiling water to cover 10 seconds; drain immediately. Plunge broccoli into ice water to stop cooking process. Combine broccoli, carrot, and cheese in a medium bowl.

Combine mayonnaise, sugar, and vinegar; add to broccoli mixture. Toss well. Sprinkle with bacon, and serve immediately. Yield: 6 servings.

CARROT-RAISIN SALAD

¾ pound carrots, scraped and
  shredded
⅓ cup raisins
⅓ cup chopped walnuts

½ cup mayonnaise or salad
  dressing
1½ tablespoons cider vinegar
1 tablespoon sugar

Combine carrot, raisins, and walnuts in a medium bowl. Combine mayonnaise, vinegar, and sugar; add to carrot mixture, and toss gently. Yield: 4 servings.

GRECIAN GREEN SALAD

8 cups torn romaine lettuce
¾ cup crumbled feta cheese
½ cup thinly sliced radishes
1 small cucumber, thinly sliced
1 sweet red or green pepper,
  seeded and chopped

½ cup olive oil
3 tablespoons lemon juice
¼ teaspoon pepper

Combine first 5 ingredients in a large bowl; toss gently.

Combine oil, lemon juice, and ¼ teaspoon pepper in a jar. Cover tightly, and shake vigorously. Pour dressing over lettuce mixture, and toss gently. Yield: 8 servings.

Mandarin Tossed Salad

4 cups torn green leaf lettuce
½ cup sliced celery
½ cup chopped green onions
2 tablespoons chopped fresh
    parsley
1 (11-ounce) can mandarin
    oranges, drained
¼ cup vegetable oil

2 tablespoons sugar
2 tablespoons tarragon wine
    vinegar
¼ teaspoon salt
¼ teaspoon hot sauce
⅛ teaspoon pepper
¼ cup slivered almonds, toasted

Combine first 5 ingredients; toss gently. Cover and chill.

Combine oil and next 5 ingredients in a jar. Cover tightly, and shake vigorously. Pour dressing over lettuce mixture, and toss gently. Sprinkle with almonds. Serve immediately. Yield: 4 servings.

Orange-Walnut Salad

½ cup white wine vinegar
½ cup vegetable oil
¼ cup sugar
¾ teaspoon salt
¾ teaspoon celery seeds
¾ teaspoon dry mustard
¾ teaspoon paprika
¾ teaspoon grated onion
1 pound fresh spinach
2 small heads Bibb lettuce
    (about 1 pound), torn

2 oranges, peeled, seeded, and
    sectioned
½ medium-size purple onion,
    thinly sliced and separated
    into rings
½ cup coarsely chopped
    walnuts
2 teaspoons butter or
    margarine, melted

Combine first 8 ingredients in a jar. Cover tightly, and shake vigorously. Set aside.

Remove stems from spinach; wash leaves thoroughly, and pat dry. Tear leaves into bite-size pieces. Combine spinach, lettuce, orange sections, and onion rings in a large bowl.

Cook walnuts in butter in a small skillet over medium heat 5 minutes or until lightly browned, stirring frequently. Add walnuts to spinach mixture. Shake dressing mixture, and pour over spinach mixture; toss gently. Yield: 8 servings.

SPINACH AND SUN-DRIED TOMATO SALAD

1 (3-ounce) package sun-dried tomatoes
1 cup boiling water
1 medium cucumber
1 small purple onion, sliced and separated into rings
8 cups torn fresh spinach
1 cup sliced fresh mushrooms
¼ cup freshly grated Parmesan cheese
Simple Salad Dressing

Place tomatoes in a small bowl; add boiling water, and let stand 10 minutes. Drain and set aside.

Cut cucumber in half lengthwise, and scoop out seeds with a spoon; cut cucumber into thin slices. Combine tomatoes, cucumber, onion, and next 3 ingredients in a large bowl; toss well. Serve with Simple Salad Dressing. Yield: 8 servings.

Simple Salad Dressing

½ cup olive oil
¼ cup red wine vinegar
1 teaspoon Dijon mustard
½ teaspoon salt
¼ teaspoon pepper

Combine all ingredients in a jar. Cover tightly, and shake vigorously. Yield: ¾ cup.

LEMONY BROCCOLI

2 pounds fresh broccoli
¼ cup water
¼ cup butter or margarine, melted
¼ teaspoon grated lemon rind
3 tablespoons fresh lemon juice
1 teaspoon dried basil
½ teaspoon salt
¼ teaspoon pepper
Garnish: lemon zest

Remove broccoli leaves, and cut off tough ends of stalks. Wash broccoli thoroughly, and cut into spears.

Bring water to a boil in a large saucepan. Add broccoli spears; cover and cook 6 to 8 minutes or until crisp-tender. Drain. Place broccoli in a serving dish; set aside, and keep warm.

Combine butter and next 5 ingredients; pour over broccoli, and toss gently. Garnish, if desired. Serve immediately. Yield: 8 servings.

APRICOT CARROTS

2½ cups sliced carrot (about
    1 pound)
¼ cup apricot preserves
1½ tablespoons butter or
    margarine
¼ teaspoon grated orange rind
⅛ teaspoon ground nutmeg
1 teaspoon lemon juice

Cook carrot, covered, in a small amount of boiling water 10 minutes or until tender; drain.

    Combine preserves and remaining ingredients in a medium saucepan; cook over low heat, stirring constantly, until preserves and butter melt. Stir in carrot; cook until thoroughly heated. Yield: 4 servings.

■ ■ ■ ■ ■ ■ ■ ■ ■ ■
This recipe presents an easy way to prepare carrots that even the kids will eat. The apricot preserves mixture glazes the sliced carrot for a sweet taste.

DILLED GREEN BEANS

2 pounds fresh green beans
1 teaspoon salt
⅔ cup sliced green onions
¼ cup vegetable oil
2 tablespoons red wine vinegar
1 tablespoon chopped fresh
    dillweed or 1 teaspoon dried
    dillweed
1 teaspoon dry mustard
¼ teaspoon freshly ground
    pepper
Garnish: fresh dillweed sprigs

Wash beans; remove ends. Add water to depth of 1 inch in a Dutch oven. Bring to a boil; add beans and salt. Cover, reduce heat, and simmer 10 to 12 minutes or until beans are crisp-tender. Drain beans, and return to Dutch oven; stir in green onions.

    Combine oil and next 4 ingredients; stir with a wire whisk. Pour oil mixture over bean mixture, and toss gently. Transfer mixture to a serving bowl, and garnish, if desired. Yield: 8 servings.

THREE-PEPPER SAUTÉ

■■■■■■■■■■

Although this recipe calls for three colors of sweet peppers, only one or two of the colors may be used if all three aren't available.

1 large sweet red pepper, seeded and cut into thin strips
1 large sweet yellow pepper, seeded and cut into thin strips
1 large green pepper, seeded and cut into thin strips
1 small onion, chopped
1 clove garlic, minced
3 tablespoons olive oil
1 teaspoon dried basil
½ teaspoon salt
¼ teaspoon pepper
Garnish: fresh basil sprig

Cook first 5 ingredients in hot oil in a large skillet over medium-high heat, stirring constantly, 5 minutes or just until tender. Stir in basil, salt, and ground pepper; garnish, if desired. Serve immediately. Yield: 4 servings.

CREOLE-SEASONED POTATOES

16 small new potatoes (about
    2 pounds)
1 tablespoon Creole seasoning
¼ cup butter or margarine,
    melted

¼ cup chopped fresh parsley
Garnish: fresh parsley sprigs

Quarter potatoes; place in a steamer rack over boiling water. Cover and steam 15 to 20 minutes or until tender. Transfer potato to a bowl, and sprinkle with Creole seasoning.

Combine butter and chopped parsley; pour over potato mixture, and toss well. Garnish, if desired. Serve immediately. Yield: 8 servings.

JAZZY MASHED POTATOES

4 large baking potatoes (about
    3 pounds), peeled and cubed
½ cup milk
½ cup sour cream

¼ cup grated Parmesan cheese
¼ cup butter or margarine
2 tablespoons fresh or frozen
    chives

Cook potato in boiling salted water to cover 20 minutes or until tender; drain and mash. Add milk and remaining ingredients, stirring until butter melts. Serve immediately. Yield: 6 servings.

Dilled Green Beans (page 221) and Three-Pepper Sauté bring a rainbow of colors to your menus.

The tangy topping on Crusty Broiled Tomatoes balances the richness of Greek Spinach Quiche (page 23).

CRUSTY BROILED TOMATOES

4 medium tomatoes
1½ tablespoons Dijon mustard
⅛ teaspoon salt
⅛ teaspoon freshly ground
    black pepper
⅛ teaspoon ground red pepper

½ cup Italian-seasoned
    breadcrumbs
½ cup grated Parmesan cheese
¼ cup plus 2 tablespoons butter
    or margarine, melted

Cut tomatoes in half crosswise. Pat cut surfaces of tomatoes with paper towels to remove excess moisture. Spread mustard evenly over cut sides of tomato halves. Sprinkle evenly with salt, black pepper, and red pepper. Combine breadcrumbs, cheese, and butter; stir well. Spoon breadcrumb mixture evenly over tomato halves.

Place tomato halves on a rack of a broiler pan. Broil 5½ inches from heat (with electric oven door partially opened) 2 to 4 minutes or until lightly browned. Serve immediately. Yield: 8 servings.

LEMON-GARLIC ZUCCHINI

4 medium zucchini, diagonally
    sliced
1 clove garlic, crushed
2 tablespoons lemon juice
2 tablespoons olive oil
1/4 teaspoon salt
1/4 teaspoon pepper
Grated Parmesan cheese
    (optional)

Combine first 6 ingredients in a large skillet; cook over medium-high heat 5 minutes or until zucchini is crisp-tender, stirring frequently. Transfer zucchini to a serving dish using a slotted spoon; sprinkle with cheese, if desired. Yield: 4 servings.

ORANGE-PECAN BAKED APPLES

6 medium baking apples
1/2 cup orange marmalade
1/4 cup chopped pecans
1/8 teaspoon ground cinnamon
1/8 teaspoon ground nutmeg

Core apples from top, cutting to, but not through, bottoms. Place apples in a shallow baking dish; add water to cover bottom of dish.

    Combine marmalade and remaining ingredients. Fill centers of apples with marmalade mixture. Bake, uncovered, at 350° for 50 to 60 minutes or until apples are tender. Yield: 6 servings.

Select apples for baking and cooking that will hold their shape and not become mushy. Granny Smith, Stayman, York, and Winesap varieties will fill the bill.

SPICED PEACHES

2 (29-ounce) cans peach halves
    in heavy syrup, undrained
1 teaspoon cornstarch
1/2 teaspoon ground cinnamon
1/2 teaspoon ground cloves
1/4 teaspoon grated orange rind
1/8 teaspoon ground nutmeg
1/8 teaspoon ground allspice

Drain peach halves, reserving syrup; set peach halves aside. Combine syrup, cornstarch, and remaining ingredients in a small Dutch oven. Bring to a boil, stirring constantly. Reduce heat; add peach halves, and simmer 1 minute. Remove from heat, and let cool. Cover and chill up to 24 hours. Yield: 6 servings.

BANANAS FOSTER

■■■■■■■■■■
When flambéing a food such as Bananas Foster, use a long-handled match. Hold the lighted match just above the liquid mixture. You want to light the fumes, not the liquid itself. Most importantly, don't lean over the pan. Stand back to ignite the mixture.

½ cup firmly packed brown sugar
¼ cup butter or margarine, melted

¼ teaspoon ground cinnamon
4 bananas, split and quartered
⅓ cup light rum
Vanilla ice cream

Combine first 3 ingredients in a large skillet; cook over medium heat, stirring constantly, until bubbly. Add banana, and cook 2 to 3 minutes or until banana is thoroughly heated, basting constantly with syrup mixture.

Heat rum in a small saucepan over medium heat (do not boil). Quickly pour rum over banana mixture, and immediately ignite with a long match. Let flames die down; serve immediately over ice cream. Yield: 4 servings.

PINEAPPLE AND FRESH CITRUS

3 oranges, peeled, seeded, and sectioned
2 pink grapefruit, peeled, seeded, and sectioned
1 fresh pineapple, peeled, cored, and cubed

½ cup flaked coconut
½ cup honey
¼ cup chopped pecans, toasted (optional)

Combine first 5 ingredients in a large bowl; toss gently. Cover and chill at least 3 hours.

Just before serving, toss gently. Sprinkle with pecans, if desired. Yield: 12 servings.

Fresh Fruit Bowl

2 cups fresh strawberries,
   hulled
2 cups fresh blueberries
2 cups seedless green grapes

2 cups watermelon cubes
2 cups cantaloupe cubes
Mandarin Dressing

Combine all fruit in a large bowl; toss gently. Cover and chill, if desired. Serve with Mandarin Dressing. Yield: 10 servings.

Mandarin Dressing

1 cup mayonnaise or salad
   dressing
1 cup marshmallow cream

1 teaspoon grated orange rind
1 teaspoon grated fresh ginger

Combine all ingredients in a small bowl, stirring gently with a wire whisk. Cover and chill, if desired. Yield: 1½ cups.

Coconut Cream Cake

1 (18.5-ounce) package white
   cake mix without pudding
1 (3½-ounce) can flaked
   coconut, divided
1⅓ cups water

2 egg whites
1 (15-ounce) can cream of
   coconut
1 (12-ounce) carton frozen
   whipped topping, thawed

Combine cake mix, 1 cup flaked coconut, water, and egg whites in a mixing bowl; beat 2 minutes at high speed of an electric mixer. Reduce speed to low; beat 1 minute.

Pour batter into a greased and floured 13- x 9- x 2-inch pan. Bake at 350° for 25 to 30 minutes or until a wooden pick inserted in center comes out clean. Cool cake in pan on a wire rack 10 minutes.

Punch holes in top of cake with a wooden pick. Pour cream of coconut evenly over warm cake; let cool completely. Spread whipped topping over cake; sprinkle with remaining flaked coconut. Cover and chill at least 4 hours. Cut cake into squares to serve. Yield: 15 servings.

■■■■■■■■■□

Coconut Cream Cake is so wonderful you'll want to serve it year-round instead of reserving it for the holiday season. This cake keeps well for several days in the refrigerator.

BUTTERMILK CHESS PIE

■■■■■■■■■■

Here's an easy recipe you'll turn to again and again because the ingredients to prepare Buttermilk Chess Pie will usually be on hand.

5 large eggs, lightly beaten
2 cups sugar
⅔ cup buttermilk
½ cup butter or margarine, melted

2 tablespoons all-purpose flour
1 teaspoon vanilla extract
1 unbaked 9-inch pastry shell

Combine first 6 ingredients; pour into pastry shell. Bake at 350° for 45 minutes or until set. Cool on a wire rack. Yield: one 9-inch pie.

QUICK BLUEBERRY COBBLER

■■■■■■■■■■

When selecting fresh blueberries, choose those that are indigo blue with a powdery silver frost coating the berries. Don't wash fresh blueberries until you're ready to use them.

5 cups fresh or frozen blueberries, thawed
1½ cups sugar
½ cup all-purpose flour
2 tablespoons lemon juice

2 tablespoons butter or margarine, melted
¼ teaspoon salt
Pastry for 9-inch pie

Combine first 6 ingredients in a medium bowl; toss gently. Spoon blueberry mixture into a lightly greased 8-inch square baking dish.

Cut pastry to fit top of dish; place over filling. Make several cuts in pastry to allow steam to escape. Bake at 425° for 30 minutes or until filling is bubbly and crust is golden. Yield: 8 servings.

WINTER FRUIT CRISP

3 medium cooking apples, sliced (about 1½ pounds)
2 cups fresh cranberries
1 (8-ounce) can unsweetened crushed pineapple, undrained
½ cup sugar
1 cup firmly packed brown sugar

¼ cup all-purpose flour
½ cup butter or margarine, softened
1 cup regular oats, uncooked
1 cup chopped pecans
Sweetened whipped cream
Ground cinnamon (optional)

Layer apple slices, cranberries, and pineapple evenly in 8 lightly greased 1½-cup individual baking dishes; sprinkle evenly with ½ cup sugar.

The buttery streusel topping sprinkled over Winter Fruit Crisp lightly sweetens the tart apples and cranberries.

Combine brown sugar and flour; cut in butter with a pastry blender until mixture is crumbly. Stir in oats and pecans. Sprinkle mixture evenly over fruit. Bake, uncovered, at 375° for 25 minutes or until bubbly and thoroughly heated. Top each serving with a dollop of whipped cream; sprinkle with cinnamon, if desired. Yield: 8 servings.

Note: Unbaked individual crisps may be covered tightly and frozen up to 1 month. Remove from freezer, and bake, uncovered, at 375° for 30 minutes or until bubbly and thoroughly heated. Serve as directed above.

Winter Fruit Crisp may be baked in a lightly greased 13- x 9- x 2-inch baking dish. Follow same directions for assembling the crisp. Bake, uncovered, at 375° for 30 minutes or until bubbly and thoroughly heated. Spoon mixture into individual bowls, and top each serving with whipped cream and cinnamon as directed above.

Chocolate lovers at your house will rave about Chocolate Mousse Parfaits. Keep a few in the freezer to serve at a moment's notice.

CHOCOLATE MOUSSE PARFAITS

½ (12-ounce) package milk
    chocolate morsels
¼ cup whipping cream
2 tablespoons water
2 teaspoons vanilla extract
1½ cups whipping cream,
    whipped

⅔ cup crushed chocolate
    wafers
Additional crushed chocolate
    wafers

Combine first 3 ingredients in a large heavy saucepan; cook over low heat, stirring constantly, until chocolate melts. Remove mixture from heat, and let cool.

Stir in vanilla, and fold in whipped cream. Layer chocolate mixture and ⅔ cup chocolate wafer crumbs evenly in 6 (4-ounce) parfait glasses. Cover and chill at least 2 hours. Sprinkle with additional chocolate wafer crumbs just before serving. Yield: 6 servings.

Note: Chocolate Mousse Parfaits may be frozen up to 1 week. Remove from freezer, and let stand 15 minutes before serving.

CHOCOLATE FONDUE

1 (12-ounce) package semisweet
   chocolate morsels
1 (6-ounce) package semisweet
   chocolate morsels

1 cup half-and-half
¾ cup sugar
1½ teaspoons vanilla extract

Combine all ingredients in top of a double boiler; cook over hot (not boiling) water, stirring constantly, until chocolate melts. Pour mixture into a fondue pot, and keep warm. Serve with fresh fruit or pound cake. Yield: 3 cups.

Note: Chocolate Fondue can be refrigerated in a tightly covered container up to 5 days. To serve, place fondue in top of a double boiler, and cook over hot (not boiling) water, stirring constantly, until mixture is smooth and thoroughly heated.

NO-BAKE BANANA PUDDING

2 (3.4-ounce) packages vanilla
   instant pudding mix
1 (8-ounce) carton sour cream
3½ cups milk

Vanilla wafers
3 large bananas
1 (8-ounce) carton frozen
   whipped topping, thawed

Combine first 3 ingredients in a large bowl; beat at low speed of an electric mixer 2 minutes or until thickened.

Line bottom and sides of a 3-quart bowl with vanilla wafers. Slice one banana, and layer over wafers. Spoon one-third of pudding mixture over bananas. Repeat layers two more times using vanilla wafers, remaining bananas, and remaining pudding. Cover and chill. Spread whipped topping over pudding just before serving. Yield: 10 servings.

No-Bake Banana Pudding is one our foods staff's favorites. The recipe is quick and easy, but folks will think you spent hours preparing it. One box of vanilla wafers will be more than enough to use in this recipe.

COFFEE ICE CREAM PIE

½ cup butter or margarine, melted
½ cup chopped pecans
2 tablespoons all-purpose flour
1 (7-ounce) can flaked coconut
½ gallon coffee ice cream, softened

1 cup whipping cream
¼ cup sifted powdered sugar
Chocolate curls
½ cup Kahlúa or other coffee-flavored liqueur (optional)

Combine first 4 ingredients; press mixture over bottom and up sides of a 10-inch pieplate. Bake at 375° for 10 to 12 minutes or until lightly browned; let cool completely on a wire rack. Spoon ice cream into prepared crust, and freeze until firm.

Beat whipping cream until foamy; gradually add powdered sugar, beating until soft peaks form. Spread whipped cream over ice cream layer; top with chocolate curls. Cut into wedges, and drizzle each serving with 1 tablespoon Kahlúa, if desired. Yield: one 10-inch pie.

ALMOND ICE CREAM BALLS

1 pint vanilla ice cream
1 (2-ounce) package slivered
  almonds, chopped and
  toasted

½ cup commercial fudge sauce
2 teaspoons amaretto or other
  almond-flavored liqueur

Scoop ice cream into 4 balls, and place on a baking sheet; freeze at least 1 hour or until firm. Coat ice cream balls with almonds; freeze until ready to serve.

Combine fudge sauce and liqueur, stirring well. Place ice cream balls in individual dessert dishes; spoon chocolate mixture evenly over ice cream. Serve immediately. Yield: 4 servings.

RAINBOW SHERBET DESSERT

2 cups whipping cream
3 tablespoons powdered sugar
1 teaspoon vanilla extract
12 coconut macaroons, crushed
   and toasted
¾ cup chopped pecans, toasted

3 cups raspberry sherbet,
  softened
3 cups lime sherbet, softened
3 cups orange sherbet, softened
Garnish: fresh strawberry
  halves

Serve Rainbow Sherbet Dessert as a refreshing end to a warm-weather dinner. The recipe makes a lot, and it's sure to please your company.

Beat whipping cream until foamy; gradually add sugar and vanilla, beating until soft peaks form. Fold in macaroons and pecans.

Spread half of whipped cream mixture in a 9-inch springform pan; freeze until firm. Layer each sherbet over frozen whipped cream mixture, allowing each layer to freeze before spreading next layer. Top with remaining whipped cream mixture. Cover and freeze until firm.

Remove dessert from pan, and place on a serving plate. Garnish, if desired. Cut into wedges to serve. Yield: 12 servings.

To add an extravagant touch, drizzle each serving of Coffee Ice Cream Pie with a spoonful of Kahlúa.

Index

Credits

Oxmoor House wishes to thank the following merchants:

Annieglass, Santa Cruz, CA
Barbara Eigen Arts, Jersey City, NJ
Bridges Antiques, Birmingham, AL
Bromberg's, Birmingham, AL
Cassis & Co., New York, NY
Christine's, Birmingham, AL
Fitz and Floyd/Omnibus International, Dallas, TX
The Holly Tree, Birmingham, AL
Los Angeles Pottery, Los Angeles, CA
Le Creuset, Yemassee, SC
Mesa International, Elkins, NH
New Environs, Birmingham, AL
Reed and Barton, Taunton, MA
Sasaki, Secaucus, NJ
Vietri, Hillsborough, NC
Villeroy & Boch, New York, NY

Photography and photo styling by Oxmoor House staff:
Photographers: Jim Bathie and Ralph Anderson
Photo Stylists: Kay E. Clarke and Virginia R. Cravens

Additional photo styling:
Iris Crawley: pages 16, 21
Debbie Maugans: pages 85, 87
Angie N. Sinclair: pages 32, 39, 42, 47